Spiritual Leadership

Spiritual Leadership

A Biblical Theology of the Role of the Spirit
in the Leadership of God's People

David Huffstutler

Foreword by Andreas J. Köstenberger

WIPF & STOCK · Eugene, Oregon

SPIRITUAL LEADERSHIP
A Biblical Theology of the Role of the Spirit in the Leadership of God's People

Copyright © 2016 David Huffstutler. All rights reserved. Except for brief quotations in critical publications or reviews, no part of this book may be reproduced in any manner without prior written permission from the publisher. Write: Permissions, Wipf and Stock Publishers, 199 W. 8th Ave., Suite 3, Eugene, OR 97401.

Wipf & Stock
An Imprint of Wipf and Stock Publishers
199 W. 8th Ave., Suite 3
Eugene, OR 97401

www.wipfandstock.com

PAPERBACK ISBN: 978-1-5326-0388-4
HARDCOVER ISBN: 978-1-5326-0390-7
EBOOK ISBN: 978-1-5326-0389-1

Manufactured in the U.S.A.   DECEMBER 7, 2016

To those who formally and informally lead the church today in local churches and parachurch ministries. May their leadership truly be a genuine work of the Spirit.

Contents

Foreword by Andreas J. Köstenberger | ix
Acknowledgments | xiii
Abbreviations | xv

1   Introduction | 1
2   The Role of the Spirit in the Leadership of Old Testament Leaders | 13
3   The Role of the Spirit in the Leadership of New Testament Leaders | 47
4   A Systematized Biblical Theology of Spiritual Leadership | 113
5   Biblical Theology and Spiritual Leadership in the Church | 146
6   Conclusion | 161

Bibliography | 163

Foreword

COMPREHENDING THE PERSON AND work of the Holy Spirit is a challenging, even mind-stretching, task. How do you wrap your brain around the teaching of Scripture regarding this unique person that is so vital in the life of the Christian—and the Christian leader in particular—and yet at times so difficult to understand?

Consider the following selection of passages:

- At creation, the writer of Genesis tells us, the Spirit was mysterious hovering over the face of the primordial waters.[1]
- Moses and the Seventy, the craftsmen working on the Tabernacle, and Israel's first king, Saul, as well as David, his successor, were all endowed with the Spirit for their respective tasks.[2]
- In one of his psalms, King David prays following his sin with Bathsheba, "Don't take your Holy Spirit away from me."[3]
- Jesus, when preaching his inaugural homily in his hometown synagogue of Capernaum, claims to be the Spirit-anointed Servant of the Lord featured in the book of Isaiah.[4]
- The risen Jesus breathed on his new messianic community (the Eleven), symbolically prefiguring the endowment of the Spirit at Pentecost.[5]

---

1. Genesis 1:2.
2. Exodus 31:3; Numbers 11:17, 25; 1 Samuel 11:6; 16:13.
3. Psalm 51:11.
4. Luke 4:18–19; cf. Isa 61:1–2.
5. John 20:22.

FOREWORD

- According to the book of Acts, and in keeping with Joel's prophecy, the Holy Spirit would empower the church for her witness to the ends of the earth.[6]
- Paul calls on believers to "walk" in the Spirit, to be "led" by the Spirit, and to "keep in step" with the Spirit. He also asserts that if anyone does not have the Spirit, he is not a true believer.[7]
- Conversely, Jude characterizes the false teachers as those who are devoid of the Spirit.[8]

This selected assortment of Old and New Testament passages with reference to the Spirit reflects a colorful array of pieces of a puzzle. But how do these pieces all fit together? And what do they teach us about God's work, particularly in the life of those he calls to a role of leadership?

In this volume, the author takes up the challenging but rewarding task of trying to assemble this puzzle, or, to change the metaphor, to connect the dots. He appropriately adopts a biblical-theological approach, paying careful attention to the unfolding revelation regarding the Spirit throughout the course of Scripture.

- Did the Spirit indwell leaders in Old Testament times as he does in the New Testament era? Or did he come on leaders only temporarily to equip them for their task?
- Is there any difference between God's work in leaders and his work in ordinary believers? What is the Spirit's role particularly in the New Testament period and in the church today?
- What are the different ways in which God has been, and continues to be, at work in and through leaders' lives?

These are the kinds of questions addressed in this helpful, well-written volume. As one who is about to embark on the project of co-authoring a monograph on a biblical theology of the Spirit, I deeply appreciate the judicious treatment the author has provided on this important issue.[9]

The present volume will prove particularly useful for pastors and church leaders. In an age when the study of leadership often lacks proper

---

6. Acts 1:8; cf. Joel 2:28–29.
7. Galatians 5:16, 18, 25; Romans 8:9.
8. Jude 19.
9. My volume will be co-authored with Gregg Allison and published by B&H Academic.

biblical grounding, it is refreshing to see a work that engages the Scriptures consistently and in depth rather than by mere occasional prooftexting.

This book is also much needed because many discussions of leadership either neglect or ignore the Spirit. This is inexcusable, however, because the Spirit is God's indispensable instrument in calling, empowering, and guiding leaders he appoints, as the Scriptures attest.

I am grateful to be able to commend this book. I am confident that those who read it will find much food for thought. Not only this, but leaders, in particular, will be able to clarify their place in God's plan and arrive at a deeper appreciation of the Spirit's work in and through their lives.

Andreas J. Köstenberger, PhD
Founder, Biblical Foundations™
Senior Research Professor of New Testament & Biblical Theology
Southeastern Baptist Theological Seminary

Acknowledgments

I would be amiss to not say that there are many individuals besides the few mentioned here who have contributed to this study in one way or another. Some, however, played a larger role than others:

- To my wife Holly, whose employment provided the funds for several years of tuition; the editor whose scholarship improved every page of this study; the mother who watched our children alone for many days while I studied; and the helpmeet who encouraged me throughout all my studies;
- To my children Calvin and Mackenna, who always hugged me as I went out the door to study but never quite understood what it meant for "daddy to work on his paper"; to my daughter Ashlyn whose unseen presence motivated me to finish this study in its first format as a dissertation before her birth; and to my daughter Gwendolyn whose unseen presence motivated me to publish my dissertation as this book before her birth as well;
- To the faculty and staff of Bob Jones University, Detroit Baptist Theological Seminary, and Southeastern Baptist Theological Seminary for their example and expectation in biblical scholarship, and especially to my major professor, Dr. Andreas Köstenberger, who mentored me in the fields of Christian leadership and biblical theology and provided me with an example of scholarly excellence;
- To Dr. Rolland McCune, and to Dr. Mark Snoeberger, former and current professors of systematic theology at Detroit Baptist Theological Seminary, whose teaching ministries gave me a hunger to study the Holy Spirit;

ACKNOWLEDGMENTS

- To my brother Dr. Joel Huffstutler, whose picture of writing as eating an elephant gave me the needed perspective to complete projects slowly over time;
- To the First Baptist Church in Troy, Michigan, and to the First Baptist Church in Rockford, Illinois, for giving me the needed time to work on my studies;
- To Dr. Michael Harding, senior pastor of First Baptist Church in Troy, Michigan, who encouraged me in word and example to be both a pastor and scholar;
- To my parents, Dale and Linda Huffstutler, and to my brothers Daniel, Joel, and Nathan, who encouraged me in my studies.
- To Dr. Bruce Compton, professor of biblical languages and literature at Detroit Baptist Theological Seminary, for encouraging me to publish my dissertation into the pages that follow.

Abbreviations

ESV	*The Holy Bible: English Standard Version.* Wheaton, Ill.: Standard Bible Society, 2001.
HALOT	Koehler, L., W. Baumgartner, and J. J. Stamm. *The Hebrew and Aramaic Lexicon of the Old Testament.* Translated and edited under the supervision of M. E. J. Richardson. 5 vols. Leiden, 1994–2000.
HCSB	*The Holy Bible: Holman Christian Standard Version.* Nashville, Tenn.: Holman Bible Publishers, 2009.
ISBE	Bromiley, Geoffrey W., ed. *The International Standard Bible Encyclopedia, Revised.* Grand Rapids, Mich.: Eerdmans, 1979–1988.
LXX	Septuagint
MT	Masoretic Text
NASB	*New American Standard Bible: 1995 Update.* LaHabra, Calif.: The Lockman Foundation, 1995.
NET Bible	*The NET Bible First Edition.* Dallas, Tex.; Biblical Studies Press, 2005.
NIV	*The Holy Bible: New International Version.* Grand Rapids, Mich.: Zondervan, 1984.
NKJV	*The New King James Version.* Nashville, Tenn.: Thomas Nelson, 1982.

1

Introduction

Statement of Thesis and Purpose

The thesis of this study argues that a biblical theology of the role of the Spirit in the leadership of God's people demonstrates a distinct work of the Spirit in biblical leaders.

The purpose of this study is to discover how a biblical theology of the role of the Spirit in the leadership of God's people demonstrates a work of the Spirit in leaders that is distinct from other works of the Spirit such as prophecy, indwelling, or regeneration. Though these other works of the Spirit cannot be discussed in detail, it can at least be demonstrated that there is a distinct work of the Spirit involved in the leadership of biblical leaders.

Definition of Key Terms and Phrases

Key terms and phrases that require definition for this study are the following: "God's people," "biblical leaders," "spiritual leadership," "the Spirit of God," and "the work of the Spirit of God in biblical leaders."

God's People

As it is used in this study, the term *God's people* generally applies to the people of God in both the OT and NT. More specifically, the people of God in the OT refers to national Israel (Deut 7:6–9) and other nations on occasion (e.g., Egypt in Isa 19:25). The people of God in the NT refers to the church (2 Cor 6:16–18), a people of God not restricted by ethnicity (cf. Rev 5:9–10). For the purposes of this paper, *God's people* or *the people of God* will refer to Israel and the church.

Biblical Leaders

The term *biblical leader* refers to anyone who has been formally recognized by God or his people to lead the people of God. As this term applies to leaders in the OT, though prophets and foreign leaders occasionally led God's people in some way (e.g., Joseph, Cyrus, Daniel), this term will be limited to those who have been officially appointed by God or God's people to be the head of Israel. With reference to men in the NT, the term *biblical leader* will apply to Jesus, the apostles, apostolic delegates, elders, and those who enjoy what is commonly called the spiritual gift of leadership.

Spiritual Leadership

The term *leadership* denotes any activity of a biblical leader that is an exercise of his authority over the people of God. This study limits its discussion to the activity of leadership that the Scriptural text explicitly or implicitly describes to be the result of the work of the Spirit. As the Spirit is involved in the exercise of a leader's leadership, this leadership may be called *spiritual*. Unless otherwise noted, this paper will not use the phrase *spiritual leadership* beyond this narrow definition.

The Spirit of God

The Hebrew term *rûaḥ* and the Greek term *pneuma* carry a range of meanings,[1] but, unless otherwise noted, the focus of this study involves uses of *rûaḥ* and *pneuma* when they mean *spirit*, and specifically *the Spirit of God*. Of the 305,500 words in the OT,[2] the term *rûaḥ* occurs 394 times,[3] and approximately 100 of these occurrences refer to the Spirit of God,[4] roughly one out of every four occurrences. The ratio of the use of *rûaḥ* in comparison to the number of all the words in the OT is 1:785. The ratio

1. See HALOT, s.v., "רוּחַ," and BDAG, s.v., "πνεῦμα."
2. Anderson and Forbes, *The Vocabulary of the Old Testament*, 3.
3. Hamilton, "God with Men in the Torah," 131–33, catalogues 389 references to *rûaḥ* in the OT. 378 are Hebrew, and 11 are found in the Aramaic portions of Daniel. See also Firth and Wegner, "Introduction," 16. Firth and Wegner assume the legitimacy of *rûaḥ* for 5 variants, bringing the total uses of *rûaḥ* to 394.
4. Wood, *The Holy Spirit in the Old Testament*, 23. Cumming, *Through the Eternal Spirit*, 17–24. Cumming carefully catalogues 88 passages "in which a Divine Person seems to be spoken of . . . contained in the Old Testament" (*Through the Eternal Spirit*, 17).

of the use of *rûaḥ* with reference to the Spirit of God in comparison to the number of all the words in the OT is approximately 1:3055.

Of the 138,162 words of the NT,[5] the term *pneuma* occurs 379 times,[6] and approximately 275 of these occurrences refer to the Spirit of God,[7] almost three out of every four uses. The ratio of the use of *pneuma* in comparison to the number of all the words in the NT is 1:365. The ratio of the use of *pneuma* with reference to the Spirit of God in comparison to the number of all the words in the NT is approximately 1:502.

These numbers indicate that, whatever meaning is in view for *rûaḥ* or *pneuma*, the use of *pneuma* in the NT (1:365) occurs more than twice as frequently as the use of *rûaḥ* in the OT (1:785). Also, for every time *rûaḥ* refers to the Spirit of God in the OT (100 of its 394 uses), the use of *pneuma* in the NT refers to the Spirit of God almost three times (275 of its 379 uses). A comparison of the ratios of the use of *rûaḥ* and *pneuma* to all the words in their respective testaments (1:3055 and 1:502) indicates that every time the OT refers the Spirit of God with the term *rûaḥ*, the use of *pneuma* in the NT refers to the Spirit of God six times.

Narrowing this data further, Chapter 2 will demonstrate that approximately 30 of the 100 OT uses of *rûaḥ* that refer to the Spirit of God are used in relation to the leadership of the leaders of Israel. Chapter 3 will demonstrate that approximately 90 of the 275 NT uses of *pneuma* that refer to the Spirit of God are used in relation to the leadership of NT leaders as defined above. Given this data, the discussion in Chapter 2 will be considerably shorter than the discussion in Chapter 3.

In defining the phrase *the Spirit of God*, it is necessary to recognize the progress and accumulation of revelation about the Spirit from one biblical era to the next. To define the Spirit according to the revelation of the OT alone would not yield the same definition as if one were to define the Spirit according to the whole of Scripture. This is not to say that the OT data about the Spirit contradicts what is found in the NT. It is to say, however, that the NT reveals developments and truth about the nature and role of the Spirit that was not given in the OT. The combined data of the OT and NT naturally yields a definition of the Spirit of God that is more complete than a definition of the Spirit of God from the OT alone.

---

5. Wallace, *Greek Grammar Beyond the Basics*, 31.
6. See Bullinger, *Word Studies on the Holy Spirit*, 209–17.
7. *EDNT*, s.v., "πνεῦμα" 3:117.

A debated topic along these lines is whether or not the OT gives enough revelation to conclude from the OT alone that the Spirit of God is a person. Some believe the OT data allow the interpreter to conclude that the Spirit in the OT is no more than an extension or personal manifestation of the one and only God. Others make a case that because the NT describes the Spirit of God as a person by quoting OT passages, these passages in the OT may have also understood the Spirit to be a person. Some suggest other lines of evidence to see the Spirit as a person in the OT as well.[8] Whatever one may say as to whether or not the OT understood the Spirit to be a person, the present writer assumes that the Spirit was understood to be a person by Jesus and the early church (cf. Matt 28:19; 2 Cor 13:14). Their understanding of the Spirit as a person may have developed from passages in the OT (see Acts 2:17–18, 33 with Joel 2:28–29).[9]

Unfortunately, this study cannot discuss the issue of the Spirit's personality in depth, and there will be other significant issues related to the doctrine of the Spirit that cannot be given the attention they deserve. However, it will at least be attempted to footnote debated matters and the writer's presuppositions when more cannot be said due to the constraints of this study. It is assumed that the Spirit of God in the OT is the same Spirit of God in the NT, and it is recognized that God's people had less revelation about the Spirit of God in the earlier ages of biblical history.

The Work of the Spirit of God in Biblical Leaders

The thesis of this paper speaks of a distinct *work* of the Spirit in biblical leaders, and it is this work that is more difficult to define than any of the terms above. In fact, one might say that the purpose of this dissertation is given to describing this work in each leader so as to gather the findings and define this work in detail toward the study's end. This being said, all that can be offered at this point are some introductory matters related to a definition of the work of the Spirit in biblical leaders.

The biblical terminology for the work of the Spirit in biblical leaders is complicated and diverse. Multiple verbs describe the work of the Spirit, and sometimes the work of the Spirit must be inferred from the context and the

---

8. For a survey of these positions, see Firth and Wegner, "Introduction," 17–21.

9. For a discussion of the NT's understanding of the Spirit as person, see Cole, *He Who Gives Life*, 65–69.

nature of a preposition that indicates some kind of connection between the Spirit, a biblical leader, and his exercise of leadership.

A few examples from the OT illustrate these points. The Spirit was "on" Moses, "put . . . on the seventy elders," and "rested on" Eldad and Medad (Num 11:17, 25).[10] Joshua was a man who the Spirit was "in" (Num 27:18). He was also "full of the spirit of wisdom" (Deut 34:9). The Spirit "clothed" (Judg 6:34), "was upon" (Judg 11:29), "began to stir" (Judg 13:25), and "rushed upon" (Judg 14:6, 19; 15:14) the judges. The Spirit likewise "rushed upon" Saul (1 Sam 10:10; 11:6) and David (1 Sam 16:13). The Spirit would "rest upon" the Messiah (Isa 11:2).

A few examples from the NT illustrate this diverse terminology as well. The Spirit "descended on" Jesus (Luke 3:22; cf. Mark 1:10) in order to "rest on him" (Matt 3:16) for the duration of his ministry. Whether he spoke "in the power of the Spirit" (Luke 4:14–15) or performed a miracle "by the Spirit of God" (Matt 12:28), it was clear that "God anointed Jesus with the Holy Spirit and with power" (Acts 10:38). In turn, Jesus would "baptize" his followers "with the Holy Spirit" (Matt 3:11; Mark 1:8; Luke 3:16; cf. John 1:33; Acts 1:8), which he did when he "poured out" the Spirit at Pentecost (Acts 2:33; cf. 11:16).

The work of the Spirit is variously described among other NT leaders as well. Jesus "breathed on" the apostles and commanded, "Receive the Holy Spirit" (John 20:22). Individual apostles and their coworkers are described as being "filled with the Holy Spirit" (Acts 4:8; 9:17; 13:9), "full of the Holy Spirit" (Acts 11:24), and "in the Spirit" (Rev 1:10; 4:2; 17:3; 21:10). "The Holy Spirit has made" elders overseers (Acts 20:28), and the first deacons were to be "full of the Spirit and of wisdom" (Acts 6:3). Apart from a reference to a particular individual, Paul also speaks of what is commonly called the spiritual gift of leadership (Rom 12:8; 1 Cor 12:28), which he describes as a "manifestation of the Spirit" (1 Cor 12:4, 7, 11).

This diversity in the biblical literature is reflected in secondary literature as well. Among other terms that could be added, biblical leaders are said to experience the Spirit's gift, power, inspiration, endowment, energy, sealing, filling, infilling, imbuement, enduement, indwelling, anointing, enabling, moving, baptism, and abiding presence.[11] This study has chosen

10. Unless otherwise noted, all biblical quotations are taken from the English Standard Version.

11. For a sampling of the various discussions on the terminology related to the Spirit, see especially the appendix in Hamilton, "God with Men in the Torah," 131–33. See also Averbeck, "Breath, Wind, Spirit and the Holy Spirit in the Old Testament," 25–37; Ryrie,

the general term *work* to capture the idea that the Spirit is in some way active in connection to the exercise of a biblical leader's leadership.

The Present State of Research on the Topic of Spiritual Leadership and the Unique Contribution of the Present Study

"As much as there is written on Christ, so little is there written on the Holy Spirit."[12] This statement by Abraham Kuyper was made over a century ago, and one could certainly not say the same today. In fact, one might wonder at the wisdom of writing another work on the Holy Spirit when so much literature on the topic already exists. At the same time, to the writer's knowledge, there is not a work written such as this study proposes to endeavor. However, many works do touch upon the topic at hand in one way or another, and it is necessary to survey what has been said up to this point.

Whole-Bible studies of the Spirit survey most or all of the passages that refer to the Holy Spirit.[13] Biblical theologies of the Spirit are also helpful to this study in that they bring out the progress of revelation concerning the Spirit and the continuity and discontinuity from one era of biblical history to the next.[14] The similarity of these works to the study at hand is that they survey most or all of the passages in this study. However, the nature of such a broad survey does not allow for an in-depth development of themes specific to the study at hand.

Other surveys limit themselves to the OT or NT in order to give a deeper analysis of a smaller number of texts. As seen above, the number of references to the Spirit of God in the OT is approximately one-third the number of references to the Spirit of God in the NT. The secondary literature shows this variance between the testaments in that OT works on the Spirit typically have room to deal with both exegetical and systematic concerns while NT works may be limited to simply an overview of each

---

The Holy Spirit, 53–55; Cole, *He Who Gives Life*, 79–83; and Firth, "The Spirit and Leadership," 259–80.

12. Kuyper, *The Work of the Holy Spirit*, ix.

13. Examples of these surveys are Horton, *What the Bible Says about the Holy Spirit*; Rea, *The Holy Spirit in the Bible*; and Thomas, *The Holy Spirit of God*.

14. Examples of biblical theologies of the Spirit are Inch, *Saga of the Spirit*; Montague, *The Holy Spirit*.

text. Some NT works further limit themselves to an examination of the Spirit within a select portion of the NT.[15]

Other works on the Spirit are systematic in nature and deal with passages that will be examined in this study, but their systematic concerns assume or do not allow for an exegetical analysis of each passage that is necessary in formulating a biblical theology of the Spirit.[16] Yet other works focus on select issues such as the Spirit's role in spiritual gifts or indwelling due to the NT data on these topics.[17] A catalyst for many of these topics is to discover the continuity and discontinuity that lies between the testaments or, as in the case of spiritual gifts, the continuity and discontinuity that lies between the early church and the church today.[18]

Numerous works contain the phrase "spiritual leadership" in their titles, and there is an abundance of literature aimed at "spiritual leaders," that is, leaders in any kind of Christian organization (church, para-church organization, etc.). As promising as these titles may be, and as helpful as these works may be for their target audience, they offer little to the study at hand. A classic work from this type of literature is *Spiritual Leadership* by J. Oswald Sanders.[19] Sanders uses Acts 6:3 to support his claim that being filled with the Spirit is essential for deacons and "those who preach and

---

15. For OT works on the Spirit, see Firth and Wegner, *Presence, Power and Promise*; Hildebrandt, *An Old Testament Theology of the Spirit of God*; Wood, *The Holy Spirit in the Old Testament*; Wright, *Knowing the Holy Spirit through the Old Testament*. For a NT work on the Spirit, see Warrington, *Discovering the Holy Spirit in the New Testament*. For an older German work on the Spirit of God in the NT, see Büchsel, *Der Geist Gottes im Neuen Testament*. Büchsel briefly surveys the Spirit of God in the OT and extrabiblical literature as well. For a survey of the Spirit in relation to Christ in the Gospels, see Hawthorne, *The Presence and the Power*. For an thorough examination of the Spirit in Pauline literature, see Fee, *God's Empowering Presence*.

16. For examples of systematic works on the Spirit, see Cole, *He Who Gives Life*; Ferguson, *The Holy Spirit*; Green, *I Believe in the Holy Spirit*; Gromacki, *The Holy Spirit*; Owen, *The Holy Spirit*; Hendry, *The Holy Spirit in Christian Theology*; Palmer, *The Holy Spirit*; Ryrie, *The Holy Spirit*; Schweizer, *The Holy Spirit*; and Scofield, *Holy Spirit in Both Testaments*.

17. For example, see Berding, *What Are Spiritual Gifts?*; and Hamilton, *God's Indwelling Presence*.

18. For the view that some spiritual gifts are no longer for today, see Edgar, *Miraculous Gifts*. For the view that all spiritual gifts are for today, see Turner, *The Holy Spirit and Spiritual Gifts Then and Now*. Numerous works could be mentioned on both sides of this issue.

19. Sanders, *Spiritual Leadership*.

teach the word of God"[20] He later notes the necessity of the Spirit's role in a leader's courage by referring to Acts 2:4 and 2 Tim 1:7.[21] He mentions the spiritual gift of leadership in Rom 12:8, but this mention is more to emphasize one's zeal in leadership rather than to explain the Spirit's relationship to gifting. He also discusses the servant of Isa 42:1 and rightly sees the fulfillment of this prophecy in Jesus (cf. Acts 10:37–38). He then claims "God offers us the same anointing," but he does not explain this statement further.[22] Apart from these occasional references, the role of the Spirit in the life of a leader is assumed and not explained in depth, if at all. Other popular works from this realm of literature are similar in that they do not address the Spirit's role in detail.[23]

One can see from the survey above that there is much literature about the Spirit that is too general to be helpful to the study at hand. Other literature addresses specific topics outside the scope of this present study. Some works, however, are similar to the topic at hand, such as John D. Harvey's *Anointed with the Spirit and Power: The Holy Spirit's Empowering Presence* (2008)[24] and Don N. Howell's *Servants of the Servant: A Biblical Theology of Leadership* (2003).[25]

Harvey's work is similar in that it gives a like-minded biblical theology of the empowering role of the Spirit. His discussion of the Spirit in the OT is similar to what will be found in this dissertation. However, unlike Harvey's work, the present study does not focus as much on the role of prophets,

20. Ibid., 31–32.
21. Ibid., 60.
22. Ibid., 24–25.
23. Another popular work along these lines is Blackaby brothers' *Spiritual Leadership*. The question is raised as to whether leadership is secular or spiritual and then goes on to speak about "Christian leadership" and "Christian leaders," indicating that his idea of *spiritual* leadership is synonymous with *Christian* leadership (*Spiritual Leadership*, 9). In answering the question, the Spirit is given no reference at all. The authors later refer to the essential enabling of the Spirit for spiritual leadership, but there is only a brief explanation of only two biblical references to the Spirit, all of which amounts to less than a page (Ibid., 42–43). The Spirit's role in guiding decisions is discussed, but Scripture is referenced only in passing and is not explained in detail (Ibid., 179–85). The works by Sanders and Blackaby are representative of this kind of literature. When speaking of *spiritual* leadership, what is really in mind is *Christian* leadership, and the Spirit is discussed as necessary for an explanation of a given principle.
24. Harvey, *Anointed with the Spirit and Power*.
25. Howell, *Servants of the Servant*. For a brief overview of a biblical theology of leadership, see Gangel, "Biblical Theology of Leadership," 13–31. It is admittedly "only the most cursory overview" ("Biblical Theology of Leadership," 13).

which allows for more attention to be given to the work of the Spirit through biblical leaders.[26] Also, Harvey's focus in the NT is more general, and the present study uniquely focuses on NT leaders as defined above.

Howell's work is similar as well. His method of biblical theology is similar to the study at hand in that his study "seeks to follow the progressive record of the drama of redemption" by looking at brief profiles of many of the leaders who will be studied in the present study.[27] Also, the present study ends with a section titled, "A Biblical Portrait of a Spiritual Leader," which is similar to Howell's closing essay, "Profile of the Servant-Leader."[28] However, Howell's focus is on the themes of servanthood and leadership, not the Spirit and leadership. Though there will be some overlap between this dissertation and Howell's study, this study's focus guarantees a product that significantly differs from what is offered by Howell.

A Brief Explanation of Biblical Theology and How This Method Is Applied in the Present Study

Just over ten years ago, D. A. Carson stated, "The history of 'biblical theology' is extraordinarily diverse. Everyone does that which is right in his or her own eyes, and calls it biblical theology."[29] Though some of the confusion over defining biblical theology has been cleared within recent years, it remains necessary for a scholar to articulate his understanding of biblical theology if he is going to attempt as much.[30] This section explains and defends biblical theology as a sound method of research methodology for the topic of spiritual leadership.

---

26. For an excellent article on this topic, see Firth, "The Spirit and Leadership," 259–80.

27. Howell, *Servants of the Servant*, 4.

28. Ibid., 295–301. This similarity is not a conscious attempt by the writer to imitate Howell's work.

29. Carson, "Systematic Theology and Biblical Theology," 91.

30. Köstenberger, "The Present and Future of Biblical Theology," 464. After a survey of various types of biblical theology, Köstenberger states, "The past decade and a half has witnessed a tremendous amount of progress in evangelical scholarship on biblical theology" (Ibid.). He continues in the next paragraph, "At the same time, there remains a need for scholars to be precise in defining what they mean when they claim to engage in biblical-theological work and to carefully distinguish between biblical and systematic theology" (Ibid.).

Briefly put, this study understands biblical theology to be "essentially a historical discipline calling for an inductive and descriptive method."[31] This definition implies a contrast between biblical and systematic theology, the latter of which approaches Scripture with preexisting categories and questions in order to relate Scripture to issues of the present day. Biblical theology begins with the text itself and lets the Bible create its own categories and conclusions according to its own themes. To clarify, this approach by no means suggests that systematic theology is unhelpful or unnecessary in any way. Perhaps this study will incidentally unearth some biblical data that are helpful for addressing any related systematic concerns.

As much as possible, this study will recognize the diversity that exists from one biblical book to the next. This study will also take into account the overarching storyline of Scripture. After an initial study of spiritual leadership in the Old and New Testaments, themes that have emerged from this study will be correlated and discussed in relation to broader themes of Scripture and the overarching narrative of Scripture as necessary. The purpose for relating these themes to their broader themes and the Scripture as a whole will be to offset any perceived exaggeration of the importance of the theme at hand.

In defense of this approach to researching the topic of spiritual leadership, several points may be made. First, according to the knowledge of the present writer, the topic of spiritual leadership has not been given a biblical-theological treatment such as this study proposes. Though the nature of this study does not allow for a detailed exegesis of every passage or an in-depth look at certain topics that could call for a dissertation in and of themselves (e.g., the nature of the work of the Spirit in the leadership of Jesus or the apostles), this study shows merit in that it uniquely gives a broad picture of spiritual leadership throughout the Bible. Second, a biblical theology of spiritual leadership creates a means of discovering the continuity and discontinuity that exists between the leaders of God's people in the Old and New Testaments, as well as areas of continuity and discontinuity from one period of biblical history to the next within the testaments. Third, a biblical theology of spiritual leadership recognizes the unity of Scripture as a whole and also allows for the diverse emphases from one biblical book to the next. Fourth, a biblical theology of spiritual leadership sources the topic of spiritual leadership first and foremost in the Scriptures. Fifth, a biblical theology of spiritual

---

31. Ibid., 445. See also the discussion the "Chicago School" of biblical theology by Klink and Lockett in *Understanding Biblical Theology*, 68–70.

leadership allows for the Bible to speak for itself as to what it expects of spiritual leaders, which could give the church and its leaders proper guidance for today. Sixth, if done properly, a biblical theology of spiritual leadership may illustrate how to practice biblical theology in general.

Delimitations and Assumptions of the Present Study

The present study is limited to demonstrating a distinct work of the Spirit in biblical leaders. In light of this narrow aim, this study cannot discuss in detail many significant topics about the Spirit. However, it will be helpful to at least make known the present writer's assumptions about a number of these topics. For example, it was briefly discussed earlier that this study assumes the personality of the Spirit. Other assumptions concerning the Spirit include but are not limited to the identification of the Spirit as God (Acts 5:3–4) and the Spirit's divine nature as shown through attributes such as eternality (Heb 9:14), omnipotence (Luke 1:35; Rom 15:19), omniscience (1 Cor 2:10–11), and omnipresence (Ps 139:7–10).

This study likewise cannot speak in any depth (if at all) to the Spirit's work in other events in the OT and NT. This work includes but is not limited to the following: creation (Gen 1:2); restraint upon the sinfulness of mankind (Gen 6:3); Jesus' incarnation (Luke 1:35); inspiration of Scripture (2 Pet 1:19–21); and works in salvation such as regeneration (John 3:3, 5), sealing (Eph 4:30), sanctification (2 Thess 2:13), and assurance (Rom 8:14–16; 1 John 3:24).

Other topics involving the Spirit will bear more on this study than others, but these topics will not be able to receive the attention they deserve as well. These topics include the New Covenant, Spirit baptism, prophecy, and indwelling. The topic of spiritual gifts will be discussed to a certain degree, but this discussion is limited to an analysis of the gift of leadership in particular.

Another delimitation of this study is the range of data to be included. The writer assumes the inspiration, inerrancy, and preservation of Scripture, as well as its being limited to the sixty-six books of the traditional protestant canon. This understanding of Scripture excludes any discussion of the Spirit in the Apocrypha[32] or writings from intertestamental Judaism.[33]

---

32. For a discussion of the Spirit in the Apocrypha, see Thomas, *The Holy Spirit of God*, 18–22.

33. For a discussion of the Spirit in writings from intertestamental Judaism, see Schweizer, *The Holy Spirit*, 29–45.

Criteria for Inclusion and Exclusion of Biblical Texts

The last introductory matter to discuss is what criteria have been used for the inclusion or exclusion of biblical texts in the present study. As this study begins, these criteria are simple. First, there must be an explicit mention of the Spirit of God with the use of either *rûaḥ* (OT) or *pneuma* (NT). Second, there must be an explicit reference to a biblical leader as defined above. Third, the text should describe the work of the Spirit as having affected the exercise of the leader's leadership.

As this study continues, however, these criteria need to be flexible to also allow for what may seem at first glance to be something other than an explicit reference to the Spirit, the Spirit's work, a biblical leader, or his leadership. Although later texts do not describe these topics in exactly the same way as previous revelation, they refer to these topics by more subtle means that would have nonetheless been clear to the original reader (e.g., quotation, echo, or allusion). This being said, a fourth criterion (if one could call it that) would be to recognize that later texts may refer to the Spirit, the Spirit's work, and the leadership of a biblical leader by some other means than the direct terminology that was used to speak of these topics at first.

Summary and Overview

This study aims to show that a biblical theology of the role of the Spirit in the leadership of God's people demonstrates a distinct work of the Spirit in biblical leaders. Chapter 2 begins the biblical theology of spiritual leadership by examining the OT, and Chapter 3 will examine the NT. As seen above, the data for Chapter 3 is roughly three times as much as that in the OT, which will be reflected in the respective length of each chapter. Chapter 4 will systematize the findings of Chapters 2 and 3 and then discuss the present study's relationship to broader theological concerns and the overarching storyline of Scripture as necessary. Chapter 5 demonstrates how a biblical theology of spiritual leadership informs and illustrates spiritual leadership in the church today. Chapter 5 ends with a biblical portrait of a spiritual leader, and a summary of the entire study is given in Chapter 6.

2

The Role of the Spirit in the Leadership of Old Testament Leaders

Introduction

THE PRESENT CHAPTER WILL demonstrate from the OT that there is a distinct work of the Spirit in biblical leaders by examining passages that describe the leadership of those who functioned as the head of Israel. Each passage below explicitly refers to a biblical leader, the Spirit of God with the use of *rûaḥ*, and how the exercise of leadership was affected by the work of the Spirit. Each passage will be surveyed briefly for its context. The focus is then given to the description of the Spirit and how the Spirit is involved in the exercise of the leader's leadership.

Moses

The Spirit is mentioned three times in relation to Moses' leadership. The first two are found in Num 11:17, 25, a context describing the Spirit's role in the leadership of the seventy elders (cf. 11:17, 25–26). The Spirit's role in the leadership of Moses and the seventy is linked together in context, which necessitates a discussion of both. The Spirit's role in Moses' leadership is described in Isa 63:11 as well.

Numbers 11:17, 25–26

During the wilderness wanderings, Moses requested death from the LORD at one point because "the burden of all this people" was "too heavy" to bear (Num 11:11, 14–15). In response, the LORD commanded Moses to assemble "seventy men from the elders of Israel" and to "bring them to the tent of meeting" (Num 11:16). The LORD then stated the reason for his directives: "I will take some of the Spirit who is upon you, and will put it upon them, and they shall bear the burden of the people with you, so that you may not bear it all alone" (Num 11:17). After Moses gathered the men, the LORD did as he promised. "Then the LORD came down in the cloud and spoke to him, and took some of the Spirit that was on him and put it on the seventy elders" (Num 11:25).

> And as soon as the Spirit rested on them, they prophesied. But they did not continue doing it. Now two men remained in the camp, one named Eldad, and the other named Medad, and the Spirit rested on them. They were among those registered, but they had not gone out to the tent, and so they prophesied in the camp. (Num 11:25–26)

After the LORD put his Spirit on the seventy, "they prophesied. But they did not continue doing it" (Num 11:25). This prophetic event seems to have tangibly confirmed to the seventy that the Spirit was on them as the Spirit was on Moses.[1] Two of the seventy prophesied in the midst of Israel, which seems to have confirmed the Spirit's presence upon the seventy to the nation.[2]

The Spirit is described as being "on" (ʿal) Moses and the seventy elders (Num 11:17, 25). At first glance, the fact that God "took" (ʾṣl) "some" (min) of the Spirit from Moses and then "put" (sym) the Spirit "on" (ʿal) the seventy may seem as if "some" of Moses' Spirit had diminished in order to be rationed out to the seventy. A simpler explanation is that the elders now had the Spirit on them just as the Spirit was on Moses.[3]

---

1. Wood, *The Holy Spirit in the Old Testament*, 110–14, understands 1 Chr 25:1–3 as the filter through which to understand prophecy passages such as Num 11:25–29, 1 Sam 10:6, 10 and 1 Sam 19:20–24. He claims the seventy were singing prophetically. It may have been, however, that they prophesied about the event at hand (cf. 1 Kgs 22:12, 18; 2 Chr 17:7, 9, 11, 17; 20:37).

2. There is debate as to whether or not these men were two of the seventy elders. See Ashley, *The Book of Numbers*, 214–15, and Budd, *Numbers*, 128–29. The point of tension is how to understand the fact that these two "were listed among the elders" (Num 11:26). The list could have referred *specifically* to the seventy, and Num 11:24 refers to the seventy in approximation (Ashley). The list could have also referred to a *general* list of elders, and the elders who prophesied in the camp were not among the seventy chosen to gather at the tent of meeting (Budd). It seems best to understand that these men were among the seventy elders, that they prophesied in the camp, that the nation noticed, and that the elders' enablement to lead was thus made public.

3. Horton states, "The infinite Spirit is not made less when He is shared with others. Ancient writers (as Origen) compared the Spirit on Moses to a lamp used to light 70 others without losing any of its brightness" (*What the Bible Says about the Holy Spirit*, 27).

The context directly connects the role of the Spirit to both the leadership of Moses and the seventy elders. The Spirit that was on Moses was given to the seventy so that both could bear the burden that Israel could sometimes be. The immediate burden at hand was leading a complaining Israel who was dissatisfied with God's regular provision of manna (Num 11:1–10). More broadly, Moses spoke elsewhere of this burden as something that involved judging legal cases that Israelites would bring against one another (Deut 1:9–18; cf. Exod 18:10–27).[4] Though Moses had previously delegated this responsibility to wise and God-fearing men (Exod 18:21, 25), it was not recorded that the Spirit had not been put on these men as God had put the Spirit on the seventy elders. Perhaps Moses could now allow "any hard case" to be solved by the seventy elders and delegate his leadership even further (cf. Num 11:26).

The description of the Spirit on Moses raises the question as to when the Spirit was first put on Moses so that he could lead Israel. Whereas the Spirit had not previously been "put . . . on the seventy elders" (Num 11:25), the Spirit was already "on" Moses (Num 11:17). The Spirit's enablement had evidently been taking place for some time. This enablement may have begun when Moses met the angel of the Lord at the burning bush on Mount Horeb.[5] There the Lord promised Moses, "Certainly I will be with you" (Exod 3:12) and immediately verified this promise to Moses by enabling Moses to perform miracles (Exod 4:1–9).[6] If this scene evidences the beginning of Moses' enablement by the Spirit, Moses' leadership was immediately confirmed in a visible way to himself just as the prophecy of the elders confirmed their leadership to themselves and Israel.

---

4. Moses declared he could not "carry" (*ns'*) the people (Num 11:14). God had laid "the burden" (*masa'*) of the people on him (Num 11:11). Similarly, referring to Exodus 18, Moses recounted how he could not "bear" (*ns'*) by himself the "burden" (*masa'*) of Israel (Deut 1:12).

5. Firth, "The Spirit and Leadership," 265; Gromacki, *The Holy Spirit*, 67; Hildebrandt, *An Old Testament Theology of the Spirit of God*, 22; Rea, *The Holy Spirit in the Bible*, 45. Firth is more tentative concerning this conclusion but leans this way due to the presence of "with" language. God's statement "I will be with you" could imply that he would enable Moses with the Spirit (see below).

6. Hildebrandt, *An Old Testament Theology of the Spirit of God*, 22.

Spiritual Leadership

Isaiah 63:11

The Spirit's enablement of Moses is also described in Isa 63:11. Isaiah encouraged Israel by recalling God's deliverance in times past and referred to the Spirit three times in doing so. One of these references correlates to Moses' leadership (Isa 63:11; cf. 63:10, 14).[7] This reference to the Spirit is found in the second of two questions which asks where God is, and this second question goes on to describe God in terms of His deliverance of Israel through the exodus event:

> Where is He who brought them up out of the sea with the shepherds[8] of His flock? / Where is He who put His Holy Spirit in the midst of [it],[9] / Who caused His glorious arm to go at the right hand of Moses, / Who divided the waters before them to make for Himself an everlasting name, / Who led them through the depths? (Isa 63:11b–13a)

God is described as bringing Israel up out of the sea, dividing the waters, and leading Israel through the depths. Within these statements, the Spirit is said to be in the midst of Israel, which is parallel in thought to God's right arm being shown mighty at the hand of Moses.[10] Thus, as

---

7. Isaiah speaks of Israel's grieving the Spirit (Isa 63:10), and he marks the continued work of the Spirit in that the Spirit gave Israel "rest," something received by Israel after the nation's entrance into and conquest of Canaan (Isa 63:14). That "the Spirit of the LORD gave them rest" (Isa 63:14) perhaps alludes to the Spirit-enabled leadership of Moses just before Israel's entrance into Canaan. The Spirit's giving of rest may also allude to Joshua's Spirit-enabled leadership of Israel during Israel's conquest of the land (cf. Num 27:18; Deut 34:9). For the Spirit's role in the life of Joshua, see below.

8. Manuscripts vary as to whether the term *shepherd* is singular or plural. Oswalt states, "On intentional grounds, while it is easy to see someone changing the pl. to the sg. to accord with the nearby references to Moses, it is difficult to imagine anyone intentionally changing the sg. to a pl. On that basis MT is preferred" (*The Book of Isaiah: Chapters 40–66*, 602).

9. Translations differ as to whether to understand the third person singular masculine suffix as a singular reference to Moses or a collective reference to the shepherds. The parallelism between "His flock" and the suffix would suggest that "it" is the proper translation, which creates a parallel between "it" and Israel. This translation allows the singular suffix to match its referent in number. Moreover, the third person singular masculine suffix is clearly used this way in Isa 63:14 to refer to the singular "cattle."

10. Goldingay does not comment on Isa 63:10–12, but his discussion applies to this text: "wherever the OT refers to God's arm or hand or finger or face or eyes, in dogmatic terms it is speaking of the activity of the Holy Spirit. . . . The Holy Spirit was there and active in OT times, but the language for expressing this activity was more varied than was later the case" ("Was the Holy Spirit Active in Old Testament Times," 18). Goldingay goes

Moses was the human agent whereby God divided the waters and led Israel through the depths of sea, so also was the Spirit the divine agent whose divine power accomplished these actions. Though Isa 63:14 speaks of God's people being led by the Spirit alone,[11] Isa 63:11 describes Moses' role in relation to the activity of the Spirit, implying the Spirit was involved in his leadership during the exodus. Moses' leadership in this instance involved performing miracles and leading God's people out of Egypt.[12]

Summary

Moses experienced the work of the Spirit in multiple ways. His miracles were performed by the power of the Spirit (Isa 63:11), and these miracles confirmed to Israel that Moses was their head who would lead them out of Egypt (Ex 4:1–9). Moses described his leadership of Israel as bearing the difficult burden that Israel could sometimes be (Num 11:11, 14; cf. 11:17), and this language could also be used to describe judging matters of difficulty that arose among the people (Deut 1:9–18). Just as the Spirit enabled Moses to lead Israel in these matters (Num 11:17), the Spirit was given to the seventy elders so that they would be enabled to do the same

---

on to demonstrate his point with examples such as the interchangeability between "the Spirit of God" in Matt 12:28 and "the finger of God" in Luke 11:20.

11. Wood, describes the Spirit's role in Isa 63:14 as a "general providential guidance of Israel" (*The Spirit of God in Biblical Literature*, 46).

12. Some argue that Isaiah's references to the Spirit being in Israel's midst and leading the nation to rest imply that the pillar of cloud and fire is the manifestation of the Spirit that Isaiah had in view and not the work of the Spirit through Moses. See Hamilton, *God's Indwelling Presence*, 39–41; Kline, *Images of the Spirit*, 13–20. As the Spirit hovered over the formless earth in Gen 1:2, so also did God hover over Israel when Israel was in the waste of the wilderness in Deut 32:10–11. The Spirit's hovering presence is assumed to be manifest through the pillar of cloud that led Israel's journey. Likewise, as the angel of presence and the cloud are distinct entities in Exod 14:19, so also the angel and the Spirit are distinct entities in Isa 63:9–11. One may assume further that Isaiah thought of the cloud as a manifestation of the Spirit in the midst of Israel. This understanding does well to bring out both the creation parallels between Gen 1:2 and Deut 32:10–11 as well as the distinction between the angel of presence and the cloud or Spirit. However, one could also conclude the relations of Gen 1:2 to Deut 32:10–11 and Exodus 14 to Isa 63:7–14 to speak more generally to the miraculous power of the Spirit, a more direct connection. The Spirit's power is explicitly in view with relation to creation (Gen 1:2) or God's miracles in the exodus event (Isa 63:10–11). The conclusion that the Spirit is the cloud and fire, however, is less direct. One must assume the Spirit was the cloud in Israel's midst (cf. Gen 1:2 with Deut 32:10–11), that this understanding was such in Isa 63:9–11, and that cloud is thus the manifestation of the Spirit in Exodus 14.

(Num 11:17, 25–26). The confirmation of their leadership was not through miracles but prophecy, also a work of the Spirit (Num 11:25–26).

Joshua

Joshua's experience of the Spirit's work in his leadership is described in Num 27:18 and Deut 34:9. It may be that Isa 63:14 alludes to the Spirit's role in his leadership as well.

Numbers 27:18

Joshua was "the attendant of Moses from his youth" (Num 11:28) and the successor of Moses as the Spirit-enabled leader of Israel. The Spirit's enablement of Joshua's leadership is first described in Num 27:15–23. Moses prayed that God would "appoint a man over the congregation" to lead after his death (Num 27:15–17). In response, God identified Joshua as Israel's next leader and specified why he was uniquely qualified to be this leader: Joshua was "a man in whom is the Spirit" (Num 27:18).

The Spirit is said to be "in" (*bĕ*) Joshua, and the content of Moses' prayer informs the reader as to how exactly the Spirit's being "in" him would be made manifest.[13] Moses prayed that Israel would "not be like sheep which have no shepherd" (Num 27:17). Also, in language suggestive of military exploit, Moses prayed for a man "who will go out and come in before them, and who will lead them out and bring them in," (Num

---

13. Just as the Spirit was already "on" Moses, the Spirit is already "in" Joshua. Scripture may or may not specify the beginning of Joshua's enablement by the Spirit for leadership. His enablement may have begun when he became Moses' aide. Exod 17:8–14 records the first mention of Joshua in which he defeated the Amalekites in battle. Like the judges, Saul, and David who followed him, Joshua's Spirit-enabled leadership over Israel especially involved conquest in battle (see below). Another suggestion is that Joshua was given the Spirit when the seventy elders were given the Spirit as well (Num 11:25, 28). If one understands Joshua to be one of the seventy elders, Joshua's enablement by the Spirit may be precisely identified in Num 11:25. Another suggestion could be that Joshua was not one of the elders, but his enablement began at this point along with the seventy as well. It would seem, however, that Joshua's unique role as Moses' assistant suggests an enablement by the Spirit that preceded Num 11:25, perhaps indicated by Joshua's military success in Exod 17:13. Hildebrandt states, "Although the endowment of *rûaḥ* is specifically noted as taking place at the same time as the seventy elders received the *rûaḥ*, Joshua's role in leadership was distinct" (*An Old Testament Theology of the Spirit of God*, 109).

27:17).¹⁴ The LORD replied to Moses and said to take Joshua, lay his hands on him before Israel, and commission him with authority (Num 27:18–20). As a result, at Joshua's "command they shall go out and at his command they shall come in" (Num 27:21).

Deuteronomy 34:9

The role of the Spirit in Joshua's leadership is explicitly mentioned next in Deut 34:9, a text which finds its background in Num 27:15–23.¹⁵ After Moses' death (Deut 34:1–8), Joshua is identified as Israel's leader and is described as one who "was full of the spirit of wisdom, for Moses had laid his hands on him" (Deut 34:9).

Many translations and scholars understand Moses' authority as "the spirit of wisdom" rather than "the Spirit of wisdom."¹⁶ However, Joshua's role as successor to the Spirit-enabled leader of Israel along with his description in Num 27:18 suggests otherwise. Also, there are other references that clearly speak of a person being "full of" or "filled with" (*ml'*) the Spirit of God (Exod 31:3; 35:31), suggesting that Joshua could be said to be "full of" or "filled with" the Spirit in Deut 34:9 as well.¹⁷ If Deut 34:9 refers to the Spirit as the source of Joshua's wisdom, this wisdom would assumably be shown through his leadership of Israel as the nation's shepherd and commander in battle (cf. Num 27:17, 21).¹⁸

---

14. Ashley states, "These expressions, although not necessarily military in reference (e.g., 2 K. 11:8), are predominantly so (e.g., Deut. 31:2–3; Josh. 14:11; 1 Sam. 18:13, 16; 29:6; 1 K. 3:7), and the military connotation is appropriate to the context. The major task of Moses' successor would be the predominantly military one of conquest and division of Canaan" (*The Book of Numbers*, 551,).

15. Firth, "The Spirit and Leadership," 267–68.

16. Ibid.

17. Harvey, *Anointed with Spirit and Power*, 19, points out that Isaiah later equates the Spirit of the LORD with the Spirit of wisdom in Isa 11:2, a text that likely finds its background in part in Deut 34:9. Exodus 31:3 may provide some background to Isa 11:2 as well, but Deut 34:9 is the more likely choice in that the wisdom of Exod 31:3 has to do with craftsmanship and not leadership. See the discussion of Isa 11:2 below.

18. Besides the passages that explicitly describe the Spirit's role in Joshua's leadership, parallels between Joshua and Moses may imply Joshua's Spirit-enabled leadership as well. Hildebrandt comments, "One of the similar miracles performed through Joshua was the parting of the water (Josh 3:17; cf. Moses in Exod 14:21–23, 29; 15:8). Both leaders interceded for the nation (Josh 7:7; cf. Deut 9:25–29), and both met the LORD on sacred ground (Josh 5:15; cf. Exod 3:5)" (Hildebrandt, *An Old Testament Theology of the*

Isaiah 63:14

It was seen above that Isa 63:11 described the Spirit's role in Moses' leadership in the exodus event. Isaiah then summarized Israel's conquest in Canaan in this way: "the Spirit of the LORD gave them rest" (Isa 63:14; cf. Josh 21:44; 23:1). Though Isaiah does not refer to Joshua, he does refer to the Spirit's guidance of Israel during the conquest of Canaan, something that took place under Joshua's leadership. This general description of the Spirit's leadership may or may not assume the role of Joshua as a leader. Horton's comments are helpful: "Through Spirit-filled leaders they were brought into victory and blessing. But the real Guide was the always the Spirit of the LORD."[19]

Summary

The LORD identified Joshua as a man in whom the Spirit resided in response to Moses' prayer for Israel's next leader (Num 27:18). The Spirit's work in Joshua's leadership would enable him to be Israel's shepherd and commander in battle (Num 27:17, 21) by giving him the wisdom to do so (Deut 34:9). When referring to Israel's conquest over Canaan, Isaiah omitted any reference to Joshua and spoke of Israel as being led by the Spirit alone (Isa 63:14).

The Judges

The next leaders of Israel whose leadership involved the work of the Spirit are the four judges Othniel, Gideon, Jephthah, and Samson. The similarity of their experiences of the Spirit allows them to be treated together below. Daniel Block summarizes the broader context of the book of Judges in which each of their records is found:

> The major part, the "Book of Deliverers" (3:7—16:31), describes the consequences of Israel's Canaanization and Yahweh's response. The collection of "hero-stories" has its own specific prologue (3:1–6) in which the reader is reminded of the problematic historical and spiritual background for the following hero-stories. The sequence of six cycles of "apostasy-punishment-cry of pain-deliverance" not only expresses the persistence of the issue; it demonstrates the

---

Spirit of God, 109).

19. Horton, *What the Bible Says about the Holy Spirit*, 66.

increasing intensity of the nation's depravity. The arrangement of the "hero-stories" reflects this process so that in the end we are left with "antiheroes" rather than truly great men of God.[20]

Within this context of Israel's increasing "Canaanization," the Spirit's work is seen in four leaders despite the fact that these leaders increasingly engage in sin as well.

Judges 3:10 (Othniel)

The first of the four judges is Othniel. "The Spirit of the LORD came upon him, so that he became Israel's judge and went to war" (Judg 3:10 NIV).[21] The explicit mention of the Spirit was necessary either to distinguish Othniel as Israel's primary leader from his present role of leadership (cf. Josh 15:17; Judg 1:3)[22] or to clue the reader to what he would otherwise not assume because "Othniel was a proselyte conscripted into leadership."[23] The Spirit "came upon" Othniel (Judg 3:10), and he thus "prevailed over" the king of Mesopotamia (Judg 3:11) and "the land had rest forty years" (Judg 3:12).

The terminology describing how the Spirit "came" (*hyh*) "upon" (*'āl*) Othniel (Judg 3:10; or Jephthah, for that matter; cf. 11:29) stands in contrast to verbs used later of Gideon (Judg 6:34) and Samson (Judg 13:25; 14:6, 19; 15:14; see below). The Spirit enabled Othniel to effectively lead Israel in battle and conquer the nation's enemies.

---

20. Block, *Judges, Ruth*, 58.

21. The ESV gives a more literal rendering: "The Spirit of the LORD was upon him, and he judged Israel" (Judg 3:10). The translation of the NIV is preferred because it communicates both the Spirit's coming ("came upon") and the result ("so that") of that coming, i.e., Othniel's successful leadership as a judge. See Firth, "The Spirit and Leadership," 270. Firth notes that "Spirit of Yahweh" is a stylistic choice to clearly point out that Yahweh and not something else is involved due to Israel's paganism during this time.

22. Firth, "The Spirit and Leadership," 271–72. Othniel served as one of Israel's greater warriors but would now be one of the nation's Spirit-enabled judges. Joshua 15:17 and Judg 1:3 record Othniel's victory over Kiriath-sepher.

23. Block, "Empowered by the Spirit of God," 57.

Spiritual Leadership

Judges 6:34 (Gideon)

The second judge is Gideon. To overcome his timidity (cf. Judg 6:15, 27; 7:11–15, 20–21),[24] "the Spirit of the LORD clothed Gideon" (Judg 6:34) who immediately rallied 32,000 men for battle (Judg 7:3).[25] This mass was whittled to a mere three hundred (Judg 7:7) in order to highlight the LORD's role in Gideon's defeat of the Midianites (Judg 7:2; cf. 7:15–25; 8:28). Though Gideon's military career ended with Israel in spiritual prostitution (Judg 8:27), "the land enjoyed peace forty years" (Judg 8:28).

Sinclair Ferguson understands the Spirit to be the one who was "clothed" (*lbš*) with Gideon, thus highlighting the "violent, naked power of God" in that "when the Spirit comes, he clothes himself with those on whose lives he descends (Jdg. 6:34; 1 Ch. 12:8; 2 Ch. 24:20)."[26] In response to this conclusion, Eugene Merrill states, "However, this rendering requires the verb to be reflexive (perhaps Piel or Niphal), not Qal as here."[27] Block seems to capture the thought best: "This idiom expresses in more dramatic form the notion expressed earlier in 3:10" (i.e., the Spirit's coming upon Othniel).[28]

The Spirit "clothed" Gideon and gave him the necessary courage to rally Israel's troops for battle. Even when his army was reduced to 300 men, the Spirit enabled Gideon to effectively administer a covert operation and achieve victory over the Midianites.

---

24. Gideon saw his clan as "the weakest in Manasseh" and himself as "the least in my father's house (Judg 6:15). In destroying the local altar of Baal, "because he was too afraid of his family and the men of the town to do it by day, he did it by night" (Judg 6:27; cf. 6:25–26). The LORD promised victory over the Midianites to Gideon (Judg 7:9) but then acknowledged Gideon's fear (7:10) and reassured him that he would have victory over the Midianites (Judg 7:11–15). Gideon may have showed his timidity again by commanding his son to kill two men instead of doing it himself (Judg 7:20–21).

25. Fleming states, "The effect of the Spirit is a sign of divine selection that will persuade the people to follow, when the king has no automatic institutional authority" ("Anointing," 35). This claim is echoed by Hildebrandt, *An Old Testament Theology of the Spirit of God*, 115.

26. Ferguson, *The Holy Spirit*, 27.

27. Merrill discusses this term in relation to "stir" in Judg 13:25: "it seems best to see the idiom [*lbš*] as an expression of the Spirit's wrapping Gideon with his power and glory" ("The Samson Saga and Spiritual Leadership," 289).

28. Block, *Judges*, 272. Likewise, Firth, "The Spirit and Leadership," 273, sees no special meaning in "clothed" in Judg 6:34.

Judges 11:29 (Jephthah)

The third of the four judges is Jepthah. "The Spirit of the Lord came upon Jephthah" (Judg 11:29 NIV),[29] and Jephthah "devastated twenty towns" and "subdued Ammon" (Judg 11:33 NIV). Unfortunately, Jephthah vowed to sacrifice the first thing to greet him upon his return home if he returned a victor and consequently sacrificed his daughter (Judg 11:30–31, 34–35, 39).[30] Thereafter, "Jephthah led Israel six years" (Judg 12:6). Unlike the accounts of Othniel and Gideon, there is no mention of rest or peace.

The Spirit "came" (*hyh*) "upon" (*āl*) Jephthah (Judg 11:29), and Jephthah then led Israel to victory in battle. The terminology describing his experience of the Spirit and military victory is similar to that of Othniel (Judg 3:10). The primary difference between the two would be that Jephthah's flaws are explicitly described, whereas Othniel's flaws are not. As for Gideon, he created an idol, but Jephthah's sin of child sacrifice appears to be worse. The omission of rest for the nation suggests that Jephthah may have achieved victory, but the Lord's deliverance of Israel was more short-lived than before.

Judges 13:25; 14:6, 19; 15:14 (Samson)

The final and fourth judge is Samson. The Spirit's role in his life is given explicit reference four times (Judg 13:25; 14:6, 19; 15:14) and implied once as well (Judg 16:20).

Judges 13:25

It is not immediately clear what Samson's resultant activity was after "the Spirit of the Lord began to stir him while he was in Mahaneh Dan" (Judg 13:25). Kevin McCune gives a brief but helpful survey of the use of the verb *p'm* (here translated "stir"):

---

29. As with the description of the Spirit's coming upon Othniel (Judg 3:10), the NIV better communicates the concept of the Spirit's coming upon Jephthah (Judg 11:29). The ESV gives a more literal translation: "Then the Spirit of the Lord was upon Jephthah" (Judg 11:29).

30. Firth, "The Spirit and Leadership," 274, comments, "It is notable that it is only when he has confessed that Yahweh is the judge that we finally reach a point where Yahweh recognizes Jephthah." Judges 11:12–28 is followed by the reception of the Spirit in Judg 11:29.

All four usages [of *pʿm*] outside of Judges 13:25 refer to someone's inner turmoil and distress. Three of them (Gen 41:8; Dan 2:1, 3) specifically relate the distress to the person's spirit, denoting deep inner conflict. The writer of Psalm 77, a lament psalm, cries out in verse four, 'I am so troubled [*pʿm*], that I cannot speak.'[31]

It would appear that Samson was provoked in his spirit by the Spirit of the LORD to be righteously distressed over the Philistine oppression of Israel.

Judges 14:6, 19; 15:14

Three other texts show Samson to be enabled by the Spirit to exercise super-human strength. First, "the Spirit of the LORD rushed upon him, and although he had nothing in his hand, he tore the lion in pieces as one tears a young goat" (Judg 14:6).[32] Second, "the Spirit of the LORD rushed upon him, and he went down to Ashkelon and struck down thirty men of the town" (Judg 14:19).[33] Third, "the Spirit of the LORD rushed upon him, and the ropes that were on his arms [which bound him as a prisoner] became as flax that has caught fire, and his bonds melted off his hands. And he found a fresh jawbone of a donkey . . . and with it he struck 1,000 men" (Judg 15:14–15).[34]

Judges 16:20

It is strongly implied in Judg 16:20 that the Spirit departed from Samson in connection with the removal of his hair, a violation of his Nazarite vow

---

31. McCune, "Theocratic Anointing in the Old Testament," 53–54. Block explains this "stirring" as a "divinely induced restlessness" in Samson used by God "to incite the Philistines and thereby disturb the comfortable *status quo* that existed between them and Israel" ("Empowered by the Spirit of God," 45).

32. Merrill states, "The verb here [*šsʿ*] . . . in the Piel means to tear to pieces" ("The Samson Saga and Spiritual Leadership," 290).

33. Merrill comments, "No weapon is named, so one is free to speculate that he might have torn them limb from limb just as he had dispatched the lion" (Ibid., 291).

34. The verb used for the Spirit's movement upon Samson in Judg 14:6, 14:19, and 15:14 is *ṣlḥ*, a verb difficult to define due to its infrequent and varied use in the qal stem. Cf. *HALOT*, "צלח," 1965. Block is helpful: "The verb *ṣālaḥ* occurs in only two other contexts, in one of which (2 Sa 19:18) its meaning is uncertain. But Amos 5:6 is instructive. Here it is used of fire breaking out and consuming everything in its path, suggesting a sudden burst of unrestrained energy" ("Empowered by the Spirit of God," 45).

(cf. Judg 13:5, 7, with Judg 16:17 and Num 6:5).[35] His enemies removed his hair (Judg 16:19), "his strength left him" (Judg 16:19), and it is said that "the LORD had left him" as well (Judg 16:20). His strength was gone, as was the LORD, which implies the Spirit's departure as well.[36]

Summary

The role of the Spirit in the life of Samson is somewhat unexpected given Samson's disregard for his Nazarite restrictions,[37] his immoral desire for pagan women (Judg 14:1; 16:1), and his passion for vengeance (Judg 14:19; 15:3–5; 16:28–30). The Spirit stirred Samson's spirit to be troubled over the Philistine oppression and then gave him unnatural strength in order to protect him from the lion (Judg 14:6) and to kill over 1,000 Philistines (Judg 14:19; 15:14). In response to Samson's request, it seems the Spirit strengthened him "just once more" (Judg 16:28) to dislodge "the two central pillars" of the Philistine temple and kill "all the lords of the Philistines . . . about 3,000 men and women" (Judg 16:27, 29–30). The absence of reference to the Spirit in Samson's final feat may have been God's tacit disapproval of his lifestyle as a whole.[38] Before his death, Samson "led Israel twenty years" (Judg 16:31). He did not give the nation rest, and he battled alone and apart from Israel's armies.

Other Judges

The Spirit's role in the leadership of the judges is only described in the stories of Othniel, Gideon, Jephthah, and Samson. The leadership of judges such as Ehud and Deborah are recorded in detail as well, but the leadership of the rest of the judges is given hardly any detail at all, let alone a description of the Spirit being at work in their leadership. Firth claims that Ehud's

---

35. Howell notes that though no power was inherent to Samson's hair, Samson's revelation to Delilah was "an arrogant rejection of his Nazarite identity" (*Servants of the Servant*, 59–60).

36. Block, *Judges*, 461–62.

37. In addition to his rejection of the vow concerning his hair, Samson also violated the command to not touch a dead body when he ate honey from the carcass of the lion that he had slain (Judg 14:8–9; cf. Num 6:6).

38. Block notes that Samson's demise was marked by "shortsighted vision," personal vengeance, and an impersonal relation to Yahweh (calling to him as "God" and not "LORD"; cf. Judg 16:23–24; Ibid., 467–68).

assassination and Deborah's role as a prophetess mark them out to be leaders, removing the need for any description of the Spirit.[39] Firth also claims that the absence of a narrative for the other judges does not allow for one to "judge their experience of the Spirit."[40]

Though many of the judges do not have narratives as do the others, there is slight evidence to suggest the role of the Spirit in the leadership of these judges. If the description of Othniel's experience as the first judge was paradigmatic for the judges to follow, it could be that they, too, experienced the Spirit's work in their leadership. Firth states, "The brief account of Othniel (Judg. 3:7–11) provides the pattern against which the other judges are measured, perhaps because this story is itself drawn almost entirely from formulae in Judges 2:11–19."[41] Though Firth sees the absence of narrative as reason to shy away from assumptions about the Spirit (see above), it could be that Judg 2:11–19 somehow implies the role of the Spirit in a way that is explicitly drawn out in the narrative of Othniel. If this is the case, the Spirit's role would be assumed in the leadership of the other judges despite the absence of narrative and any description of the Spirit's role in their leadership.

It may be that a statement in Judg 2:18 implies the role of the Spirit in the leadership of all the judges: "the LORD was with the judge." In the discussion of Samson above, it was concluded that the loss of both Samson's strength and the LORD (Judg 16:20; "the LORD had left him") could be understood as the departure of the Spirit as well. Though terminology referring to the Spirit may be absent, the concept of the LORD being with a leader could include the idea of the Spirit's work through his leadership as well.

The fact that the Spirit is explicitly mentioned in relation to Gideon, Jephthah, and Samson may strengthen the thought that the Spirit's role is implied in the leadership of the other judges. It would seem the sins of cowardice (Gideon), child-sacrifice (Jephthah), or immorality and disregard for one's vows (Samson) would disqualify one from leading Israel and thus disqualify him from enjoying the work of the Spirit in his leadership as well (as eventually was the case with Samson). The Spirit's mention for these three may have been necessary in order for readers to know that the Spirit's work was still present despite their disobedience.[42] At the same time, these

---

39. Firth, "The Spirit and Leadership," 270–71.
40. Ibid., 270.
41. Ibid., 271.
42. Firth states that Judges continues to develop a theme begun in the Pentateuch:

conclusions can only be tentative. The Spirit's role is explicitly described in the leadership of only four of the judges.[43]

Summary

The Spirit enabled Othniel to lead Israel in battle and effectively conquer her enemies (Judg 3:10). The Spirit not only enabled Gideon to do the same, but to do so in spite of his timid and fearful nature (Judg 6:34). Jephthah was enabled by the Spirit to lead Israel to conquer her enemies as well (Judg 11:29). Samson was moved by the Spirit to be righteously distressed over Israel's oppression (Judg 13:25), but his sinful choices led him into situations in which only he himself could attack the Philistines (Judg 14:19; 15:14; cf. 14:6). His persistent disobedience eventually forfeited him the enablement of the Spirit (Judg 16:20). Other judges may have been enabled by the Spirit as well (cf. Judg 2:18), but there is no explicit description of the Spirit in their leadership. Most of these judges are not even given a lengthy narrative that would provide the data to make a conclusion one way or the other.

For the judges whose leadership is described as involving the work of the Spirit, this work is somewhat surprising when one considers their acts of disobedience. Gideon created an idol, Jephthah sacrificed his daughter, and Samson was disobedient in multiple ways. The Spirit's role in their leadership was given on occasion for defeating the enemies at hand. When acting according to the Spirit's enablement, these men carried out the purposes of God. Apart from this enablement, however, the Spirit's work in these leaders is difficult to see, if one can see it at all.[44]

"The experience of the Spirit is generally not when they begin to lead but when their leadership needs to be recognized" (Ibid., 276–77).

43. Deborah was a prophetess (Judg 4:4), a role which assumes the Spirit's work in prophecy (cf. 2 Pet 1:20–21). In view of the discussion above, the question would be whether or not the Spirit's work extended to her leadership over Israel as well. Her role shares similarities to prophet-leaders such as Joseph and Daniel, and it could be that the Spirit was at work through her leadership as well. (See the discussion of Joseph and Daniel in Chapter 4.)

44. It should be noted that, despite their flaws, Gideon, Samson, and Jephthah are said to be among those who are "commended through their faith" (Heb 11:32, 39). Apart from their description in Hebrews, there seems to be little to no evidence to otherwise make this conclusion.

Saul

Saul's experience of the Spirit is similar to the judges before him and yet unique in some ways as well. Four passages describe the role of the Spirit in the leadership of Saul.

First Samuel 10:6–7, 10

The first mention of Saul and the Spirit is found in the record of Saul's call to be the first of Israel's kings. Samuel anointed Saul to be king (1 Sam 10:1) and told Saul of three signs that would confirm to him that he indeed had been called to be Israel's first king.[45] The third sign involved the Spirit's work through Saul to prophesy: "the Spirit of the LORD will rush upon you, and you will prophesy with them and be turned into another man" (1 Sam 10:6).[46] Similar to the prophecy that confirmed the leadership of the seventy elders under Moses (cf. Num 11:25–26), this prophecy would function to confirm that Saul had received the Spirit for leadership: "Now when these signs meet you, do what your hand finds to do, for God is with you" (1 Sam

---

45. Hildebrandt, *An Old Testament Theology of the Spirit of God*, 120. The three signs were as follows: (1) encountering two men who would announce to Saul that his lost donkeys had been found (1 Sam 10:2); (2) encountering three men who respectively carried three goats, a jug of wine, and three loaves of bread, two of which would be given to Saul (1 Sam 10:3–4); and (3) the Spirit's mighty coming as evidenced by prophecy (1 Sam 10:6). Firth, "The Spirit and Leadership," 297, notes that the third sign is fully narrated, showing its importance.

46. Some understand Saul's being "changed into another man" to refer to regeneration. E.g., Wood, *The Holy Spirit in the Old Testament*, 134, claims Saul to be a believer on the basis of being Israel's first king. Others, however, understand Saul's change differently. Pettegrew, *The New Covenant Ministry of the Holy Spirit*, 23, explains 1 Sam 10:6 in terms of empowerment for service, not regeneration. Hildebrandt is more specific: "The nature of the 'changed heart' may refer to the courage and strength that are part of the charisma needed to perform a deed of valor" (*An Old Testament Theology of the Spirit of God*, 121). He parallels Saul to Gideon in that they both courageously rallied troops for battle (Judg 8:20; 1 Sam 11:8). Rea, *The Holy Spirit in the Bible*, 56, points out that Israel's soldiers were described similarly in 1 Sam 10:26. Whether or not Saul was regenerate is hard to say. Despite a eulogy in which David spoke of Saul and Jonathan in positive terms (2 Sam 1:19–27), Saul's life showed a pattern of sin, his actions were out of accord with the desires of God's heart (cf. 1 Sam 13:14), and his epitaph in 1 Chr 10:13–14 spoke of him as one punished by God for disobedience. Saul's experience of the Spirit for prophecy was genuine but does not necessarily involve regeneration, as was the case with the pagan prophet Balaam (Num 24:2; cf. 31:8, 16; 2 Pet 2:15; Rev 2:14). See Simpson, *The Holy Spirit*, 171–78.

10:7).⁴⁷ After the first two signs had taken place (cf. 1 Sam 10:9), "a group of prophets met him, and the Spirit of God rushed upon him, and he prophesied among them" (1 Sam 10:10). Though the spectators were unsure why Saul was prophesying (1 Sam 10:11–12), Saul would have taken this event to be a confirmation of his call to be Israel's first king. The terminology of the Spirit's having "rushed" (ṣlḥ) "upon" (ʿal) Saul (1 Sam 10:6, 10) is the same as found in the description of Samson (Judg 14:6, 19; 15:14).

First Samuel 11:6

The second mention of the Spirit's role in relation to Saul's leadership is similar to that of the judges. When told of the threat of the Ammonites' looming invasion of Jabesh-gilead (1 Sam 11:5), "the Spirit of God rushed upon Saul when he heard these words, and his anger was greatly kindled" (1 Sam 11:6). Saul consequently dismembered a yoke of oxen and sent the pieces to the Israelites as an example of what would happen to those who would not join him. As a result, "they came out as one man" (1 Sam 11:7), and Saul led Israel to victory (1 Sam 11:11). These actions were in accord with Samuel's instructions: "do for yourself what the occasion requires, for God is with you" (1 Sam 10:7).

A number of similarities exist between Saul and Israel's previous leaders, particularly the judges.⁴⁸ As with Samson (Judg 14:6, 19; 15:14), the Spirit "rushed upon" Saul to act upon his righteous anger (1 Sam 11:6). Similar to the story of Gideon (Judg 6:34–35; cf. 7:3), the Spirit's work in the leadership of Saul resulted in rallying Israel for battle (1 Sam 11:7). Also similar to Gideon (Judg 6:15, 72; 7:10), the Spirit's work through Saul included courage to overcome his cowardice (cf. 1 Sam 9:21; 10:21–22; 15:17).⁴⁹ As with Othniel (Judg 3:10), Gideon (7:15–25; 8:28), Jephthah (11:33), and Joshua (Num 27:17–18), the Spirit's work through Saul included the effective leadership necessary to achieve victory in battle (1 Sam 11:11).

---

47. Harvey, *Anointed with Spirit and Power*, 22. See also Csövek, *Three Seasons of Charismatic Leadership*, 56. Csövek notes that 1 Sam 10:6–10 echoes Moses' experience in that Saul was given personal confirmation of his newfound leadership over Israel (1 Sam 10:1–10; cf. Exod 4:1–9). Csövek also notes the similarity in terminology that describes both Moses and Saul in an earlier passage (Ibid., 49). Saul would come to rescue Israel from oppression (1 Sam 9:16) just as Moses in times past (cf. Exod 3:7–9).

48. Cf. Wright, *Knowing the Holy Spirit through the Old Testament*, 41–42; Firth, "The Spirit and Leadership," 277.

49. Rea, *The Holy Spirit in the Bible*, 56.

Spiritual Leadership

First Samuel 16:14

The third mention of the Spirit's role in relation to Saul describes the Spirit's departure from Saul. A recurring theme in Saul's kingship is his persistent disobedience.[50] He disobeyed instructions from the prophet Samuel more than once (1 Sam 13:8–9, 13–14; 15:3, 9–11; cf. 28:18),[51] attacked the innocent city of Nob (1 Sam 22:18–19), and consulted the witch of Endor (1 Sam 28:3–25; cf. Deut 18:10–11; 1 Chr 10:13). As a result, Saul's kingdom would not continue (1 Sam 13:14; 15:28), which meant that God had rejected Saul from being Israel's king (1 Sam 15:23, 26; 16:1). It seems clear that this rejection of Saul stands behind why "the Spirit of the LORD departed from Saul" (1 Sam 16:14), especially when the preceding verse describes that the Spirit "rushed upon" David (1 Sam 16:13). David would be Israel's next king, an individual who was repeatedly noted for his obedience and devotion to God (cf. 1 Sam 13:14; 1 Kgs 3:14).

It was concluded above that the loss of Samson's strength and the fact that "the LORD had left him" (Judg 16:20) implied the departure of the Spirit from Samson. This conclusion is strengthened by the description of the Spirit's departure from Saul. Just as "the LORD left" Samson (16:20), so also "the Spirit of the LORD departed from Saul" (1 Sam 16:14). The verbs describing departure are one and the same (*swr*). What is implied for Samson is explicitly described for Saul.

This conclusion is further strengthened by a later description of Saul as well. "Saul was afraid of David because the LORD was with him but had departed from Saul" (18:12). Whether "the Spirit of the LORD" in 1 Sam 16:14 or "the LORD" in 1 Sam 18:12, both are said to have "departed from Saul," and the verb of departure (*swr*) is the same in both statements.[52] It is apparent that "the LORD" at times may assume the role of the Spirit when used with reference to the leader of Israel. For both Samson and Saul, the Spirit departed as a result of their persistent disobedience to the LORD.

---

50. For a summary of Saul's acts of disobedience, see Howell, *Servants of the Servant*, 84–86.

51. Ibid., 68. Howell reasons that Saul's severe punishment in 1 Samuel 13 stemmed from his high accountability as the national leader of Israel. This is similar to Moses' story in Numbers 20.

52. Apart from the subject, word order, and the gender of the verb, the clause is much the same. First Samuel 16:14 states *wĕrûaḥ yhwh sārâ mēʿim šāʾûl*. The clause in 1 Sam 18:12 is *ûmēʿim šāʾûl sār. . . yhwh*.

Though Samson was unaware of this departure (Judg 16:20), this was not the case for Saul (1 Sam 18:12).[53]

The Spirit's departure from Saul is evidenced in numerous ways. Saul lost courage for battle (1 Sam 17:11), wisdom during battle (1 Sam 14:24), and success in battle (1 Sam 31:1–10). He went against God's purposes in attempting to kill David (1 Sam 19:1; 20:31; 26:1–2; et al) and thought little to nothing of killing innocents in his attempt to do so (1 Sam 22:18–19). Moreover, he was terrorized by an evil spirit as well (1 Sam 16:14; cf. 16:15, 16, 23; 18:10; 19:9).[54]

First Samuel 19:20–24

The final description of the Spirit's role in relation to Saul acts as a counterpart to Saul's experience of the Spirit in 1 Sam 10:10 (cf. 1 Sam 10:6). Though Saul would eventually lose his kingdom (1 Sam 13:14; 15:28) and had already lost the Spirit (1 Sam 16:14), he still held his throne for a time. During this time, he repeatedly attempted to kill David and came close to capturing David at Naioth in Ramah. He sent three groups of messengers, each of which did not capture David but ended up prophesying with Samuel and his prophets instead (1 Sam 19:20–21). Saul himself then attempted to capture David, and "the Spirit of God came upon him also, and as he went he prophesied until he came to Naioth in Ramah" (1 Sam 19:23).[55] He then "stripped off his clothes, and he too prophesied before Samuel and lay down naked all that day and all that night" (1 Sam 19:24).[56]

---

53. Howard, "The Transfer of Power," 476.

54. Wood, *The Holy Spirit in the Old Testament*, 127–36, identifies the spirit as a demon. A more common position is to not understand the spirit as a demon, but some form of torment imposed by God upon Saul as a punishment. See Block, "Empowered by the Spirit of God," 51–52; Firth, "Is Saul Also Among the Prophets," 298–302; Hildebrandt, *An Old Testament Theology of the Spirit of God*, 170–72; Howard, "The Transfer of Power from Saul to David in 1 Sam 16:13–14," 481–83; Kaiser, et al., *Hard Sayings of the Bible*, 211–12.

55. Wood, *The Holy Spirit in the Old Testament*, 110–16, sees Saul as engaging in singing, a form of prophecy. He cites 1 Chr 25:1–3 as the filter through which to understand difficult prophecy passages such as Num 11:25–29, 1 Sam 10:6, 10 and 1 Sam 19:20–24. Wood explains Saul and his messengers as needing to prophesy in order to praise God and approve of David as His choice for king. A number of authors follow Wood or take a similar view. See also Horton, *What the Bible Says about the Holy Spirit*, 24, and Howell, *Servants of the Servant*, 75–76.

56. Firth, "Is Saul Also Among the Prophets? Saul's Prophecy in 1 Samuel 19:23,"

As earlier (1 Sam 10:11–12), the proverbial question was asked, "Is Saul also among the prophets?" (1 Sam 19:24). The difference between Saul's two episodes of prophecy seems to be that, whereas the first prophecy verified the Spirit's enablement for his kingship, this prophecy suggests his kingship's end.[57] In attempting to capture David and keep the throne, Saul was overtaken by the Spirit of God in spite of his evil desires. He then prophesied and allowed David to escape. God was no longer with him in the sense that the Spirit ceased to enable him to do as the occasion required (cf. 1 Sam 10:7; 18:12).

Summary

Saul experienced the Spirit's work in multiple ways. He was enabled by the Spirit to prophesy at the beginning and end of his kingship (1 Sam 10:10; 19:23–24). Like the seventy elders, his prophecy at the beginning of his leadership confirmed that the Spirit would enable him to effectively lead the nation (1 Sam 10:6–7). The Spirit enabled him to lead Israel to victory in battle (1 Sam 11:6–7). Because of his persistent disobedience, Saul lost the Spirit's enablement (1 Sam 16:14). Stated another way, the LORD was no longer with Saul (cf. 1 Sam 18:12).

David

The Old Testament mentions the Spirit three or four times in relation to David, two of which are found in the context of his leadership, 1 Sam 16:13 and Ps 51:11.[58]

302–04, brings out the fact that the niphal and hithphael uses of *nbʾ* ("to prophesy") suggest Saul and his messengers were unable to control their prophetic activity The hithpael is used of Saul and his messengers in 19:20, 21 (2x), 23, and the niphal is used of the prophets in 19:20. The hithpael is also used of Saul in 10:6, highlighting the change to be God's control over him. The niphal is never used negatively. Hildebrandt helpfully comments that the prophecy of 1 Sam 19:20–24 serves to show (1) "that Saul and his men are restrained"; (2) Saul is "stripped not only of his kingly robes but of his dignity and ability to function as ruler over the people"; and (3) David is contrasted with Saul (*An Old Testament Theology of the Spirit of God*, 171–72). Dumbrell, "Spirit and Kingdom of God in the Old Testament," 7, discusses this variance between the forms as well.

57. Cf. Hildebrandt, *An Old Testament Theology of the Spirit of God*, 171–72.

58. The third mention of the Spirit is found in David's last words and specifies the source of David's words: "The Spirit of the LORD spoke by me" (2 Sam 23:2). The fourth

First Samuel 16:13

The first mention of the Spirit in relation to David's leadership is found immediately before the description of the Spirit's departure from Saul (1 Sam 16:14). In carrying out God's instructions to anoint a king to replace Saul (1 Sam 16:1–12), "Samuel took the horn of oil and anointed him in the midst of his brothers; and the Spirit of the LORD came mightily upon David from that day forward" (1 Sam 16:13). Though the Spirit of the LORD is similarly described as having "rushed" (*ṣlḥ*) "upon" (*'el*) David as with Saul (cf. 1 Sam 10:6, 10; 11:6),[59] David's enablement is unique in that the Spirit is described as having rushed upon David "from that day forward," suggesting an ongoing enablement by the Spirit.[60] This enablement is similar to that of Moses (cf. Num 11:17; see above) and perhaps Joshua (cf. Num 27:18; see above) and stands in contrast to leaders such as Samson and Saul who are

---

mention of the Spirit is reflected in some translations of 1 Chr 28:12 which speaks of the plans of the temple as having been given to David by means of the Spirit (NIV, NKJV). For authors who support this translation, see Harvey, *Anointed with Spirit and Power*, 24–25; Horton, *What the Bible Says about the Holy Spirit*, 50; Inch, *Saga of the Spirit*, 50; and Rea, *The Holy Spirit in the Bible*, 51. While it seems that the Spirit did reveal to David the plans for the temple (cf. 1 Chr 28:19), David did not build the temple himself, and this activity of the Spirit is limited to the reception of revelation and not the exercise of leadership in some way.

59. The Spirit's rushing "upon" David is described with the preposition *'el* and not the typical preposition *'al* used with the Spirit's rushing "upon" Samson and Saul (cf. Judg 14:6, 19; 15:14; 1 Sam 10:6, 10; 11:6). There is no great significance to this switch of prepositions since *'el* "often alternates with לְעַ [*'al*]" (HALOT, s.v., "אֶל," 50). The Spirit's activity is not always described with a verb but may be said to simply be "on" (*'al*) someone, as is the case with Moses and the seventy elders (Num 11:17, 25a). The preposition "on" (*'al*) may be used with other verbs than "rush" (*ṣlḥ*) to describe the activity of the Spirit as well. The Spirit "rested" (*nwḥ*) "on" (*'al*) the seventy elders (Num 11:25b, 26). The Spirit "came" (*hyh*) "on" (*'al*) Othniel (Judg 3:10) and Saul and his messengers (1 Sam 19:20, 23). It seems that whatever the combination of verb and preposition may be (or the lack thereof of one or the other), the experience of all of these leaders is similar to one another, implying that the difference in terminology is no great matter.

60. Wood, *The Holy Spirit in the Old Testament*, 51. Block states, "The Spirit which came upon David in this instance was never retracted" ("Empowered by the Spirit of God," 52). Hamilton gives another suggestion and states, "This could mean that the Spirit was continually upon David, or it could mean that the Spirit continued to 'rush to' him and inspire him at significant moments" ("God with Men in the Prophets and the Writings," 185). The Spirit's repeated description in the leadership of Samson and Saul, however, would suggest that if David experienced multiple "rushings," the text would have described as much. Also, the description of the Spirit's work in the leadership of Moses and Joshua is of an ongoing nature as well, giving precedent to conclude that David experienced the same.

recorded to have experienced the work of the Spirit multiple times and in multiple ways.⁶¹ After this instance, the Spirit is not explicitly mentioned again in the OT narratives in relation to David's leadership.

This ongoing nature of the Spirit's enablement is also evidenced by variations of the statement that "the Lord was with David."⁶² In demonstrating this point, it is helpful to remember that the *Spirit's* departure from Saul in 1 Sam 16:14 was described as the *Lord's* departure in 1 Sam 18:12. In contrast to the Lord's departure from Saul, 1 Sam 18:12 states of David that "the Lord was with him." First Samuel 18:12 implies that the concept of God's presence being with a leader or departing from a leader includes the notion of God's Spirit being upon the leader or departing from the leader as well.⁶³ In the case of David, 1 Sam 18:12 clearly implies that the statement "the Lord was with him" could be understood as if the text stated that "the Spirit of the Lord was on him for the purpose of leading Israel."

The question at this point would be whether or not one could take any phrase describing the Lord being "with" a leader to mean that the leader had been enabled by the Spirit to lead the nation. For both Saul and David, the Spirit's role in their leadership had been explicitly described, which allowed for later "shorthand" descriptions that assume the Spirit's role without directly referring to the Spirit (e.g., the Lord being "with" them). In contrast, one should not necessarily infer the Spirit's role in the leadership of a given leader if the leader has no prior description of the Spirit's involvement in his leadership. For example, the judges are generally described as enjoying the Lord's presence during their leadership (Judg 2:18; "the Lord was with the judge"), but only four of the judges are explicitly recorded to have been enabled by the Spirit.⁶⁴ It cannot be definitively concluded from Judg 2:18 alone that the other judges enjoyed this enablement as well. For

61. Howard states, "There are no references to its coming upon him again. Indeed, later we see that David feared its withdrawal (Ps 51:11 [13]), implying a more permanent or sustained empowerment, different from the usual pattern seen in the OT" ("The Transfer of Power from Saul to David in 1 Sam 16:13–14," 475).

62. Firth, "The Spirit and Leadership," 279.

63. Howard, "The Transfer of Power from Saul to David in 1 Sam 16:13–14," 476.

64. It would seem appropriate, however, to infer the Spirit's role in the leadership of Moses in Exod 3:12. The context of Exod 3:12 involves God's presence ("I will be with you") with a leader (Moses). The lack of a preceding description of the Spirit's role in the leadership of Moses leaves one tentative in concluding the Spirit's role from Exod 3 and thereafter. However, in light the discussion of 1 Sam 18:12 above, it seems the description of the Spirit's being on Moses in Num 11:17 may imply that the Spirit's enablement of Moses' leadership began in Exod 3:12.

David, the Spirit was clearly said to have "rushed upon" him "from that day forward" (1 Sam 16:13), and 1 Sam 18:12 seems to assume the Spirit's ongoing enablement with the phrase "the Lord was with him."

If this is the case, it may be that other statements involving David's leadership and the Lord's being with David imply or assume the Spirit's role as well. Some of these statements are people's prayers that God would be with David,[65] but other statements directly assert that the Lord was with David. One of Saul's servants declared of David that "the Lord is with him," possibly implying the Spirit's role in David's being "skillful in playing, a man of valor, a man of war, prudent in speech" (1 Sam 16:18).[66] David is also described as having "success in all his undertakings, for the Lord was with him" (1 Sam 18:14). Likewise, in speaking of David's military accomplishments, "David became greater and greater, for the Lord, the God of hosts, was with him" (2 Sam 5:10). Finally, just as Nathan declared to David, "the Lord is with you" (2 Sam 7:3; cf. 1 Chr 17:2),[67] so also God said the same of David to Nathan. In speaking of the Davidic covenant to Nathan, the Lord summarized His presence in the life of David in terms of military achievement: "I have been with you wherever you went and have cut off all your enemies from before you" (2 Sam 7:9; cf. 1 Chr 17:8). It seems reasonable to infer the role of the Spirit in David's leadership in each of these statements, or at least in the statements that describe David's leadership in terms of how

65. Saul blessed David before he battled Goliath, "Go, and may the Lord be with you" (1 Sam 17:37). Jonathan blessed David when David was fleeing from Saul for his life: "And may the Lord be with you as He has been with my father" (1 Sam 20:13). The woman in disguise blessed David before he made a judgment concerning her situation: "And may the Lord your God be with you" (2 Sam 14:17).

66. Firth, "The Spirit and Leadership," 260, connects the Spirit's anointing in 1 Sam 16:13 with the phrase "the Lord is with him" in 16:18. Rather than simply being another description of David ("*and* the Lord is with him"), the descriptive comment may serve to explain the descriptions before it ("*for* the Lord is with him"). The Lord's presence in this context may be clearly and generally described as "divine favor." See Tsumura, *The First Book of Samuel*, 430. Given the precedent in this study thus far, it does not seem a stretch to attribute some of these qualities to the enablement of the Spirit. While David's description of being "a handsome man" refers to an external characteristic, his ability as a warrior may be attributed to the enablement of the Spirit as was the case with the judges discussed above. Also, as Bezaleel and Oholiab were made skillful by the Spirit to craft Israel's tabernacle (Exod 31:3, 6), so it may be the Spirit gave David skill as a musician. Similarly, as Joseph's discernment and wisdom came from the Spirit of God (Gen 41:33, 39), so also David's discernment in speech may be said to come from the Spirit as well.

67. Wood, *The Holy Spirit in the Old Testament*, 56, sees David as a craftsman (1 Chr 28:11–12). Howell, *Servants of the Servant*, 90, suggests that 2 Sam 7:7 would seem to argue against this, however.

previous leaders led by the Spirit as well (e.g., victory in battle, courage, etc.). To clarify, this conclusion does not mean that statements describing God's presence "with" a leader are perfectly synonymous or limited to the enablement by the Spirit to lead.

Unlike Saul, David was qualified to lead Israel in light of his obedience and devotion to the LORD. Like Samson, Saul's persistent disobedience led to the loss of the Spirit's enablement for his leadership. In condemning Saul for his disobedience to the LORD's commandments, Samuel described Saul's replacement as one who would be "a man after His own heart" in contrast to Saul who broke the LORD's commandments (1 Sam 13:14; cf. 15:23). The anointing of David by Samuel and the Spirit in 16:13 makes it clear that David is both a man after God's own heart and one whose tenure as king would be generally characterized by obedience (cf. 1 Kgs 9:4; 14:8; 2 Kgs 15:4–5).

Psalm 51:11

The second mention of the Spirit in relation to David's leadership is found in Ps 51:11.[68] Assuming the validity of the superscription, the context of Psalm 51 is David's repentance to God for his sins of adultery with Bathsheba and the murder of her husband Uriah (cf. 2 Sam 11:1–27; cf. 11:27; 12:9; 1 Kgs 15:5). The consequences of these sins for David were severe: he would be engaged in constant warfare with his enemies (2 Sam 12:10); his wives would be sexually defiled (2 Sam 12:11; cf. 16:22); and the son conceived through his adultery would die (2 Sam 12:14). In light of Ps 51:11, it may be concluded that David also feared that he would lose the enablement of the Spirit for his leadership as did his predecessor Saul (1 Sam 16:14).[69]

---

68. Estes, "Spirit and Psalmist in Psalm 51," 129–34, surveys three historical options for interpreting 51:11. First, the psalmist is a prophet who has sinned and does not want to lose the Spirit. Second, the psalmist is a royal figure, perhaps David, and does not want to lose the Spirit as did Saul. Third, the psalmist does not want to lose the Spirit's sanctifying influence, "undoubtedly the majority position" ("Spirit and Psalmist in Psalm 51," 131). Estes then suggests a fourth option, understanding Ps 51:11 to be referring to the psalmist's own spirit in light of the surrounding references to his spirit. While each view has its merits, there seems to be no compelling reason to dismiss the context described in the superscription and that the psalmist is King David.

69. Cole, *He Who Gives Life*, 121; Dumbrell, "Spirit and Kingdom of God in the Old Testament," 5; Gromacki, *The Holy Spirit*, 72; Hamilton, *God's Indwelling Presence*, 32–33; Hamilton, "God with Men in the Prophets and the Writings," 174; Ryrie, *The Holy Spirit* (Chicago: Moody, 1997), 57; Wood, *The Holy Spirit in the Old Testament*, 51; Grudem, *Systematic Theology*, 636. Ferguson, *The Holy Spirit*, 24–25, sees Ps 51:11 referring to both the

David thus prayed to God, "Cast me not away from your presence, and take not your Holy Spirit from me" (Ps 51:11).

David's qualification of the Spirit by the attribute of holiness ("Holy Spirit") suggests that his unholy sins yielded the potential for God to remove his Spirit from David. David had seen this phenomenon in the life of Saul, a leader who himself became aware of his loss of the Spirit as a result of his disobedience (1 Sam 16:14; 18:12).[70]

At the same time, David's concern was for Israel as well. The Spirit's role in his life affected him personally for the purpose of leading the nation as a whole. Parallel in thought to the removal of God's Spirit is being cast away from the LORD's presence, a phrase that is only used elsewhere with reference to God's corporate rejection of his people and not just an individual (2 Kgs 13:23; 17:20; 24:20; 2 Chr 7:20; Jer 7:15; 52:3).[71] It is no surprise, then, to find David end Psalm 51 with an appeal to God on behalf of the nation (Ps 51:18–19).[72] God's goodness to the nation as a whole would be expressed in part by continuing the Spirit's work through the nation's king in order for the nation to have effective, competent leadership (Ps 51:11).

Summary

In addition to the Spirit giving David revelation from time to time (2 Sam 23:2; 1 Chr 28:12), the Spirit granted David an ongoing enablement to lead as king when the Spirit departed from Saul (1 Sam 16:13–14; cf. 18:12). Though David committed significant sin and feared the loss of the Spirit like his predecessor Saul, David's repentance and request for the Spirit not to depart allowed his enablement to continue (Ps 51:11).

Kings after David

There is debate as to whether or not the Spirit enabled the kings after David to effectively lead the nation Israel since the Spirit is not explicitly mentioned to have enabled any of these kings. Some authors explain why the Spirit is mentioned in relationship to some leaders (e.g., Moses, David), but

---

Spirit's enablement for leadership *and* sanctification. It is not a choice for one or the other.

70. Howard, "The Transfer of Power," 476.

71. McCabe, "Were Old Testament Believers Indwelt by the Spirit," 261.

72. Ibid., 260.

they do not go further to discover whether or not the Spirit enabled the kings after David as well.[73] Others conclude that the absence of the Spirit's mention denies that there can be any certainty as to whether or not these kings were enabled by the Spirit.[74] Others conclude the Spirit enabled the Davidic kings until the captivity.[75]

Though the Spirit is not explicitly mentioned in relation to any king after David in the historical books, some kings are described in terms reminiscent of how the Spirit worked through previous leaders. These kings are Solomon and the eight good kings of the Southern Kingdom.[76] Like Joshua (Deut 34:9), Solomon was endowed with wisdom (1 Kgs 3:28; cf. 4:29–34; 5:12; 10:6–9, 23–24).[77] Similar to the description of David that "the LORD was with him" (1 Sam 18:12; cf. 1 Sam 16:13–14), Asa was promised by the prophet Azariah, "The LORD is with you while you are with him" (2 Chr 15:2). Similar statements describe Asa (2 Chr 15:9), Jehoshaphat (2 Chr 17:3), and Hezekiah (2 Kgs 18:7). As Joshua, the judges, Saul, and David experienced military success, so also did Asa (2 Chr 15:15), Jehoshaphat (20:30), Amaziah (25:11–12), Uzziah (26:6–15), Jotham (27:5), and Hezekiah (2 Kgs 18:7–8).

---

73. Wood claims that the Spirit is mentioned in relationship to Moses, Joshua, Saul, and David because they "were fully national figures" who "faced the most demanding tasks of any other national figures" (*The Holy Spirit in the Old Testament*, 62–63). Wood continues, "Of the nineteen kings of the southern kingdom, eight were considered 'good,' but apparently their tasks were not considered great enough to qualify" (i.e., for being described as something enabled by the Spirit; Ibid.). Firth, "The Spirit and Leadership," 269, suggests that the mention of the Spirit in relationship to a leader was necessary only when the individual's newfound status as a leader needed to be made known. Davidic kings need no mention of the Spirit since they were guaranteed their kingship by hereditary right.

74. E.g., Neve, "Realized Eschatology in Psalm 51," 266.

75. Pettegrew, *The New Covenant Ministry of the Holy Spirit*, 24. McCune, "Theocratic Anointing in the Old Testament," 32–37, anchors this understanding of anointing in the existence of the theocracy and ties anointing to the Davidic covenant.

76. The eight good kings of the Southern Kingdom are described as having a reign generally marked by obedience to God. These kings are Asa (1 Kgs 15:11), Jehoshaphat (1 Kgs 22:43; 2 Chr 20:32–33), Joash (Jehoash; 2 Kgs 12:2–3; 2 Chr 24:2), Amaziah (2 Kgs 14:3–4; 2 Chr 25:2), Uzziah (Azariah; 2 Kgs 15:3–4; 2 Chr 26:4), Jotham (2 Kgs 15:34–35; 2 Chr 27:2), Hezekiah (2 Kgs 18:3; 2 Chr 29:2), and Josiah (2 Kgs 22:2; 2 Chr 34:2).

77. McCune, "Theocratic Anointing in the Old Testament," 66. In discussing Solomon, Howell, *Servants of the Servant*, 104, points out that wisdom and discernment are attributed to Joseph in Gen 41:33, 39. A case may be made to claim that Gen 41:38 sources this wisdom in the Spirit of God (see Chapter 4).

Despite these similarities, the fact remains that the Spirit's role is not described as being involved in the leadership of any of these kings. Though the Spirit's role was implied in descriptions of Samson (Judg 16:20), Saul, and David (1 Sam 18:12), for each of these leaders, the Spirit's involvement in their leadership had been previously described. While a case may be easily made to state that Solomon received his wisdom by the Spirit of God (cf. Deut 34:9; Isa 11:2), the evidence is slim to conclude that the kings thereafter were enabled by the Spirit to lead.

Even if the Spirit's role could be inferred from these similarities, the later disobedience of these kings would cause one to wonder if this enablement was as short-lived as it was for Samson and Saul.[78] Moreover, when the Spirit of God is described to be somehow involved during the kingships of the kings after David, it is through the prophets who gave counsel or rebuke. The Spirit "came" (*hyh*) "upon" (*'al*) Azariah to counsel Asa (2 Chr 15:1–2), the Spirit "came" (*hyh*) "upon" (*'al*) Jahaziel to counsel Jehoshaphat (2 Chr 20:14–15), and the Spirit "clothed" (*lbš*) Zechariah to rebuke Israel and Joash (2 Chr 24:20–21). These three episodes show that, though the Spirit's role was described in the leadership of Saul and David, "the role of the Spirit during the monarchal period was most closely associated with the prophets and seen in their ministry."[79] Apart from Solomon, it is difficult to conclude that the Spirit enabled the leadership of the kings after Saul and David.

A brief examination of Isa 63:7–14 further implies either that the Spirit did not enable these kings or that, if the Spirit did give such an enablement, it would eventually come to an end. Isaiah prophesied of a future time[80]

---

78. Solomon (1 Kgs 11:1–13), Asa (2 Chr 16:1–6, 12–13), Jehoshaphat (1 Kgs 22:48; 2 Chr 20:35–37), Joash (2 Chr 24:15–22), Amaziah (2 Chr 25:14–16), Uzziah (2 Chr 26:5), Hezekiah (2 Kgs 20:12–18; 2 Chr 32:25), and Josiah (2 Chr 35:20–24) are said to have sinned in some significant way.

79. Inch, *Saga of the Spirit*, 43. See also Horton, *What the Bible Says about the Holy Spirit*, 50–54, and Rea, *The Holy Spirit in the Bible*, 71–75.

80. Smith notes the eschatological nature of Isaiah 55–66 and states, "It is appropriate to question if this future setting has anything to do with the present location of the prophet and his audience" (*Isaiah 40–66*, 517). If the events of Isa 63:7–14 did have something to do with the present audience, this audience would have been Isaiah's readers during the days of Hezekiah (cf. Isa 1:1; 36:1) or Hezekiah's wicked son Manasseh (cf. Isa 37:38). Isaiah 37:38 refers to the beginning of the Assyrian King Esarhaddon's reign, which is commonly understood to have begun in 681 B.C., six or seven years after the death of Hezekiah (688/87 B.C.). If this text was not added by a later author to show fulfillment to Isaiah's prophecy, it would have been written by Isaiah himself, which would have meant it was written during the reign of Hezekiah's son Manasseh (cf. 2 Kgs 21:1;

when Israel would lament[81] and look back to "the days of old" (Isa 63:9, 11). These were the days when Moses was the Spirit-enabled leader of Israel (Isa 63:11–12; see above), after which "the Spirit of the LORD gave them rest" (Isa 63:14).[82] The Spirit's work is thus described as something of the past.

The lament follows this description with a plea that God would restore his favorable presence to Israel once again. Israel pleas that God would "look down" (Isa 63:15), "return" (Isa 63:17), "come down" (Isa 64:1), and stop hiding from Israel in silence and anger (Isa 64:7, 9, 12). It could be that this lament over God's limited presence assumes that God was withholding his Spirit from the king of Israel as well (cf. Isa 63:11, 14). If this is the case, this would mean that the Spirit was not at work through the leadership of whoever would be the future king in the setting of Isa 63:7–14.

Isaiah likely spoke of Israel's approaching captivity, a result of God's casting the nation away from his presence because of the nation's sins (cf. 2 Chr 17:20; 24:20). If God had cast away the nation as a whole, it would follow that the Spirit had been withdrawn from the king as well (cf. Ps 51:11, 18–19). Though the nation would find itself in such a desperate situation, Isaiah did not leave Israel without hope.

The Prophesied King of Isaiah

Isaiah gave numerous prophecies of a time when the LORD would return and restore Israel to a time of blessing and peace. Included within these prophecies are at least five texts that describe a king whose experience of the Spirit would be like no other: Isa 11:2; 42:1; 48:16; 59:21; and 61:1.

Isaiah 11:2

Isaiah predicted the coming of a descendant of David whose reign would be unlike any other king (Isa 11:1–10).[83] He would rule with perfect judgment

---

2 Chr 33:1). Cf. Oswalt, *The Book of Isaiah*, 670; Smith, *Isaiah 1–39*, 633; Watts, *Isaiah 34–66*, 47–48.

81. Oswalt, *The Book of Isaiah*, 603–04.

82. The general description of the Spirit giving Israel rest may or may not imply the Spirit's enablement of the leaders who led Israel into this rest. (See the above discussion of Joshua.)

83. Hailey, *A Commentary on Isaiah*, 120–21. Hailey points out that the stump of Jesse in Isa 11:1 speaks to the fallen condition of the Davidic dynasty. David is not even

(Isa 11:3) and restore creation to an Eden-like existence (Isa 11:6–9).[84] One of the primary reasons for such an incredible rule would be the role of the Spirit in the leadership of this king as described in Isa 11:2:

> And the Spirit of the LORD shall rest upon him, / the Spirit of wisdom and understanding, / the Spirit of counsel and might, / the Spirit of knowledge and the fear of the LORD.

Structurally, Isa 11:2 gives a sevenfold description of the Spirit. Geoffrey Grogan states that this structure "would suggest that the Messiah was to be perfectly endowed by the Spirit with everything requisite to his kingly task."[85] Grogan goes on to explain that the first description of the Spirit being "of the LORD" precedes "three pairs of qualities attributed to the Spirit," totaling seven in all.[86] "Wisdom and understanding" (11:2) would be granted by the Spirit to this king just as they were to Joshua (Deut 34:9) and Solomon (1 Kgs 3:12, 28; cf. 4:29). Hillary Marlow defines "counsel and might" as "the ability to devise a plan or strategy and the heroic power to carry it out" (Isa 11:2; cf. 9:6),[87] an ability possessed by every Spirit-enabled leader from Moses and thereafter. Finally, "knowledge and the fear of the LORD" (Isa 11:2) speak to the king's obedience to God (cf. 2 Sam 23:3; Prov 1:7),[88] something required for every king of Israel (cf. Deut 17:19). The Spirit's work through this king enables him to carry out a worldwide rule of perfect knowledge and righteousness (Isa 11:3–5).

It is also significant that the Spirit "shall rest" (*nḥ*) upon this king. This verb is used in relation to the Spirit only two other times in the OT. The Spirit which was on Moses "rested" upon the seventy elders (Num 11:25), and sons of the prophets noted that the Spirit "rests on Elisha" as well (2

---

named. The "shoot" that comes from the stump figuratively represents the coming of a Davidic descendant.

84. Hamilton, *God's Indwelling Presence*, 103–04, notes that Isa 11:6–9 pictures the reversal of the curse in Gen 3:15.

85. Grogan, "Isaiah," in *Proverbs–Isaiah*, 544. Motyer, *Isaiah*, 103, agrees with this sevenfold scheme. For a survey of early interpretations of Isa 11:2, see Schlütz, *Isaias 11, 2 (Die Sieben Gaben des Hl. Geistes)*.

86. Grogan, "Isaiah," 44.

87. Marlow, "The Spirit of Yahweh in Isaiah 11:1–9," 226. See also Grogan, "Isaiah," 544, and Young, *The Book of Isaiah: Chapters 1–18*, 382. Both Grogan and Young link this phrase to Isa 9:6, a verse which terms a Davidic descendant (cf. Isa 9:7) as both "Wonderful Counselor" and "Mighty God."

88. Marlow, "The Spirit of Yahweh in Isaiah 11:1–9," 227.

Kgs 2:15),[89] two contexts which Marlow describes as "significant transfers of power."[90] By using this verb, Isaiah may have been likewise indicating a significant transfer of power. Perhaps the significance was that the LORD would enable a Davidic king with His Spirit to rule after He had forsaken the nation as a whole and thus the king as well (cf. 2 Kgs 17:20; 24:20; cf. Ps 51:11; see above).

Isaiah 42:1

In the first of four passages commonly known as the "Servant Songs,"[91] Isaiah records the words of the LORD who states, "Behold, My Servant . . . I have put My Spirit upon Him" (Isa 42:1). The Servant is also "My chosen one in whom My soul delights" and the LORD's agent who would "bring forth justice to the nations" (Isa 42:1).

Several authors note parallels between the statements in this verse and other accounts describing the installation of a king (cf. 1 Sam 9:15–16; 16:1–13; Ps 89:3; Zech 3:8; 6:12).[92] What is unique of Isaiah's Servant is that he is an individual[93] whose rule is both worldwide and yet marked with gentleness and peace (Isa 42:2–4).

Isaiah 48:16

The identity of the one enabled by the Spirit in Isa 48:16 is not quite as apparent as the identity of the Davidic king of Isa 11:2 and the royal servant of

---

89. The text states that "the spirit of Elijah rests on Elisha," which seems to be shorthand for directly or indirectly referring to the Spirit's role in the prophetic ministry of Elijah.

90. Marlow, "The Spirit of Yahweh in Isaiah 11:1–9," 226. See also Weisman, "The Personal Spirit as Imparting Authority," 227–28, and Hildebrandt, *An Old Testament Theology of the Spirit of God*, 128.

91. Chisholm states, "Most scholars recognize the presence of four servant songs in Isaiah 40–55: (1) 42:1–7; (2) 49:1–13; (3) 50:4–9; and (4) 52:13–53:12" ("The Christological Fulfillment of Isaiah's Servant Songs," 393–94).

92. Blenkinsopp, *Isaiah*, 2:211–12; Childs, *Isaiah*, 324; and Cole, *He Who Gives Life*, 134.

93. For all of the servant songs and the identity of their referent(s), see an excellent summary of the issues by Childs, *Isaiah*, 420–23. For this passage, Grogan is helpful: "Isaiah 42:6 shows that we cannot, without qualification, identify the servant here with the nation, but we can certainly say that in him the servant mission of Israel finds perfect expression" ("Isaiah," 738).

Isa 42:1. Isaiah records the words of one who speaks for himself: "now the Lord God has sent Me, and His Spirit" (Isa 48:16b). Though the identification of the speaker seems vague at first glance, there is reason to conclude that the speaker is the Servant described in Isaiah 49. In a previous passage, Isaiah described how God used the foreign king Cyrus for Israel's good (Isa 44:28–45:1). Isaiah 48:14–15 again refers to God's work through Cyrus. The description of Cyrus in Isa 48:14–15 speaks of Cyrus in the third person, and Isa 48:16 then abruptly changes to the first person, suggesting that a new figure is in view.[94] Though the speaker is anonymous at first, his identity later becomes clear in Isaiah 49 (i.e., in the Servant Song at the beginning of the chapter).[95]

Edward J. Young notes that though the phrase "and his Spirit" could grammatically be a second subject alongside "the Lord God," it is better understood as an object and "the conjunction would probably have the force *together with*, and the teaching would be that the servant did not come alone but that his entire ministry was in the power of the Spirit."[96] If this explanation is correct, though the statement concerning the servant in Isa 48:16 is brief, it could have caused the reader to recall what was said in Isa 11:2 and Isa 42:1 and reaffirmed the importance of the role of the Spirit in the reign of this coming king.

Isaiah 59:21

In Isa 59:21 the Lord speaks to an individual who bears the Spirit and consequently speaks with prophetic authority:

> And as for me, this is my covenant with them," says the Lord: "My Spirit that is upon you, and my words that I have put in your mouth, shall not depart out of your mouth, or out of the mouth of your offspring, or out of the mouth of your children's offspring," says the Lord, "from this time forth and forevermore." (Isa 59:21)

Isaiah 59:21 is similar to Isa 48:16 in that it shifts away from the third person in order to indicate some type of transition. The text is not completely broken from its preceding verse, however. Though God speaks to

---

94. Childs, *Isaiah*, 373.
95. Ibid., 377–78. Hailey, *A Commentary on Isaiah*, 401, argues similarly to Childs.
96. Young, *The Book of Isaiah: Chapters 40–66*, 259. So also Grogan, "Isaiah," 772, and Blenkinsopp, *Isaiah*, 2:294.

"them" in the beginning of Isa 59:21, He states, "My Spirit which is upon you," and the singular pronominal suffix translated "you" could refer back to the singular "Redeemer" of Isa 59:20.[97]

After the Redeemer is told by God that the Spirit would be upon him, he is described in prophetic terms. God states, "My words which I have put in your mouth shall not depart from your mouth" (Isa 59:21). This announcement by God may echo Deut 18:18 and possibly Deut 30:14 or Josh 1:8 as well.[98]

Isaiah 61:1

Isaiah 61:1–3 records the words of one who announces himself in terms of royalty and as one who is enabled by the Spirit for his God-given task. The speaker parallels his claim "The Spirit of the LORD God is upon me" with the statement "the LORD has anointed me" (Isa 61:1).[99]

As to his royalty, the description of this anointing by the Spirit is reminiscent of Saul and David's anointing by oil and subsequent experience of the Spirit (1 Sam 10:1, 6; 11:6; 16:13; 2 Sam 23:2).[100] Rather than speaking of both a physical anointing with oil and then a subsequent anointing by the Spirit, the speaker of Isa 61:1 describes himself as only anointed by the Spirit.

As to what Hildebrandt terms as his "twofold task," the speaker acts to carry out his tasks of "proclamation" and "action,"[101] indicating he is a prophet in addition to being an anointed king.[102] He will "bring good news to the poor," "proclaim liberty to captives and the opening of the prison

---

97. Hailey, *A Commentary on Isaiah*, 459–60.

98. Young, *The Book of Isaiah: Chapters 40–66*, 441–42. Deuteronomy 18:18 states, "I will raise up for them a prophet like you from among their brothers. And I will put my words in his mouth, and he shall speak to them all that I command him." Deuteronomy 30:14 states, "But the word is very near you. It is in your mouth and in your heart, so that you can do it." Joshua 1:8 states, "This Book of the Law shall not depart from your mouth." Also, the similarities between the Spirit-enabled Redeemer of Isa 59:20–21 and the speaker of Isa 48:16b and Isa 61:1 imply that their identity is one and the same. See Blenkinsopp, *Isaiah*, 3:200–203, and Motyer, *Isaiah*, 370–71.

99. Hamilton states, "Thus to be anointed of Yahweh . . . is to possess the Spirit of Yahweh" (*God's Indwelling Presence*, 104).

100. Chisholm, "The Christological Fulfillment of Isaiah's Servant Songs," 401.

101. Hildebrandt, *An Old Testament Theology of the Spirit of God*, 133.

102. Hildebrandt states, "It is quite likely that the offices of prophet and king are here merged so that the proclamation of the good news and the actions performed are brought about by the same figure" (Ibid.).

to those who are bound," and "proclaim the year of the LORD's favor" (Isa 61:1–2a). He will also "proclaim . . . the day of vengeance of our God" and will thereby "comfort all who mourn" with "the oil of gladness" and "the mantle of praise" so that "the LORD . . . may be glorified" (Isa 61:2–3).

The combined roles of both prophet and king show this text to be a culmination of the texts above. This figure is both the Spirit-anointed king (cf. Isa 11:2) who is also the Spirit-enabled prophet (cf. Isa 59:21) and Spirit-enabled Servant who will proclaim God's favor to the world (Isa 42:1; 48:16; cf. 49:8; 50:4–5).[103]

Summary

The prophesied king of Isaiah would be a Davidic descendant whose enablement by the Spirit would be like no other ruler before him. The repeated descriptions of his obedience suggest he would perfectly obey the LORD, which would guarantee he would not lose the Spirit's enablement like Samson or Saul of old (Isa 11:2–3). The LORD's placement of the Spirit upon this individual would inaugurate his reign (Isa 42:1) and anoint him as a prophet to proclaim the LORD's favor to the world (Isa 61:1–2a). The Spirit would grant him wisdom and power of such a nature that would allow him to rule the world in perfect righteousness (Isa 11:2–5). Though his rule would be marked by gentleness and peace (Isa 42:2–4), he would proclaim and execute justice against his enemies as well (Isa 11:4; 61:2b–3).

Conclusion

The examination of the passages above allows one to conclude that the OT presents a distinct work of the Spirit in biblical leaders. This work may be more precisely described as the Spirit granting the necessary wisdom to a leader in order for him to lead God's people in carrying out the various purposes of God. This work of the Spirit in leadership was described in various ways: bearing the burden of the people (Num 11:17); shepherding (Num 27:17); leading in battle (Num 27:17, 21; Judg 6:34; 11:29; 13:25; 1 Sam 11:6–7); and exercising authority with wisdom (Deut 34:9). Though David was enabled by the Spirit to lead and seen as a paradigm for kings to follow (1 Sam 16:13; cf.

---

103. Young, points out that "this passage is a compound of 11:2; 42:1; 49:8 and 50:4, 5 in that what in those passages was promised now occurs" (*The Book of Isaiah. Chapters 40–66*, 458).

1 Kgs 3:14), the prophesied king of Isaiah would be enabled by the Spirit to lead like no other. His wisdom and power from the Spirit would enable him to execute justice throughout the world (Isa 11:2–4).

To describe this work further, the work of the Spirit in leadership was given *selectively* in that the OT describes the Spirit being given to some leaders but not to others. When this work of the Spirit was granted to a leader, it was of either a *continuous* (e.g., Moses) or *occasional* (e.g., the four judges) nature. Disobedience could forfeit a leader's enablement by the Spirit (e.g., Saul).

What helps to clarify this study's thesis further is that some leaders experienced multiple works of the Spirit, and though these works were related to the Spirit's work in leadership, these works of the Spirit were distinct from the Spirit's granting of wisdom for the purpose of leadership. The Spirit enabled some to perform miracles (Moses, Joshua), prophesy (the seventy elders, Saul), and speak the revelation of God (David), but these activities were of a more supernatural character than the Spirit's granting of wisdom to leaders for the purpose of leading God's people.

3

The Role of the Spirit in the Leadership of New Testament Leaders

Introduction

A BIBLICAL THEOLOGY OF the Spirit's role in the leadership of God's people carries many themes from the OT into the NT. Other themes and developments emerge from a study of the NT as well. The present chapter will demonstrate from the NT that there is a distinct work of the Spirit in biblical leaders by examining passages that describe the leadership of Jesus, the apostles, apostolic delegates, elders, deacons, and what is commonly called the spiritual gift of leadership. Each passage below explicitly refers to the Spirit and a biblical leader or the spiritual gift of leadership.[1] Each passage will be surveyed briefly for its context and examined as to whether or not the Spirit is involved in the exercise of the leader's leadership.

Jesus

There is much to say of Jesus and the Spirit, and this section can hardly hope to say all that should be said. Though Jesus is dissimilar from all leaders in that he is both man and God, his experience of the Spirit is nonetheless similar to both OT and NT leaders in several ways. His relationship to the Spirit is also related to the work of the Spirit in all Christians, leaders included. He is both the one to whom the Spirit was given and the one who would give the Spirit.

---

1. To clarify, deacons were not identified as biblical leaders in the outset of this study. However, they are included in this study in order to better understand their role in distinction from elders in the church.

The One to Whom the Spirit Was Given

Each of the four Gospels records the Spirit's descent upon Jesus at his baptism (Matt 3:16; Mark 1:10; Luke 3:22; John 1:32–33). Scattered references in the Gospels describe the work of the Spirit during his ministry (Matt 12:18, 28; Luke 4:14, 18; John 3:34), and the book of Acts describes the work of the Spirit in Jesus after his resurrection (Acts 1:2) and throughout his ministry as a whole (Acts 10:38). Two passages describe the work of Jesus and the Spirit in concert with one another during the days of the early church (1 Cor 12:4–5; Rev 2:7, 11, 17, 29; 3:6, 13, 22).

Matthew 3:16; Mark 1:10; Luke 3:22; John 1:32–33

John the Baptist regularly baptized people in the Jordan River (Matt 3:5–6). When Jesus came to be baptized, John prevented him at first (Matt 3:14) but then consented when Jesus explained his baptism would "fulfill all righteousness" (Matt 3:15).[2] After the crowds and Jesus had been baptized, Jesus was standing and praying in the river (Luke 3:21).[3] The heavens opened (Mark 1:10), and both Jesus and John saw the Spirit descend upon Jesus like a dove and remain on him (Matt 3:16; John 1:32). The voice of God the Father then came from heaven and said, "This is my beloved Son, with whom I am well pleased" (Matt 3:17).[4]

All of the Gospels state that the Spirit "descended" or was "descending" upon Jesus "like a dove." It is also said that Jesus saw the Spirit "coming to rest on him" (Matt 3:16) and that John would "see the Spirit . . . remain" on him as well (John 1:33). Though the terminology is not the same, the concept of "resting" and "remaining" is parallel in concept to what is said

---

2. This statement perhaps implied Jesus' need to cleanse himself ceremonially as an Israelite in light of the sins of Israel as a whole. Cf. Bock, *Jesus according to Scripture*, 87; Hawthorne, *The Presence and the Power*, 119–21.

3. Hawthorne, *The Presence and the Power*, 141, points out that the construction of *en tō* with an infinitive (*en tō baptisthēnai*) in Luke 3:21 indicates Jesus was baptized and praying after the crowds were baptized. Marshall, *The Gospel of Luke*, 152, suggests Jesus could have been baptized with the crowds but was then praying after the baptisms had taken place. Either way, Luke is describing a private event in which only John and Jesus are present. Mark 1:9–11 and John 1:32–34 portray Jesus' baptism as a private event as well. Cf. Bock, *Jesus according to Scripture*, 86.

4. Peter, James, and John heard this same statement later at Jesus' Transfiguration (Matt 17:5), a statement which Peter attributed to the Father (2 Pet 1:17).

THE SPIRIT IN THE LEADERSHIP OF NEW TESTAMENT LEADERS

of the Messiah in Isa 11:2: "the Spirit of the LORD shall rest upon him."[5] The preposition *epi* is used to describe the Spirit's resting "on" Jesus (Matt 3:16; Luke 3:22)[6] and echoes the description of the Spirit resting on the messianic king (Isa 11:2), servant (Isa 42:1), and royal prophet (Isa 61:1) of Isaiah.[7] If these echoes are intentional, Jesus is being identified as Isaiah's king, servant, and prophet.

In addition to these echoes, the two statements spoken by the voice from heaven in Luke 3:22 explicitly identify Jesus as both a royal figure and Isaiah's servant. The first statement is a quotation from Ps 2:7: "You are my . . . Son."[8] Psalm 2 is "a royal psalm celebrating God's choice of the Davidic dynasty," implying that the quotation of Ps 2:7 by the Father indicates the approval of Jesus as the Davidic king over Israel.[9] Moreover, the Father stated Jesus to be his son who was "beloved" (*agapētos*; Matt 3:17; Mark 1:11; Luke 3:22), a word not found in Ps 2:7. This addition may reflect the fact that Jesus was "the unique Son, the one who has a special and unparalleled relationship with the Father."[10]

The second statement in Luke 3:22 is an allusion to Isa 42:1: "with you I am well pleased."[11] This statement as found in Isa 42:1 immediately precedes what the Father could have said of Jesus at his baptism, "I have put my Spirit upon him." The Father clearly identifies Jesus as the prophesied

---

5. Matthew uses *erchomai* for what is variously translated as "resting" (ESV) or "lighting" (NASB). John uses *menō* for "remained" (John 1:32) and "remain" (John 1:33). The verb for "rest" in Isa 11:2 is *anapauō* (LXX). See John Owen, *The Holy Spirit* (Carlisle, Pa.: Banner of Truth Trust, 1998), 64–65.

6. Mark 1:10, however, uses the preposition *eis*. Hawthorne, *The Presence and the Power*, 127, suggests Matthew and Luke chose *epi* in order to reflect the terminology of Isaiah. He further suggests that Mark chose this preposition to show that "Jesus was now filled with the Spirit as he was never filled before" (Ibid.).

7. The LXX uses the preposition *epi* in each of these references.

8. The word "beloved" does not come from Ps 2:7 (see below). Mark records this phrase with the second-person personal pronouns as well ("You are . . . with you"). Matthew, however, records the quotation in third-person ("This is . . . with whom"). Bock clarifies, "Matthew relates the point for his readers as a time when God marked out Jesus for the task. Matthew gives the historical effect of the event" (*Jesus according to Scripture*, 87–88).

9. Chisholm, Jr., "The Christological Fulfillment of Isaiah's Servant Songs," 403.

10. Hawthorne, *The Presence and the Power*, 129. Marshall, *The Gospel of Luke*, 156, states of *agapētos*, "It means 'beloved', but when applied to a son or daughter means 'only.'"

11. This statement reflects the same terminology of Matthew's quotation of Isa 42:1. The text of Matt 3:17 states, "with whom I am well pleased" (*en hō eudokēsa*). Matthew 12:18 directly quotes Isa 42:1: "with whom my soul is well pleased" (*eis hon eudokēsen hē psychē mou*).

servant of Isaiah, someone who would establish justice around the world (cf. Isa 42:2–4).[12]

Jesus' baptism was not necessarily an event in which he exercises leadership, but rather an event in which he is marked out by the Father as a leader. He declared Jesus to be Israel's king and Isaiah's servant who would rule the world, and the Father put the Spirit upon him to carry out these tasks. While more could be said at this point, the subsequent work of the Spirit in Jesus' leadership is further described in numerous passages examined below.

Matthew 12:18

Matthew 12:18 quotes Isa 42:1, a verse to which the Father alluded when speaking of his pleasure with Jesus at Jesus' baptism (Matt 3:17; see above). It was concluded above that the Father's reference to Isa 42:1 at Jesus' baptism identified Jesus as Isaiah's prophesied Servant. Matthew 12:18 repeats this quotation with reference to Jesus and reinforces Jesus' identity as Isaiah's Servant.[13] Beyond this identification, however, Matt 12:18 is only part of 12:18–21, a passage which quotes most of Isa 42:1–4 in order to show how Jesus' actions in Matt 12:15–16 fulfilled the description of the Servant in Isa 42:1–4.[14] The immediate point of Matthew's quotation of Isaiah is to show the gentle character of Jesus' ministry. The repetition of the Father's pleasure with his Son (Matt 12:18; cf. 3:17; 17:5) implies that this passage also served to explain not just the events recorded in Matt 12:15–16, but Jesus' ministry as a whole.[15] This being the case, it could be said that Matthew's reference to the Spirit (Matt 12:18; cf. Isa 42:1) indicates that the Spirit enabled Jesus' actions in Matt 12:15–16 as well as his ministry as a whole.

In the preceding context, Jesus had just healed the withered hand of a man in a synagogue (Matt 12:9–13). His reason for doing so was to

12. Russell, "The Anointing with the Holy Spirit in Luke-Acts," 48–49.

13. Cf. France, *The Gospel of Matthew*, 471; Keener, *A Commentary on the Gospel of Matthew*, 361; Thomas, *The Holy Spirit of God*, 54.

14. Matthew does not quote the entirety of Isa 42:1–4 in Matt 12:18–21. He omits the first two lines of Isa 42:4 (cf. Matt 12:21). See Grindel, "Matthew 12,18–21," 115. Also, it is not clear what text is the source for Matthew's quotation. Luz states, "The wording of the formula quotation from Isa 42:1–4 agrees neither with the MT nor the LXX" (*Matthew 8–20*, 190). Luz suggests that Matthew gave his own free quotation or quoted from a "targum-like text" (Ibid.).

15. Neyrey, "The Thematic Use of Isaiah 42, 1–4 in Matthew 12," 460.

demonstrate that "it is lawful to do good on the Sabbath" (Matt 12:12; cf. 12:10). In response to what they perceived to be a violation of Sabbath law, "the Pharisees went out and conspired against him, how to destroy" Jesus (Matt 12:14). Once Jesus became "aware of this" plot to kill him, he "withdrew from there" (Matt 12:15). Thereafter, "many followed him, and he healed them all and ordered them not to make him known" (Matt 12:16). Jesus' rejection, withdrawal, healing, and order to silence are the actions which Matthew understands to be the fulfillment of Isa 42:1–4.

Jesus' withdrawal from the Pharisees (Matt 12:15a) revealed that he would not needlessly oppose his enemies through either verbal or physical retaliation. This action fulfilled Isa 42:2 in that Jesus did "not quarrel or cry aloud" (Matt 12:19a).[16] The Pharisees also brought fulfillment to Isa 42:2 in that they did not "hear his voice in the streets" (Matt 12:19b), that is, they refused to acknowledge his message.[17]

Jesus also showed compassion and healed the many people who followed him (Matt 12:15b). Rather than needlessly quarreling with his opposition, Jesus helped those in need, a mark of gentleness foretold in Isa 42:3. Figuratively speaking, Jesus' actions would be so gentle that he would not break a reed that had already been damaged ("a bruised reed he will not break") or put out the wick of a candle that was barely keeping its flame ("a smoldering wick he will not quench").[18] Luz notes, "Obviously he preserves what is crushed and lets imperfect shine."[19]

Jesus then ordered those who were healed to refrain from making him known. The gentle character of his ministry extended to not announcing his identity in a dramatic fashion. Jesus was concerned with the proclamation of his message rather than people knowing who he was.[20]

Other details in Matthew's quotation of Isaiah do not find fulfillment in the immediate context, though they would find fulfillment in time to come. Jesus' proclamation would eventually extend to the Gentiles (Matt 12:18), and he would execute justice in time as well (Matt 12:20).[21]

16. Bock, *Jesus according to Scripture*, 185; Morris, *The Gospel According to Matthew*, 308; Nolland, *The Gospel of Matthew*, 493–94; Rea, *The Holy Spirit in the Bible*, 127–28.

17. Blomberg, *Matthew*, 200.

18. Morris, *The Gospel According to Matthew*, 310–11; Nolland, *The Gospel of Matthew*, 494.

19. Luz, *Matthew 8–20*, 194.

20. Hagner, *Matthew 1–13*, 338.

21. Hagner points out that the mention of justice in Matt 12:20 implies "the delay of judgment" (Ibid.). Justice will not take place until Jesus has carried out his initial

The Spirit's work through Jesus is identified in Matt 12:18, and this work applies to all that is described in Matt 12:18–21, which itself is a commentary of Matt 12:15–16. The immediate point of Matthew's quotation is to show the gentle nature of Jesus' ministry in Matt 12:15–16, and it is implied that the Spirit's work through Jesus enabled him to carry out his ministry as a whole.

Matthew 12:28

Matthew 12:28 is found in the midst of Jesus' defense of the divine authority and power behind his ministry (Matt 12:22–32). Jesus had cast out the demon of a man who was blind and mute, resulting in the man's ability to speak and see (Matt 12:22). When the people asked if Jesus was the Messiah, "the Son of David" (Matt 12:23), the Pharisees responded by claiming his power came from the "prince of demons" (Matt 12:24). Jesus explained the faulty logic of such a claim (Matt 12:25–27) and then pointed to the true source of his ability to cast out demons: "But if it is by the Spirit of God that I cast out demons, then the kingdom of God has come upon you" (Matt 12:28).

Whether the phrase is "the Spirit of God" (Matt 12:28) or "the finger of God" (Luke 11:20), the point is that "the power is from God."[22] The exercise of Jesus' authority over demons is possible by the power of the Spirit, and this miracle evidenced the establishment[23] or imminency[24] of God's kingdom. Though space does not allow for even a brief summary of the nature of the kingdom as presented by Matthew or others, it may be at least said that the kingdom was somehow present. Though the kingdom had not arrived in the sense of its consummate form, Jesus the king exercised his authority over the kingdom of darkness.[25]

This passage in particular demonstrates Jesus' authority and power as a leader. He was the agent of God's kingdom who exercised power and

---

ministry of gentle proclamation. At the same time, while not denying a future judgment to come, Neyrey, "The Thematic Use of Isaiah 42, 1–4 in Matthew 12," 464, identifies multiple scenes of judgment even within Matthew 12. Jesus executes judgment in the sense that he condemns his hearers multiple times (e.g., 12:31–32, 38–42).

22. Morris, *The Gospel According to Matthew*, 316. Cf. Bruce, "The Holy Spirit in the Acts of the Apostles," 169.

23. France, *The Gospel of Matthew*, 480.

24. Keener, *A Commentary on the Gospel of Matthew*, 364.

25. Hagner, *Matthew 1–13*, 343.

authority over the kingdom of darkness by means of the Spirit of God. The demons were subject to his commands, implying his authority over the ruler of demons as well.

Luke 4:14

In considering Luke 4:14, it is helpful to remember that Luke 3:16–17 records the descent of the Spirit upon Jesus at his baptism. Jesus is then described as being "full of the Holy Spirit" and being "led by the Spirit in the wilderness for forty days, being tempted by the devil" (Luke 4:1–2).[26] After the record of the temptation of Jesus (Luke 4:3–13), Luke 4:14–15 summarizes Jesus' ministry in Galilee and states, "Jesus returned in the power of the Spirit to Galilee, and report about him went through all the surrounding country. And he taught in their synagogues, being glorified by all" (Luke 4:14–15).

The phrase "in the power of the Spirit" is used to explain how Jesus "returned . . . to Galilee" (Luke 4:14). It could be that the Spirit's role in this description primarily involved guiding Jesus back to Galilee,[27] but it also said immediately thereafter that "a report about him went out through all the surrounding country" (Luke 4:14). While this report may have been a reaction to Jesus' teaching alone (the only activity identified in Luke 4:15), Jesus' return in the "power" of the Spirit implies the presence of miracles.[28] Luke 4:14–15 serves as a summary statement for Jesus' ministry in general and would thus apply to what follows in Luke 4:16–41,[29] which includes a reference to the exercise of Jesus' power to cast out demons (Luke 4:36). At the same time, Luke 4:14–15 does not explicitly mention miracles, but it does focus on Jesus' teaching (cf. Luke 4:15).[30] The following discussion of Luke 4:18 focuses on this theme.[31]

---

26. Shepherd, *The Narrative Function of the Holy Spirit*, 130–31, explains the descriptions of Jesus in Luke 4:1 and 4:14 as implying his role as a prophet.

27. Bock, *Luke 1:1—9:50*, 392.

28. Lenski explains the Spirit's power as being expressed "by word and by deed" (*The Interpretation of St. Luke's Gospel*, 243). See also Nolland, *Luke 1:9–20*, 186.

29. Green, *The Gospel of Luke*, 203. Green notes that Luke 4:14–15 functions as an *inclusio* with 4:42–44. Luke 4:14 likewise functions as an inclusio with Luke 4:1. Cf. Shepherd, *The Narrative Function of the Holy Spirit*, 132.

30. Bock, *Luke 1:1—9:50*, 391–93.

31. It could be added that Luke does not require the idea of power to include the use of miracles. It was said of John the Baptist that he would minister "in the spirit and power

Spiritual Leadership

Luke 4:18

While in Galilee, Jesus went to his hometown Nazareth and spoke in the synagogue (Luke 4:16). This event was an example of Jesus' regular teaching in the synagogues introduced in Luke 4:14-15. Jesus opened the scroll of Isaiah and read from Isa 61:1-2a:

> The Spirit of the Lord is upon me, / because he has anointed me / to proclaim good news to the poor. / He has sent me to proclaim liberty to the captives / and recovering of sight to the blind, / to set at liberty those who are oppressed, / to proclaim the year of the Lord's favor. (Luke 4:18-19)

Jesus then sat down to explain the text and claimed, "Today this Scripture has been fulfilled in your hearing" (Luke 4:20-21).[32]

It was concluded previously that Isa 61:1-3 was one of several passages in Isaiah that spoke of the Spirit being upon a royal figure who would come and administer perfect justice for the world. If Isa 11:2, 42:1, and 61:1 all speak of the same person, the Lord's anointing with the Spirit in Isa 61:1 and Luke 4:18 is not merely for the purpose of prophecy, but also a royal anointing so that the Anointed would be enabled to rule in perfection. Luke later recorded the words of Peter when he spoke of Christ as the royal "Anointed" who was "anointed" by the Father (Acts 4:26-27; cf. 10:38).[33]

Jesus' claim that the Spirit was upon him refers back to the Spirit's descent upon him at his baptism (Luke 3:21-22).[34] The Spirit thereafter gave Jesus guidance (Luke 4:1) and empowered his ministry of teaching in the synagogues (Luke 4:14-15). Jesus himself then specifically clarifies that the Spirit's work through him at the present was primarily for the purpose of proclamation. The Father had anointed Jesus with the Spirit to "proclaim good news to the poor," to "proclaim liberty to the captives and recovering

---

of Elijah" (Luke 1:17). For John the Baptist, this power was shown not through miracles but proclamation alone. Cf. Stein, *Luke*, 76-77, 149.

32. The perfect tense of "fulfilled" indicates certain present fulfillment. Cf. Bock, *Luke 1:1—9:50*, 412.

33. Stein, *Luke*, 156.

34. Shepherd, *The Narrative Function of the Holy Spirit*, 135-36.

of sight to the blind,"[35] and to "proclaim the year of the Lord's favor" (Luke 4:18–19).[36] These descriptions emphasize Jesus' role as a prophet.[37]

Though some would limit Luke 4:18–19 to refer only to Jesus' ministry as a prophet,[38] there is good reason to understand this text to refer to Jesus' ministry as the Messiah as well.[39] Luke 4:18–19 is a quotation of most of Isa 61:1–2a,[40] but the final line of Luke 4:18 is a partial quotation of Isa 58:6 as well, probably an alteration of Jesus' words by Luke in order for his readers to see Jesus' role as the Messiah.[41] The significance of this inclusion is that Jesus does not only "proclaim liberty to the captives" (Luke 4:18, fourth line; cf. Isa 61:1), but he is also the one "to set at liberty those who are oppressed" (Luke 4:18, sixth and last line; cf. Isa 58:6). In other words, Jesus proclaims liberty as a prophet, and he grants liberty as the Messiah as well.[42] Though Jesus would grant physical and spiritual deliverance during his ministry, his role as the Messiah was yet to be seen in full. Jesus' quotation of Isa 61:2 excluded the reference to "the day of vengeance of our God," implying his proclamation about God's vengeance was yet to come, as well as its execution.[43]

Jesus' role as a leader is obviously unique. He alone is the Messiah who granted deliverance to the physically and spiritually oppressed. He saw

---

35. Luke records that Jesus granted sight to those who were blind physically (Luke 18:35–43) and spiritually (1:77–79; 8:10; 10:23–24; cf. Acts 26:18). It is not necessary to choose whether this sight was one or the other. Luke's understanding of the poor seems to be broader than material concerns as well. See Bock, *Luke 1:1–9:50*, 409, and Stein, *Luke*, 156.

36. Scholars often refer to the year of Jubilee as being the thought behind "the day of the Lord's favor" (cf. Lev 25:8–12). Bock, points out that any reference to the Jubilee would be to give a "picture of forgiveness and spiritual liberation" (*Luke 1:1–9:50*, 406).

37. Hawthorne, *The Presence and the Power*, 163.

38. Ibid., 163–64. Hawthorne argues in detail against certainty as to whether anointing refers to the ministry of Jesus as a priest or king (cf. Luke 4:24). Bock, *Luke 1:1–9:50*, 406–07, notes that it may have been that the audience may have understood only prophetic overtones, but Luke meant more by altering Jesus' quotation (see below) and recording Jesus' miracles, acts which provoked the recognition of him as the Messiah (cf. 4:38–31; ibid., 407).

39. Cho, *Spirit and Kingdom in the Writings of Paul*, 172–73; Shepherd, *The Narrative Function of the Holy Spirit*, 136.

40. Luke 4:18 does not include the phrase "to bind up the brokenhearted" (Isa 61:1).

41. Stein, *Luke*, 156

42. Bock, *Luke 1:1–9:50*, 409; Lenski, *The Interpretation of St. Luke's Gospel*, 248.

43. Bock, *Luke 1:1–9:50*, 411; Nolland, *Luke 1:9–20*, 198; Stein, *Luke*, 155–57.

himself as a prophet who proclaimed good news, liberty, and the Lord's favor. He was enabled by the Spirit to carry out these tasks.

John 3:34

John the Baptist explained that Christ's ministry superseded his own (John 3:25–30). After recording these words, John the Evangelist then commented on this topic further (John 3:31–36). John 3:34 explains why Jesus' testimony is superlative to all who have come before him and why God is shown to be true through him: "For he whom God has sent utters the words of God, for he gives the Spirit without measure" (John 3:34; cf. 3:31–33).

While it is possible for the grammar of John 3:34 to identify Jesus as the giver of the Spirit,[44] multiple reasons suggest it is the Father who gives the Spirit to Jesus.[45] John 1:32–33 has already described the event in which the Spirit was given to Jesus.[46] Also, the following statement in John 3:35 would echo the grammar and concept of the final clause of John 3:34. Just as the Father "gives the Spirit without measure" to the Son (John 3:34), so also "the Father loves the Son and has given all things into his hand," the Spirit included (John 3:35).[47] Finally, the Spirit was given "without measure," which means that the Spirit's work through Jesus to reveal the words of God was not limited in any way. Previous prophets revealed only so much according to the measure of the Spirit they were given.[48] Jesus' unique relationship with the Father allowed him this limitless experience of the Spirit, something no other person could claim (cf. John 1:14, 16, 18).[49]

What was recorded in John 1:32–33 is mentioned again here in John 3:34. The promise of the Spirit's coming in Isaiah's prophecies (Isa 11:2; 42:1; 61:1) had been fulfilled in Jesus,[50] and John 3:34 focuses in particular on the Spirit's work through Jesus to perfectly reveal the Father.

---

44. Keener, *The Gospel of John*, 1:582.

45. Even if Christ is the one who gives the Spirit "without measure," this thought would assume that Christ himself has the Spirit without measure to give the Spirit to others in like fashion.

46. Keener, *The Gospel of John*, 1:583

47. Bruce, *The Gospel of John*, 97; Carson, *The Gospel According to John*, 213; Keener, *The Gospel of John*, 582–83.

48. Carson, *The Gospel According to John*, 213.

49. Borchert, *John 1–11*, 194.

50. Carson sees John 3:34 as a restatement of John 1:32–33, noting, "The same truth is repeated in new form," i.e., "John the Baptist had already testified that he had seen the

Acts 1:2

Luke introduces the book of Acts by referring to his gospel in which he wrote about "all that Jesus began to do and teach, until the day he was taken up, after he had given commands through the Holy Spirit to the apostles whom he had chosen" (Acts 1:1–2).

The "commands through the Holy Spirit" that Jesus gave (Acts 1:2) were given prior to being "taken up" into heaven (cf. Acts 1:9–11). Luke likely referred to the commands that Jesus gave in Acts 1:4: "And while staying with them he ordered them not to depart from Jerusalem, but to wait for the promise of the Father."

Most commentators explain that the phrase "through the Holy Spirit" is grammatically awkward and could modify Jesus' giving of commands or his choosing of the apostles.[51] However, the context immediately records the giving of these commands (cf. Acts 1:4), and it seems more likely that Luke would refer to Jesus' present giving of commands as taking place by the Spirit than his past choosing of the apostles (cf. Luke 6:13).[52] As in Luke 4:1 and 4:14, though the terminology is different, the resurrected Jesus is presented again as being full of the Spirit,[53] perhaps to prepare the reader for Jesus' giving of the Spirit in Acts 2:33.[54]

While Luke describes Jesus in Acts 1:2 in terms similar to previous descriptions (cf. Luke 4:1, 14), the significance of this passage is that Jesus is still seen to experience the work of the Spirit in his ministry after his resurrection.

Acts 10:38

Peter explained the "good news of peace through Jesus Christ" to a number of Gentiles (Acts 10:36; cf. 10:34–43).[55] After some opening comments

---

Spirit descend *and remain* on Jesus (1:32–33), in fulfilment of Isaiah's prophecy (Is. 11:2; 42:1; 61:1)" (italics original; *The Gospel According to John*, 213).

51. E.g., see Barrett, *The Acts of the Apostles*, 1:67–69. Bock, *Acts*, 53–54, mentions a third view as well, which sees the phrase as explaining *why* Jesus had to choose the apostles, that is, because the apostles were about to be given the Spirit. Jesus gave commands to the apostles *because of* (*dia*) the Holy Spirit. Bock points out that this use of *dia* would be rare and does not fit the context.

52. Cf. Peterson, *The Acts of the Apostles*, 103.

53. Bock, *Acts*, 54; Shepherd, *The Narrative Function of the Holy Spirit*, 154–55.

54. Peterson, *The Acts of the Apostles*, 103.

55. Ibid., 333–34.

(Acts 10:34–36), Peter summarized significant events that "happened throughout all Judea" (Acts 10:37; cf. 10:37–43), including the ministry of Jesus: "God anointed Jesus of Nazareth with the Holy Spirit and with power. He went about doing good and healing all who were oppressed by the devil, for God was with him" (Acts 10:38).

Acts 10:38 looks back to Luke 3:21–22 when the Father anointed Jesus with the Spirit at his baptism. It was pointed out above that Jesus' miracles and teaching were the result of this anointing (cf. Luke 4:14–15, 36).[56] Jesus then claimed that he had been anointed with the Spirit by quoting Isa 61:1 (Luke 4:18). His own understanding of his anointing was that the Spirit would work through him for the purpose of proclamation and deliverance.[57]

Rather than focusing on the teaching ministry of Jesus as Luke did earlier (cf. Luke 4:14–15, 18–21), the result of the Spirit's work is now described as Jesus' "doing good and healing all who were oppressed by the devil" (Acts 10:38). The first of these two participles, "doing good," is from the word *euergeteō*, which is found only here in the NT. A related word, *euergesia*, is translated "good deed" in Acts 4:9, and the good deed in view was the healing of a crippled man's feet and ankles (cf. Acts 3:6–9). This use of *euergesia* in Acts suggests that the use of *euergeteō* in Acts 10:38 could refer to Jesus' ministry of "doing good" through miracles. This conclusion is strengthened by the fact that this participle is placed side-by-side with the participial phrase "healing all who were oppressed by the devil." Just as Jesus went about "doing good," so also it could be said that Jesus healed the oppressed. Though the focus of Jesus' healing the oppressed involved physical healings, this description of his ministry could have had notions of spiritual healing as well. His miraculous healings testified to his identity and the authenticity of his message.

A final point of interest is the clause that explains further why Jesus was able to do good and heal: "for God was with him" (Acts 10:38). It was seen in the previous chapter that the description of God being "with" an individual could imply the work of the Spirit through this individual, especially if the Spirit's work through the individual had been previously described. In Acts 10:38, Jesus' healing ministry is described as the result of having been anointed with the Spirit, and it is then described as the result of God having been "with him." The anointing of the Spirit and God's being with Jesus are two ways to describe the same enabling by the Spirit that was given to Jesus.

---

56. Larkin, *Acts*, 166; Peterson, *The Acts of the Apostles*, 337.

57. Hawthorne, *The Presence and the Power*, 132–33.

As clarified in the previous chapter, the description of God's being "with" a leader does not demand that the Spirit be at work through the leader in some way, but it could certainly imply as much when the Spirit's work through the leader has been previously described as taking place.

The description of the role of the Spirit in Jesus' ministry in Acts 10:38 is significant to this study for at least two reasons. First, the entire ministry of Jesus is summarized in terms of what took place as a result of God anointing him with the Spirit. Second, the phrase "God was with him" echoes the terminology used to describe some Spirit-enabled leaders in the OT (cf. 1 Sam 18:12),[58] reinforcing the conclusion that leaders may sometimes be described as being enabled by the Spirit without directly referring to the Spirit.

First Corinthians 12:4–5

First Corinthians 12–14 is Paul's lengthy response to the Corinthians' question about spiritual gifts (cf. 1 Cor 12:1). In stressing the variety of gifts given to the body, Paul referred to the Spirit, Son, and Father as all being involved in giving these gifts:

> Now there are varieties of gifts, but the same Spirit; and there are varieties of service, but the same Lord; and there are varieties of activities, but it is the same God who empowers them all in everyone. To each is given the manifestation of the Spirit for the common good. (1 Cor 12:4–7)

Just as Paul notes that the Spirit is the one to grant "varieties of gifts" (1 Cor 12:4), so also does he state that "the Lord" is the one to grant "varieties of service" (1 Cor 12:5), a phrase parallel in concept to "varieties of gifts."[59] Paul then mentions "varieties of activities" (parallel to the two phrases noted above) and identifies "God" as the one "who empowers them all in everyone" (1 Cor 12:6). The "Lord" is the Lord Jesus Christ, creating a reference to the Trinity by identifying the Spirit, Lord, and God.[60]

More will be said of spiritual gifts below, but it may at least be said for the moment that Paul is not teaching that the Spirit, Son, and Father grant gifts, services (ministries), and activities apart from one another. Rather,

---

58. Bock, *Acts*, 398, states that this "clause gives the reason Jesus worked with such power."

59. Carson, *Showing the Spirit*, 33–34, notes that these phrases are not exactly synonymous, but Paul's point is not necessarily to highlight the differences.

60. Thomas, *Understanding Spiritual Gifts*, 26.

each member of the Trinity is in concert with the other in granting spiritual gifts to the members of the body.[61] Though the Lord Jesus Christ sent the Spirit at Pentecost (cf. Acts 2:33), it may also be said that he continued and continues to grant spiritual gifts through the Spirit to those who truly confess him as Lord (cf. 1 Cor 12:3).

Revelation 2:7, 11, 17, 29; 3:6, 13, 22

Revelation 2–3 contains John's record of Jesus' words to seven churches. Jesus closes his message to each church with these words: "He who has an ear, let him hear what the Spirit says to the churches" (Rev 2:7, 11, 17, 29; 3:6, 13, 22).

What is clear is that Christ considered his words to the churches to be the words of the Spirit.[62] What Jesus said in Revelation 2–3 is an example of fulfillment to what he promised previously promised the apostles. He would send them the Spirit to "declare . . . the things that are to come" (John 16:13; cf. 16:12–15).[63]

The One Who Gives the Spirit

Not only is Jesus the one to whom the Spirit is given, he is also the one who gives the Spirit. This fact shows Jesus' experience of the Spirit to be patently distinct from any other leader in this study. A brief survey of the passages on this topic is sufficient for the present section, and these passages will be discussed in further detail when examining the apostles below.

All of the Gospels record the prophecy that the one to come after John the Baptist would baptize his followers with the Spirit (Matt 3:11; Mark 1:8; Luke 3:16; John 1:33). Before and after his death, Jesus promised he would send the Spirit (Luke 24:49; John 15:26; 14:16–17, 26; 16:7, 13–15 Acts 1:5, 8).[64]

---

61. Carson, *Showing the Spirit*, 33–34.

62. Beale, *The Book of Revelation*, 234.

63. The phrase "things that are to come" does not demand that the revelation given by Christ through the Spirit would be limited to eschatological events. See the discussion of John 16:12–15 below.

64. These passages involve both Jesus and those to whom the Spirit is sent. The parallel passages in Matt 10:20, Mark 13:11, and Luke 12:12 promise the Spirit's work through the apostles in the context of persecution, but Jesus does not specify in these passages that he would be the one to send the Spirit. When coupled with Luke 21:15 ("I will give you a mouth and wisdom"), however, it would seem that the Spirit's work through the apostles

After his resurrection and before his ascension, Jesus breathed on the disciples and gave the imperative, "Receive the Holy Spirit" (John 20:22). Whatever may be said of the situation in John 20:22,[65] the events of Acts 2:1–4 and Peter's explanation thereafter (cf. Acts 2:14–36) certainly indicate that Jesus sent the Spirit after his ascension into heaven. Peter explained the events of Acts 2:1–4 in this way: "Being therefore exalted at the right hand of God, and having received from the Father the promise of the Holy Spirit, he [i.e., Jesus] has poured out this that you yourselves are seeing and hearing" (Acts 2:33). Peter's listeners were "seeing and hearing" the phenomena of Acts 2:1–4, specifically that the disciples "began to speak in other tongues as the Spirit gave them utterance" (Acts 2:4). Peter explained this event as a fulfillment of Joel 2:28–32 in that God's promise "I will pour out my Spirit" had taken place (cf. Acts 2:17–18). Joel spoke of God as the one who would pour out the Spirit, and it was Christ that Peter identified as the one who "poured out this," that is, the Spirit (Acts 2:33).[66]

Summary

Jesus was anointed by the Spirit at his baptism (Matt 3:16; Mark 1:10; Luke 3:22; John 1:32–33) and was identified by the Father as the king of Israel (Matt 3:17; cf. Ps 2:7) and the prophesied Servant of Isaiah (Matt 3:17; cf. Isa 42:1). This anointing began a multi-faceted work of the Spirit that characterized Jesus' entire ministry (Matt 12:18; Luke 4:14–15; Acts 10:38). The NT records the work of the Spirit in Jesus' teaching (Luke 4:14–15), performance of miracles (Matt 12:28; cf. Luke 4:14, 36), and granting spiritual and physical deliverance to the oppressed (Luke 4:18–21; cf. Isa 58:6;

---

takes place by the direction of Jesus. These passages and others that specifically speak of the Spirit being sent to the apostles are discussed in further detail below.

65. The nature of Jesus' action and words in John 20:22 is highly debated. See below.

66. Though the terminology shifts from baptism to pouring, Peter would later speak of this event as the baptism of the Spirit (Acts 11:15–16). It would appear that outpouring and baptism are one and the same activity. Peter's description in Acts 11:15–17 refers to the reception of the Spirit by the Gentiles in Acts 10:44–48. The terminology used in Acts 10:44–48 recalls the events of Acts 2:1–4. Acts 2:4 states, "And they were all filled with the Holy Spirit and began to speak in other tongues." As seen above, Peter explained this filling and utterance as the result of Jesus' having "poured out this," the Spirit (Acts 2:33; cf. 2:17–18). Similarly, "The gift of the Holy Spirit was poured out even on the Gentiles. For they were hearing them speaking in tongues and extolling God" (Acts 10:46). Peter then referred to this outpouring as a fulfillment of Jesus' promise of Spirit baptism (Acts 11:15–17). Cf. Bruce, *The Acts of the Apostles*, 269.

61:1–2a). Though Jesus is the Messiah who will execute his enemies and bring about worldwide peace (Isa 11:2–5), his ministry before his death did not include these activities but was of a gentle nature (Matt 12:18). He was a prophet who proclaimed the good news of salvation (Luke 4:18–21; cf. Isa 61:1–2a) and perfectly revealed the Father (John 3:34).

Jesus experienced the work of the Spirit after his resurrection (Acts 1:2) and sent the Spirit upon his followers just as he and others promised he would do (Acts 2:1–3, 17–18, 33; cf. Matt 3:11; Mark 1:8; Luke 3:16; 24:49; John 1:33; 15:26; 16:7; Acts 1:5, 8). He gave revelation to John and others through the Spirit (Rev 2:7, 11, 17, 29; 3:6, 13, 22; cf. John 16:12–15) and continues to grant the work of the Spirit in spiritual gifts to those who confess him as Lord (1 Cor 12:3–5).

The Apostles as a Group

The NT describes the Spirit's work in the apostles in the Gospels, mostly in Acts, and the letters. This section will begin by examining passages that involve the Spirit and the apostles as a group.

The Ones to Whom the Spirit Would Be Given

Jesus promised that the Spirit would be given to the apostles in the context of persecution (Matt 10:20; Mark 13:11; Luke 12:12), that the Spirit would be given after he left (John 14:16–17; 14:25–26; 15:26–27; 16:4b–11; and 16:12–15; cf. 20:22), and that the Spirit would be given on the day of Pentecost (Luke 24:49; Acts 1:4–5, 8).

Matthew 10:20; Mark 13:11; Luke 12:12

Matthew, Mark, and Luke each record a promise by Jesus to the apostles about the Spirit's work in the context of persecution.[67] The record of Mark more or less represents its parallels in Matthew and Luke:[68] "And when they

---

67. Matthew 10:19–20; Mark 13:11; Luke 12:12 are similar to what Jesus says in John 15:26–27. The difference, however, would be that Matthew, Mark, and Luke speak of a desperate situation involving persecution. Cf. Thiselton, *The Holy Spirit*, 44; France, *The Gospel of Mark*, 518.

68. Bock points out that these parallels are "conceptual" (*Jesus According to Scripture*, 266). These passages vary in setting and other details as well. See below.

bring you to trial and deliver you over, do not be anxious beforehand what you are to say, but say whatever is given you in that hour, for it is not you who speak, but the Holy Spirit" (Mark 13:11). The Spirit's words would allow them "to bear witness before them" of the gospel (Mark 13:9–10).

Though the substance of this promise is similar from one Gospel to the next, there are some differences to be noted.[69] The setting in Matthew's record is Jesus' commissioning of the twelve to preach to the cities of Israel (Matt 10:5–8). The setting given by Mark involves only four of the disciples, and the timing of the promise's fulfillment would be in the last days (Mark 13:3–4). The setting in Luke records Jesus' words to the twelve disciples when they were surrounded by thousands of people (Luke 12:1), and it is not specified when this persecution would take place.

There are some differences in how this promise is stated as well. Matthew speaks of the "Spirit of the Father,"[70] and Mark and Luke refer to the "Holy Spirit." Matthew and Mark record that it is not the one on trial who speaks, but the Spirit. Luke states that the Spirit will "teach you in that very hour what you ought to say."[71] These differences do not change the substance of the promise.

The similarities among these passages are obvious. There is a warning that the apostles will be forced to give a defense for their message before synagogues and Gentile rulers (Matt 10:17–18; Mark 13:9; Luke 12:11). However, they should not be anxious (Matt 10:19; Mark 13:11; Luke 12:11). The Spirit will give them the words to speak (Matt 10:20; Mark 13:11; Luke 12:12). Matthew and Mark add that this persecution would involve physical violence (Matt 10:17; Mark 13:9), rejection by one's own family (Matt 10:21; Mark 13:12), hatred, and salvation to the one who endures (Matt 10:22; Mark 13:13).

The parallel passage of Mark 13:9–13 is Luke 21:12–19,[72] and though there is no reference to the Spirit by Luke, this passage repeats the promise

---

69. Bock comments, "The Spirit will instruct them with specific content in that hour" (*Luke*, 2:1143). Though expressed differently from Matthew and Mark, the concept is one and the same. The Spirit would give the disciples words to say.

70. Fitzmyer, *The Gospel According to Luke X–XXIV*, 963, suggests Matthew may intentionally have referred to the Father in keeping with the references to the Father in 10:29, 32, 33.

71. Bock, *Luke*, 2:1144.

72. Matthew 24:9–14 is a parallel passage as well but omits the details of any help by the Spirit or Christ during the point of trial before any authorities. See Bock, *Jesus According to Scripture*, 341–42.

of help in the time of persecution. Jesus speaks to the apostles (cf. Luke 20:25) of the last days (cf. Luke 21:8) and promises that persecution will come (Luke 21:12). When it does, Jesus commands that no thought would be given to one's defense (Luke 21:14) because he himself would "give . . . a mouth and wisdom" that could not be refuted (Luke 21:15), just as the LORD promised Moses, "I will be with your mouth and teach you what you shall speak" (Exod 4:12).[73] What is said of the Spirit in Mark is said of Jesus in Luke.[74] As the Spirit would speak for the apostles, so also Jesus would give them a mouth and wisdom to answer their interrogators. Jesus would assumedly direct the words of the apostles through the Spirit.

These passages describe how the Spirit would work through the apostles in the context of persecution. When brought before authorities to give a defense for their message and actions, there was no need for anxiety—the Spirit would give them the words to say in defense of their message of the gospel. This work took place after Jesus commissioned the twelve to speak in the cities of Israel, and, as will be seen below, the book of Acts records that this ministry of the Spirit certainly took place after Jesus' ascension into heaven.[75]

The Five Paraclete Passages

There are five "*Paraclete* passages"[76] in the Farewell Discourse (John 14–17) in which Jesus describes how the Spirit would work through the apostles: John 14:16–17; 14:25–26; 15:26–27; 16:4b–11; and 16:12–15.[77] The audience consists of the eleven apostles (cf. John 13:31),[78] and it will be seen

---

73. Keener, *Matthew*, 324. In response to Moses' request that the LORD would "send someone else" (Exod 4:13), the LORD allowed Aaron to go with Moses and stated of them both, "You shall speak to him and put the words in his mouth, and I will be with your mouth and with his mouth and will teach you both what to do" (Exod 4:15).

74. Bruce, "The Holy Spirit in the Acts of the Apostles," 168; Irving Francis Wood, *The Spirit of God in Biblical Literature* (New York: A. C. Armstrong & Son, 1904), 132.

75. Fitzmyer, *The Gospel According to Luke X–XXIV*, 965; Keener, *Matthew*, 324.

76. The term *Paraclete* is a transliteration of *paraklētos*, which is translated "Helper" by the ESV in John 14:17, 26; 15:26; and 16:7. For a lengthy discussion of the lexical and background information of this term, see James M. Hamilton, Jr., *God's Indwelling Presence*, 64–72. Beasley-Murray, *John*, 256, points out that Jesus' role as *paraklētos* in 1 John 2:1 does not necessarily correspond to how Jesus speaks of the Spirit in John 14:16–17.

77. Cf. Beasley-Murray, *John*, 256; Köstenberger, *John*, 37.

78. Köstenberger states, "Now that the new messianic community has been cleansed

that they are primarily in view for the multi-faceted ministry of the Spirit described in the Farewell Discourse.

JOHN 14:16–17

Jesus promised the apostles that the Father "will give you another Helper, to be with you forever, even the Spirit of truth.... You know him, for he dwells with you and will be in you" (John 14:16–17).

The promise "he... will be in you" has excited a considerable amount of debate over the issue of whether or not Old Testament believers were indwelt by the Spirit.[79] While this passage has some bearing upon how the Spirit works through *all* believers after Pentecost,[80] it is the present author's understanding that John 14:16–17 primarily involves a ministry of the Spirit that would be unique to the *apostles*. Two phrases from John 14:16–17 support this understanding.

First, Jesus promises that the Father will send "the Spirit of truth" and later explains the relationship between the Spirit, truth, and the apostles further in the following four *Paraclete* passages. John 15:26 and 16:13 also speak of "the Spirit of truth," and it is particularly the apostles (John 15:26, "you have been with me from the beginning") who will "bear witness" to the truth about Jesus (John 15:26) and receive new truth about him as well (John 16:13; see below), not believers in general.

Second, the phrase "he dwells with you and will be in you" may be taken to primarily apply to the apostles as well. Ferguson explains:

> The distinction in view here is not between his presence with and his dwelling in the disciples as such, but between the ministry of the Spirit in Christ (i.e., 'with you' in this sense) and his subsequent ministry as the Spirit of Christ in the disciples ('in you'). By

---

and the traitor [Judas Iscariot] has been removed, Jesus' final instruction of his followers can begin" (*John*, 422).

79. The inference for some is that the Spirit could not be said to be "in you" for believers prior to Pentecost in the sense that they were permanently indwelt by the Spirit. For a survey of positions on this issue, see Hamilton, *God's Indwelling Presence*, 9–24.

80. Köstenberger, *John*, 437, points out that there is a "secondary sense" in which the Spirit works in all believers. He states that the Spirit "... fulfills similar roles in believers today. He illumines the spiritual meaning of Jesus' words and works both to believers and, through believers, to the unbelieving world."

this new mode of indwelling, Christ's ministry will be continued and advanced.[81]

The Spirit's being "in" the disciples would continue and advance the ministry of Christ by empowering the disciples to be effective witnesses to the gospel, just as the Spirit was already doing so by empowering Christ to do the same. As the Spirit was "with" them through his ministry through Christ, so also the Spirit would continue this ministry by being "in" the apostles. The Spirit's presence for the purpose of empowerment and revelation are primarily in view, not indwelling or sanctification.[82]

JOHN 14:26

In John 14:26 Jesus states to the eleven, "But the Helper, the Holy Spirit, whom the Father will send in my name, he will teach you all things and bring to your remembrance all that I have said to you."

Jesus' statement repeats some of the same thoughts found in John 14:16–17. The Spirit is the Helper and would be sent by the Father. John 14:26 adds that the Spirit would "teach" the apostles "all things" and "bring to your remembrance all that I have said to you."

While the *Paraclete* passages do include the promise of new revelation (John 16:13; see below), John 14:26 is not one of these passages. Jesus stated that the Spirit's activity would be to "teach" and "bring to your remembrance." The content of this teaching would be "all things," and the remembrance would be "all that I have said to you." At first glance, it would seem that the Spirit would teach something new and then also bring to remembrance what Jesus had already said. However, a closer look at the text indicates that both instances of the word "all"[83] should be qualified by

---

81. Ferguson, *The Holy Spirit*, 186–87.

82. McCabe, "Were Old Testament Believers Indwelt by the Spirit," 220–21. This is not to say that these two ministries of the Spirit can exist apart from one another (cf. 1 Cor 12:3–7, 11).

83. The term *pas* is used twice, first translated "all things" and then "all," which is followed by the phrase "that I have said to you" (*ha eipon hymin*).

the phrase "that I have said to you,"[84] which means that the Spirit's roles in teaching and remembrance both involve what Jesus has *already* said.[85]

John 14:26 contains the one use of *hypomimnēskō* ("bring to your remembrance") in John, but its simpler form *mimnēskomai* is used in John 2:17, 22 and 12:16. These passages illustrate how the Spirit would have brought Jesus' words to remembrance and then taught them their significance.[86] The disciples remembered Ps 69:9 and Jesus' statement about the temple being raised in three days, and this recall of information allowed them to see the significance of these statements as they applied to the situation at hand (John 2:17, 22). Likewise, the disciples remembered Zech 9:9 and understood its significance in light of Jesus' triumphal entry into Jerusalem (John 12:15–16). Beasley-Murray helpfully notes that the Spirit "not only enables them to *recall* these things but to perceive their significances, and so he *teaches* the disciples to grasp the revelation of God brought by Jesus in its richness and profundity."[87]

John 15:26

In John 15:26–27 Jesus states, "But when the Helper comes, whom I will send to you from the Father, the Spirit of truth, who proceeds from the Father, he will bear witness about me. And you also will bear witness, because you have been with me from the beginning."

This passage promises again that the Spirit would be sent to the apostles, and Jesus says that it would be he who sends the Spirit from the Father (John 15:26). Jesus then states that the Spirit "will bear witness about me" (John 15:26) and that the apostles "also will bear witness" (John 15:27). It is not specified in this passage how exactly the Spirit would bear witness along with the witness of apostles. It can at least be assumed that their

---

84. Keener, *The Gospel of John*, 978. Keener points out the similarity of this ministry by the Spirit to believers today. The Spirit teaches believers the significance and meaning of what has previously been said in God's Word (1 John 2:20, 27). For the apostles, the Spirit would teach them the significance and meaning of what had previously been said by Jesus. See also Pettegrew, *The New Covenant Ministry of the Holy Spirit*, 71.

85. Köstenberger states that this teaching does not involve revealing "qualitatively new or independent revelation" but "all that I have said to you" (*John*, 442). In other words, the Spirit brings to mind Jesus' words and then teaches the disciples to understand "the true meaning and significance of the revelation imparted by Jesus" (Ibid.).

86. Beasley-Murray, *John*, 261.

87. Ibid.

witness would be not as separate entities, but in harmony with one another.[88] This witness could be similar to what Jesus promised to the disciples in times of persecution. At such a time, the Spirit would give them the words necessary to witness to the truth of the gospel (cf. Mark 13:9–11).[89] In fact, John 15:26–27 is found in the midst of warnings of persecution (cf. John 15:18–25; 16:1–4a). Jesus expressly says of his preceding words (John 15:26–27 included) that they were stated for the apostles to remember in times of persecution so that they would persevere (John 16:1–4a).[90]

JOHN 16:7

In John 16:7 Jesus stated to the apostles, "It is to your advantage that I go away, for if I do not go away, the Helper will not come to you. But if I go, I will send him to you."

Jesus repeated the promise that he would send the Spirit. He added that his departure and the Spirit's coming would be more beneficial to the disciples than if he had stayed. In the following verses (John 16:8–11), the Spirit is not necessarily described as to how he would work through the disciples but how he would aid them in their witness to the world (cf. John 15:26–27). As the apostles bore witness about Jesus, the Spirit would bear witness with them by convincing[91] the world of three matters: its sinful

---

88. Borchert, *John 1–11*, 160.

89. Beasley-Murray claims this passage is "one in intention" with Mark 13:9, 11 and Luke 12:11–12 (*John*, 277). He points out that Mark 13:10 indicates that the content of this speaking would be the gospel.

90. Pierson, *The Acts of the Holy Spirit*, 98, couples this passage with Mark 16:20 and Hebrews 2:4 in order to show the multiple means of attestation by the Spirit—through the witness of the apostles and the miracles wrought by their hands. In keeping with the other *Paraclete* passages, it seems that the witness primarily involves the proclamation of truth about Jesus.

91. Aloisi, "The Paraclete's Ministry of Conviction," 56–60. After a lengthy discussion of the use of *elenchō*, Aloisi summarizes, "The emphasis in John 16:8 seems to be on showing people their sin and convincing them that they stand guilty before God. This convicting or convincing work involves the Holy Spirit bringing the world to a self-conscious 'conviction' of its sin and guiltiness" (Ibid., 60).

unbelief in Jesus (John 16:9);[92] its absence of righteousness (John 16:10);[93] and its consequent judgment to come (John 16:11).[94]

John 16:12–15

John 16:12–15 is the fifth and final *Paraclete* passage.

> I still have many things to say to you, but you cannot bear them now. When the Spirit of truth comes, he will guide you into all the truth, for he will not speak on his own authority, but whatever he hears he will speak, and he will declare to you the things that are to come. He will glorify me, for he will take what is mine and declare it to you. All that the Father has is mine; therefore I said that he will take what is mine and declare it to you. (John 16:12–15)

Whereas the apostles were earlier promised that the Spirit would bring to mind *past* revelation and teach them the significance of this revelation (John 14:26; see above), the apostles are promised that the Spirit would give them *new* revelation in John 16:12–15.[95] Jesus had "many things" to say that he refrained from saying (John 16:12), and these things would be said to the apostles later by revelation from the Spirit. This revelatory process is described in multiple ways: "he will guide you into all the truth" (John 16:13); "whatever he hears he will speak" (John 16:13); "he will declare to you the things that are to come" (John 16:13); "he will take what is mine and declare it to you" (both John 16:14 and 16:15).

The content of this revelation would focus on Jesus (cf. John 16:14, "He will glorify me") and could have included further explanation as to the person and role of Jesus as well as future events (John 16:13, "the things that are to come").[96] Whatever the specific revelation would be, the apostles

---

92. Carson, *The Gospel According to John*, 619; Keener, *The Gospel of John*, 1034.

93. See Aloisi, "The Paraclete's Ministry of Conviction," 61–63, and Köstenberger, *John*, 472. Jesus' ascension implies his approval by the Father, showing him to be righteous and the world to be unrighteous in its condemnation of him.

94. Keener, states that the judgment is that Satan "has been judged in Jesus' glorification and shown to be wrong" (*John*, 1034).

95. For a contrasting view, see Harvey, *Anointed with Spirit and Power*, 100. Harvey takes "guide you into all the truth" as "guide you in the truth" (John 16:13), making the point that this truth is what "their Lord and Savior had already made known unto them," not something new. He ties this understanding to John 14:26.

96. Köstenberger, *John*, 473 74. Cf. Borchert, *John*, 169–70.

would receive it and in turn communicate it in their witness to others (cf. John 15:26–27).

Summary of Paraclete Passages

The coming Spirit would help the apostles as Jesus helped them during his earthly ministry (John 14:16–17). The Spirit would also bring to mind what Jesus had previously said to the apostles and teach them the significance of his words (John 14:26). The Spirit would bear witness with the witness of the apostles (John 15:26–27) by convincing the world of its sin, righteousness, and judgment (John 16:7–11). The Spirit would also give new truth to the apostles that Jesus had not previously revealed (John 16:12–15). This ministry of the Spirit would be an advance in his work through the apostles (John 16:7).

John 20:22

After Jesus' resurrection, Jesus appeared in a locked room where ten of the remaining eleven apostles were hiding from the Jews (John 20:19; cf. 20:24).[97] In the midst of Jesus' words of commission to the apostles (John 20:21–23), Jesus "breathed on them and said to them, 'Receive the Holy Spirit'" (John 20:22). It is helpful to see Jesus' action and statement in context:

> Jesus said to them again, "Peace be with you. As the Father has sent me, even so I am sending you." And when he had said this, he breathed on them and said to them, "Receive the Holy Spirit. If you forgive the sins of any, they are forgiven them; if you withhold forgiveness from any, it is withheld." (John 20:21–23)

At the least, this giving of the Spirit in some sense involves the commission of the apostles to bear witness about Jesus. Jesus stated to the disciples, "As the Father sent me, even so I am sending you" (John 20:21). Jesus then breathed on them and told them to receive the Spirit (John 20:22). Jesus had stated earlier that he would give the disciples the Spirit for the

---

97. It may have been that others were present as well. Bock states, "The parallel to this scene in Luke 24:36–49 suggests that this is a larger group. However, it is also possible that Jesus in giving the commission has the Eleven especially in mind" (*Jesus According to Scripture*, 545). The note concerning Thomas's absence from the apostolic Twelve seems to imply this conclusion (Luke 20:24). Cf. Köstenberger, *John*, 571.

purpose of help, revelation, and bearing witness about him (John 14:16–17, 26; 15:26–27; 16:7–11, 12–15), and it would seem that John 20:22 indicates some type of fulfillment of these promises.

That the reception of the Spirit in John 20:22 involves the disciples' witness is also made clear in John 20:23. After his command for the disciples to receive the Spirit (John 20:22), Jesus gave the disciples the authority to declare whether or not their hearers had been forgiven of their sins (John 20:23). This declaration assumes the disciples' witness about Jesus and their discernment of whether or not their hearers responded with faith to this witness.[98]

A much-debated complexity arises when the interpreter attempts to harmonize this passage with the disciples' reception of the Spirit in Acts 2. There are roughly three positions in this debate, and each of these positions could be examined further for differences among their proponents as well. This giving of the Spirit is either John's version of what took place at Pentecost, an actual giving of the Spirit that was something distinct from Pentecost, or something symbolic of Pentecost.[99]

The last of these three options seems best for at least two reasons. First, if John and Luke both record their own version of Pentecost, they would be in conflict with one another as to the details of the event. The most obvious contradiction would be that Jesus had not ascended yet in John 20:22, whereas Jesus had indeed ascended by the time Pentecost took place in Acts 2 (cf. Acts 1:9–11). Beyond this, after the events of John 20:22 took place, the disciples were not immediately bearing witness thereafter as they were recorded to do so as in the book of Acts from the day of Pentecost and thereafter. Rather, they continued to stay indoors (John 20:26), and seven of them were later found fishing (John 21:1–3).[100]

Second, the context of the book of John as a whole suggests that an actual reception of the Spirit in John 20:22 would put John in conflict with himself. The mention of Jesus giving the Spirit to the disciples in John 20:22 naturally recalls the *Paraclete* passages in the Farewell Discourse,[101] but John 20:22 could not be an actual fulfillment of these passages because

98. Carson, *The Gospel According to John*, 655–56.

99. For a survey of eight positions as to how to harmonize this text with Pentecost in Acts 2, see Pretlove, "John 20:22—Help from Dry Bones," 94–96. For a summary of seven majors views as to how to interpret the passage as a whole, see Bennema's chart in "The Giving of the Spirit in John 19–20," 104.

100. Köstenberger, *John*, 575.

101. Cf. Beasley-Murray, *John*, 380–82.

Jesus was physically present (John 16:7). It seems that John alluded to their fulfillment at Pentecost by recording an actual event in which Jesus gave an "acted prophecy" of the Spirit's coming by breathing on the disciples and telling them to receive the Spirit.[102]

The Promise of Pentecost

Luke records three promises of the Spirit's coming at Pentecost by Jesus to the apostles (Luke 24:49; Acts 1:4–5; 1:8). After an examination of each of these promises, a summary will be given.

LUKE 24:49

Luke's last recorded words of Jesus in his Gospel (cf. Luke 24:44–49) contain a promise that the Spirit would come to the apostles: "And behold, I am sending the promise of my Father upon you. But stay in the city until you are clothed with power from on high" (Luke 24:49).[103]

Though Jesus did not mention the Spirit directly, his mention of "the promise of my Father" would have been understood as a reference to the Spirit. Just as Jesus would send "the promise of my Father" (Luke 24:49), John records Jesus' words that the Spirit would come from the Father (John 14:16, 26; 15:26; cf. 16:15). Jesus also gave a command to "stay in the city until you are clothed with power from on high" (Luke 24:49). This promise to be "clothed" (*endyō*) echoes the description of Gideon who was likewise "clothed" (*endyō*) with the Spirit (Judg 6:34, LXX),[104] suggesting it would be the Spirit who clothed the apostles. This power is said in a parallel promise to come from the Spirit: "you will receive power when the Holy Spirit has come upon you" (Acts 1:8).

---

102. Cole, *He Who Gives Life*, 191.

103. It is not entirely clear from Luke 24:36–49 whether the apostles or a larger group of disciples were given this promise. Cf. Bock, *Jesus According to Scripture*, 402. Jesus walked with two disciples (Luke 24:13), one of whom was named Cleopas (Luke 24:18), and these disciples reported of their conversation with Jesus to the eleven disciples (Luke 24:33–34). Then "they" were talking about these things, and Jesus appeared (Luke 24:36). Whether or not others were present, the parallel promises of the Spirit in Acts 1:5, 8 are directed primarily towards the apostles, which suggests that the apostles were primarily in view here as well (see below).

104. Rea, *The Holy Spirit in the Bible*, 54.

Acts 1:4–5

The book of Acts begins by describing Jesus who "had given commands through the Holy Spirit to the apostles whom he had chosen" (Acts 1:2). These commands are recorded in Acts 1:4–5 and promise the coming Spirit: "And while staying with them he ordered them not to depart from Jerusalem, but to wait for the promise of the Father, which, he said, 'you heard from me; for John baptized with water, but you will be baptized with the Holy Spirit not many days from now.'"

Acts 1:4–5 essentially repeats the content of Luke 24:49.[105] The apostles are told to remain in the city (Jerusalem), and there they were to wait for the promise of the Father, the Holy Spirit. Acts 1:5 adds that the time to wait would be "not many days from now," which would be the day of Pentecost ten days later (cf. Acts 2:1).[106] The primary difference between Luke 24:49 and Acts 1:4–5 is the description of the Spirit and his coming activity. Whereas Luke 24:49 records Jesus' promise that the disciples would be clothed with power, Acts 1:5 records Jesus' promise that they would "be baptized with the Holy Spirit" (cf. Matt 3:11; Mark 1:8; Luke 3:16; John 1:33). The Spirit's coming at Pentecost was the fulfillment of this promise (cf. Acts 11:15–16).

Acts 1:8

The disciples "had come together" (Acts 1:6) one last time before Jesus' ascension (cf. Acts 1:9–11) and, in keeping with the anticipation of the coming Spirit, asked Jesus if the kingdom would be restored to Israel (Acts 1:6). Jesus did not say whether or not the kingdom would be restored (Acts 1:7) but reiterated that they would receive the Spirit: "But you will receive power when the Holy Spirit has come upon you, and you will be my witnesses in Jerusalem and in all Judea and Samaria, and to the end of the earth" (Acts 1:8).

Acts 1:8 repeats the promise of the coming Spirit as foretold in Acts 1:4–5 but reflects the promise as it is stated in Luke 24:49. In both Luke 24:49 and Acts 1:8, Jesus promised the apostles that the Spirit would come

---

105. Bruce, "The Holy Spirit in the Acts of the Apostles," 169–70.

106. Peterson, *The Acts of the Apostles*, 131. Pentecost took place fifty days after the Passover, forty of which had taken place since Christ's resurrection (Acts 1:3). The disciples waited only ten days.

"upon" them and that they would have "power,"[107] enabling their witness to the nations to be effective (cf. Luke 24:47–48).[108]

Summary

Luke 24:49 and Acts 1:8 promise the apostles that the Spirit would come upon them and empower them to be effective witnesses of the gospel to the nations. Acts 1:5 describes the coming of the Spirit as it had been prophesied by John the Baptist, that they would be baptized with the Spirit. While the coming of the Spirit at Pentecost would certainly not be limited to the apostles, it does seem that the apostles are primarily in view with reference to the power that would be given for the purpose of effective witness.

The Ones to Whom the Spirit Was Given

Luke mentions the Spirit in both his record of the Spirit's coming at Pentecost (Acts 2:4) and Peter's explanation of the event thereafter (Acts 2:17–18, 33). Numerous references record the work of the Spirit in relation to the apostles, but only one reference clearly connects the work of the Spirit to the leadership of the apostles as a whole (Acts 5:32).

Pentecost

A description and explanation of Pentecost are found in Acts 2:4, 2:17–18, and 2:33. Though the significance of Pentecost is much greater than what is being explored for the study at hand, the apostles are primary characters in these passages. Each passage will be examined in isolation, and all three passages will be considered together for what they say of the work of the Spirit through the apostles and their leadership.

---

107. Peterson states, "The qualifying clause explains that this will happen 'when the Holy Spirit comes on you'" (Ibid., 110).
108. Bock, *Acts*, 64; Peterson, *The Acts of the Apostles*, 110; Pierson, *Acts of the Holy Spirit*, 27.

ACTS 2:4

When the disciples were gathered together in a house (Acts 2:1–2),[109] there was the sound of a great wind and "tongues as of fire" that "rested on each one of them" (Acts 2:2–3). Acts 2:4 records what took place next: "And they were all filled with the Holy Spirit and began to speak in other tongues as the Spirit gave them utterance."

Acts 2:4 contains one of Luke's several descriptions of people being "filled with the Holy Spirit."[110] The activity of being "filled" is designated by the verb *pimplēmi* which, when the filling is with the Spirit, often describes a work of the Spirit that brings about a dramatic event.[111] In this instance, the filling of the Spirit brought about the speaking in tongues. These "tongues" were actual, recognized languages that are identified in Acts 2:8–11,[112] and the content of their speech was "the mighty works of God" (Acts 2:11).[113]

---

109. Others were likely present with the apostles at Pentecost. Those in the upper room (Acts 1:13) numbered "about 120" (Acts 1:15). As the narrative continues, the chapter ends with the eleven disciples seeking a twelfth to replace Judas Iscariot (Acts 1:21–26). Because of the mention of the 120 and a shift in focus on the apostles, it is not entirely clear who is the implied subject of *ēsan* ("*they* were") in Acts 2:1. However, it seems the 120 are likely in view. Peterson states, "When Luke says *they were all together in one place*, the collection of terms, reminiscent of Acts 1:14–15, is quite emphatic *(pantes homou epi to auto)*" (*The Acts of the Apostles*, 132). Nonetheless, the apostles and Peter in particular are given special attention in Acts 2 (cf. Acts 2:14). For an alternative view, see Gromacki, *The Holy Spirit*, 146–48, for a detailed discussion for where the place could have been and that "they" in Acts 2:1 refers to the twelve apostles.

110. Cf. Luke 1:15, 41, 67; Acts 4:8, 31; 9:17; 13:9. Acts 4:8, 9:17, and 13:9 are discussed below.

111. The verb *pimplēmi* is to be distinguished from the verb *plēroō* and its cognate *plērēs* (cf. Acts 6:3, 5; 7:55; 11:24). When individuals in Acts are "filled with" (*pimplēmi*) the Spirit, a dramatic event typically takes place. When individuals are "full of" (*plērēs*) the Spirit, it generally refers to their character in some way. See Bruce, *The Acts of the Apostles*, 114; Peterson, *The Acts of the Apostles*, 133–34; Pettegrew, *The New Covenant Ministry of the Holy Spirit*, 189–205; and Schnabel, *Acts*, 115. Köstenberger states, "The difference between the references to being 'filled with' and being 'full of' the Spirit appears to be essentially one of event (in the case of the former) versus general characteristic (in the case of the latter). Acts 7:55, however, where Stephen, 'full of the Spirit,' describes a vision (cf. also 6:15) indicates that this distinction is not a rigid one" ("What Does It Mean to Be Filled with the Spirit," 237).

112. Bruce, *The Acts of the Apostles*, 114–15. Bruce points out that 1 Cor 14:2–23 describes tongues of "a different character." No interpreters were needed in Acts 2.

113. Peterson, *The Acts of the Apostles*, 135, sees this content as similar to the prophecies recorded in Luke 1:46–55, 67–79; 2:28–32.

Spiritual Leadership

Acts 2:17–18

After the disciples spoke in tongues and had attracted a sizeable crowd (Acts 2:5–13), Peter was "standing with the eleven" and "lifted up his voice" to explain to the crowd the nature and significance of the events that had just taken place (Acts 2:14; cf. 2:1–4).[114] He explained their utterances as a fulfillment of Joel 2:28–32. Peter's quotation of Joel 2:28–29 in Acts 2:17–18 explains the Spirit's work in Acts 2:1–4:

> And in the last days it shall be, God declares, / that I will pour out my Spirit on all flesh, / and your sons and your daughters shall prophesy, / and your young men shall see visions, / and your old men shall dream dreams; / even on my male servants and female servants / in those days I will pour out my Spirit, and they shall prophesy. (Acts 2:17–18)

The fulfillment of Joel's prophecy was that the Spirit had been poured out, a type of prophecy was the result,[115] and those who called upon the Lord would be saved.[116]

Acts 2:33

After quoting Joel's prophecy that God was the one who would pour out the Spirit (Acts 2:17–18; cf. Joel 2:28–29), Peter spoke of "this Jesus" (Acts 2:32) who, upon "having received from the Father the promise of the Holy Spirit, he has poured out this that you yourselves are seeing and hearing" (Acts 2:33).

Acts 2:33 records Peter's identification of Jesus as the one who poured out the Spirit in Acts 2:1–4. This identification shows Jesus to be God (cf. Acts 2:17–18) and the fulfillment of the prophecies that Jesus would send

---

114. The disciples were first in a house (Acts 2:2), and then Peter addressed a crowd (Acts 2:14–40) with the result that "there were added that day about three thousand souls" (Acts 2:41). Bruce, *The Acts of the Apostles*, 51, suggests that the disciples walked out into public while speaking in tongues and drew a crowd which followed them to the temple, a place large enough to accommodate the size of the crowd that heard Peter's address.

115. Harvey, *Anointed with Spirit and Power*, 115. The only difference between the tongues of Acts 2:4 and prophecy is that the speakers in Acts 2:4 did not previously know the languages they were speaking.

116. Peter's quotation of Joel does not demand that all of the details of this prophecy had to be fulfilled at Pentecost. For instance, the meteorological details of Joel's prophecy could still take place in the future. See Treier, "The Fulfillment of Joel 2:28–32," 13–26.

the Spirit to baptize his followers and to empower the apostles to be effective witnesses of the gospel (see below).

The Spirit and the Apostles at Pentecost

The Spirit was sent, resulting in observable phenomena (Acts 2:1–3) and a dramatic event (Acts 2:4). Peter explained the Spirit's coming as a fulfillment to Joel's prophecy (Acts 2:17–18; cf. Joel 2:28–29) through Jesus who sent the Spirit (Acts 2:33).

Several comments may be made. First, the Spirit's coming at Pentecost fulfilled the prophecy of Spirit baptism that was to come upon believers in general. Both John the Baptist and Jesus prophesied that the Messiah would baptize his followers with the Spirit (cf. Matt 3:11; Mark 1:8; Luke 3:16; John 1:33; Acts 1:5).

Second, the baptism of the Spirit fulfilled Joel's prophecy of the outpouring of the Spirit. Peter's explanation of Pentecost in Acts 2:17–18, 33 describes the event as an outpouring of the Spirit (Acts 2:17–18, "I will pour out my Spirit"; Acts 2:33, "he has poured out this"). Peter later described Pentecost as the baptism of the Spirit. In Acts 10:44–48, Luke recorded that the Spirit "fell on all who heard the word" (Acts 10:44) and "was poured out even on the Gentiles" (Acts 10:45). Recounting this event later, Peter stated that "the Holy Spirit fell on them just as on us at the beginning" (Acts 11:15), which Peter then identified as the baptism of the Spirit (Acts 11:16). In another setting, Peter likewise stated, "God . . . bore witness to them [the Gentiles], by giving them the Holy Spirit just as he did to us" (Acts 15:8). Whatever may be the reason for the absence of the metaphor of "baptism" with the Spirit in the OT,[117] the various descriptions of Pentecost in Acts evidently identify the Spirit's baptism and outpouring as being one and the same.

This work of the Spirit is not for leaders such as the apostles alone but is experienced by others as well (cf. Acts 8:14–17; 10:44–48; 19:1–6). Correlating Luke's narrative of this work by the Spirit with the description by that of Paul (cf. 1 Cor 12:12–13), it seems that Luke describes the Spirit's baptism in stages in order to show the geographic spread of the gospel from

---

117. See Pettegrew, *The New Covenant Ministry of the Holy Spirit*, 46–47. At the least, it may be said that this change of metaphor was by God and not an invention of John the Baptist (cf. John 1:33). Pettegrew claims, "John changed his metaphor to baptism because of his dramatic ministry of baptizing people in water" (Ibid., 46).

Jerusalem to the world.[118] Paul's statement "in one Spirit we were all baptized into one body" (1 Cor 12:13) indicates that baptism with the Spirit is something simultaneous with being spiritually united to the body of Christ.[119] The instances in Acts that describe a chronological gap between belief in the gospel and baptism with the Spirit are limited to a transitional period in redemptive history and should not be expected today.

Third, Luke's use of *pimplēmi* in Acts 2:4 indicates the Spirit brought about a dramatic event (speaking in tongues) *in addition* to the baptism of the Spirit. Baptism with the Spirit and the Spirit's enabling to speak in tongues are two different workings of the Spirit. The latter evidenced that the former had taken place for the very first time.

Fourth, Acts 2:33 identifies Jesus as the one who sent the Spirit, which implies that, in addition to the fulfillment of the prophecy of Spirit baptism, the fulfillment of Jesus' promises in the Farewell Discourse had begun as well. He promised that he himself would send the Spirit (John 15:26; 16:7), and that the Spirit would work through the apostles to recall and reveal the content of the gospel so that they would be effective witnesses of the truth (John 14:16–17, 26; 15:26–27; 16:7, 12–15). With the sending of the Spirit in Acts 2:1–4, this work had now begun. The apostles would powerfully articulate the gospel, and they would certainly do so as given utterance by the Spirit when standing on trial before their opponents (cf. Matt 10:20; Mark 13:11; Luke 12:12; John 15:18–25; 16:1–4a).

Fifth, it seems fair to conclude that Peter's message was a fulfillment of Jesus' promises in the Farewell Discourse. Peter "bore witness" (*diamartyromai*) about Jesus Christ (Acts 2:40; cf. 1:8; John 15:26–27), and the Spirit convinced the hearers of their sin and judgment (Acts 2:37; cf. John 16:7–11).

The Spirit's coming at Pentecost does not describe a work of the Spirit unique to spiritual leaders except that Jesus showed his leadership in a unique way in that he sent the Spirit from heaven to his followers. Even if Acts 2:1–4 describes events that were limited to the apostles, these events are parallel in nature to the experience of the Gentiles in Acts 10:44–48 and Acts 19:1–6. Nonetheless, Acts 2:33 identifies Christ as the one to send the Spirit, implying that the fulfillment of the *Paraclete* passages had begun. The Twelve would witness by the power of the Spirit (cf. Acts 1:8) and be

118. Carson, *Showing the Spirit*, 148–50.

119. Erickson, *Christian Theology*, 894–95. The body is Christ (1 Cor 12:12), and to be baptized into the body is to be baptized into him. Referring to 1 Cor 12:13, Erickson states, "Baptism by the Spirit appears to be, if not equivalent to conversion and new birth, at least simultaneous with them" (Ibid., 895).

given utterance by the Spirit to answer before their opposition. As will be seen below, the book of Acts records several instances of this type of work of the Spirit in individual leaders.

After Pentecost

After the Spirit's arrival at Pentecost, the Spirit's work was described in multiple ways. It is helpful to note several instances in which the apostles are present and the work of the Spirit is somehow manifest, but this work is not necessarily related to the exercise of their leadership. After a survey of these passages, Acts 5:32 will show at least one context in which only the apostles are in view when the work of the Spirit is described.

A Survey of the Work of the Spirit and Leaders in General

The Spirit's coming at Pentecost inaugurated a new age in redemptive history. Numerous activities are described by the NT authors as having taken place at the impulse of the Spirit, much of which involves NT leaders such as apostles, their delegates, and elders. The work of the Spirit in deacons is described as well. While some of this activity is unique to these leaders, some of this activity is not. For instance, there are occasions when groups of people receive the Spirit after apostles lay their hands upon them, and there are other occasions when the laying on of hands is by someone who is not an apostle and the Spirit is then given to an apostle. The Samaritans received the Spirit after the apostles Peter and John laid their hands upon them (Acts 8:14–17), which is similar to the reception of the Spirit by the Ephesian disciples when the apostle Paul laid his hands on them (Acts 19:1–6). Conversely, an otherwise unmentioned disciple named Ananias laid his hands upon the apostle Paul who would then "be filled with the Holy Spirit" (Acts 9:17). Ananias' participation shows that the reception of the Spirit in Acts is not limited to the laying on of the apostles' hands alone.[120]

Other events describe the work of the Spirit in both the apostles and others. The apostles Peter and John (Acts 4:19) and "their friends" (Acts

---

120. This is not to say that the context of Acts 9:17 does not describe a unique filling of the Spirit for the apostle Paul. See below.

4:23)[121] "were all filled with the Holy Spirit and continued to speak the word of God with boldness" (Acts 4:32).[122] Yet other events describe the work of the Spirit in someone whose resultant activity is directed towards an apostle. The disciples in Tyre "through the Spirit . . . were telling Paul not to go on to Jerusalem (Acts 21:4). The prophet Agabus likewise declared, "Thus says the Holy Spirit," and prophesied to Paul of the opposition awaiting him in Jerusalem (Acts 21:11).

Even the Spirit's revelation of new truth that was foundational to the church was not limited to the apostles (cf. John 16:12–15). Paul stated that the gospel in all its detail "has now been revealed . . . by the Spirit"[123] not to him or the apostles alone, but "to his holy apostles and the prophets" (Eph 3:5).[124]

121. Larkin identifies these friends as "perhaps the original 120 of the pre-Pentecost upper room days" (cf. 1:13–15; *Acts*, 78). Bruce, *The Acts of the Apostles*, 156, points out that the same term (*idios*) is used in Acts 24:23 as those who could visit Paul in prison. Peterson adds that the focus is on the apostles, but Acts 4:33 and Acts 5:12 suggest "a wider fellowship of friends and supports" (*The Acts of the Apostles*, 198). Peterson then only refers to the apostles as receiving "a fresh filling of the Spirit" in order "to continue their work of testifying to the resurrection of the Lord Jesus (v. 33)" (Ibid., 203). It does seem to be the entire community up to this point, and they may play a role in communicating God's Word after they have been filled. Cf. Bock, *Acts*, 203, 209–210.

122. It is significant that Luke uses *pimplēmi* to describe the Spirit's "filling" of the church, a verb typically reserved for a special work of the Spirit in individuals (cf. Luke 1:15, 41, 67; Acts 4:8; 9:17; 13:9). This would be one of the two instances in Luke-Acts in which the filling of the Spirit involves a group of people and not just an individual (cf. Acts 2:4). Referring to Acts 4:31, Köstenberger states, "[T]he Spirit now empowers not merely individual spokesmen of God but the entire Church as God's witnessing community" ("What Does It Mean to Be Filled with the Spirit," 238). See also Turner, "Spirit Endowment In Luke/Acts," 55, and Wood, *The Spirit of God in Biblical Literature*, 186–88.

123. The phrase "by the Spirit" is said to modify either the prophets alone, both apostles and prophets, or the verb that precedes these two groups. Cf. Hoehner, *Ephesians*, 442. Lincoln helpfully notes that, as with the construction in Eph 2:22 ("by the Spirit" modifies the verb though phrases intervene between the two), "by the Spirit" refers back to the verb "has . . . been revealed" (*Ephesians*, 180). Cf. also Arnold, *Ephesians*, 190–91; Thielman, *Ephesians*, 200.

124. This phrase ("his holy apostles and prophets") does not describe the apostles alone with the use of two terms (i.e., apostles and prophets, meaning something like "apostles who are prophets"). Rather the two terms refer to two distinct groups, the prophets being distinct from the apostles. Thielman, *Ephesians*, 199, points out that the placement of "his" (*autos*) between "apostles" and "and" (*tois hagiois apostolois autou kai prophētais*) implies a distinction between apostles and prophets. Though it could seem that apostles and prophets are one and the same group as mentioned together in Eph 2:20, Eph 4:11 clearly distinguishes between the two groups, implying Paul saw apostles and prophets as distinct here in Eph 3:5 as well. See Hoehner, *Ephesians*, 442. Wallace,

In other passages, the Spirit's work is described, but it is not clear whether leaders such as the apostles or their delegates are the ones who experience this work. The author of Hebrews states that the gospel that "was declared at first by the Lord . . . was attested to us by those who heard, while God also bore witness by signs and wonders and various miracles and by gifts of the Holy Spirit distributed according to his will" (Heb 2:3–4). It could be that "those who heard" the gospel from the Lord were apostles because they were authenticated as God's spokesmen by means of "signs and wonders and various miracles," which Paul identifies as "the signs of a true apostle" (2 Cor 12:12).[125] At the same time, this supernatural activity was extended to men such as Stephen (Acts 6:8), Philip (Acts 8:13), and Barnabas (Acts 14:3). "Those who heard" likely included the apostles, others who performed miracles, and perhaps other eyewitnesses as well (cf. Luke 1:2).[126] Whoever is in view, it is natural to infer from this passage that the "signs and wonders and various miracles" were performed by those who received the gospel directly from Jesus himself, which would indicate these works of the Spirit were not expected to take place by the hands of the author and readers of Hebrews.[127] It may be said that these works of the Spirit were unique to the era of the early church, and, insomuch as they were performed primarily by Jesus, the apostles, or their delegates, they were typically limited to these leaders.

Another passage along these lines is 1 Pet 1:12 which refers to "those who preached the good news to you by the Holy Spirit sent from heaven."

"The Semantic Range of the Article-Noun-Καί-Noun Plural Construction in the New Testament," 59–84, discusses Eph 2:20, 3:5 and 4:11 and makes this fact clear as well as the fact that these prophets are NT prophets, not the prophets of the OT.

125. Cf. Hughes, *A Commentary on the Epistle to the Hebrews*, 79. Paul states of himself to the Corinthians, "The signs of a true apostle were performed among you with all perseverance, by signs and wonders and miracles" (2 Cor 12:12 NASB).

126. Allen observes that miraculous gifts were performed by the apostles and Christ to testify to the "foundational nature" of their ministry in the church (Eph 2:20; cf. Acts 2:22; 14:3; Rom 15:18–20; 2 Cor 12:12; *Hebrews*, 195; see also 198–99). Cockerill, *The Epistle to the Hebrews*, 122, echoes this thought.

127. See Wallace, "Hebrews 2:3–4 and the Sign Gifts," paragraph 12. Whoever "those who heard" are, they were the ones to do the signs, wonders, and miracles, not the listeners. It is natural to infer that these phenomena would disappear with the passing of these eyewitnesses. This would make sense, given their purpose of testifying to the fact that something new had taken place, namely, the definitive revelation of God had come in the person of his Son Jesus Christ (Heb 1:1–2). Also, if Gal 3:5 was written by Paul roughly a generation before Hebrews was written, Heb 2:3–4 is written by a second-generation Christian towards the close of the era of apostles.

Though the apostles were initially the primary witnesses of the good news, "those who preached . . . by the Holy Spirit" could be any evangelist or messenger who gave their Spirit-empowered witness to Peter's readers.[128]

Acts 5:32

Though many passages refer to the Spirit and leaders but do not connect the Spirit to the exercise of their leadership, several passages do, and one passage that speaks of the Spirit's work through the apostles as a whole is Acts 5:32. While standing before rulers of Israel, Peter and the apostles gave a defense for their message and many miracles (Acts 5:12–32). In their closing words, Peter and the apostles stated, "And we are witnesses of these things, and so is the Holy Spirit, whom God has given to those who obey him" (Acts 5:32).

The Holy Spirit is stated to be a witness in addition to the witness of the apostles. Acts 5:32 indicates a fulfillment of what Christ promised the apostles in John 15:26–27. They Spirit would "bear witness" about Christ (John 15:26), and the apostles would do so as well (John 15:27).[129] What is not precisely stated is how exactly the Spirit functioned as a witness. It could be that the Spirit was a witness by means of the Spirit's agency in producing their "many signs and wonders" (Acts 5:12; cf. 5:32; Heb 2:3–4).[130] The Spirit could have also convinced those who heard the gospel of their sinfulness, their need for Christ's righteousness, and their coming judgment (John 16:8–11).[131]

The Spirit's witness is only briefly mentioned, which leaves the surrounding context to indicate how the Spirit was a witness. The apostles worked miracles, and listeners were convinced of the gospel. The Spirit's witness could be said to be involved in both of these activities.

Summary

The Spirit gave the apostles the words to speak in defense of the gospel (cf. Mark 13:9–10) when standing before others in the context of persecution,

---

128. Davids, *The First Epistle of Peter*, 64; Jobes, *1 Peter*, 103.
129. Bruce, "The Holy Spirit in the Acts of the Apostles," 179.
130. Cf. Pierson, *Acts of the Holy Spirit*, 59.
131. Bock, *Acts*, 248.

both before (Matt 10:20; cf. 10:5–8) and after (cf. Mark 13:11; see below) the death of Christ. Jesus promised the apostles that he would send the Spirit to empower them, witness with them, and recall and reveal truth after he ascended to heaven (John 14:16–17, 26; 15:26; 16:11, 12–15; cf. 20:22; Acts 1:4–5, 8). That he had sent the Spirit for these purposes was initially confirmed by other works of the Spirit such as fire, wind, and the speaking of tongues (Acts 2:1–4). From that point forward, the promises concerning the *Paraclete* began to be fulfilled (cf. Acts 5:32).

The Apostles and Their Delegates

Several NT passages describe the work of the Spirit in individual apostles, groups within the apostles (e.g., Peter and John), groups including apostles and their delegates, and individual apostolic delegates. Some of these passages describe something similar to the experience of people who are not leaders, and some of these passages describe a work of the Spirit that is distinct to these leaders. This section will discuss these leaders according to the order of the designations given above.

Individual Apostles

The fact that the work of the Spirit is described as taking place in the life of one of the apostles and not the others obviously does not demand that other apostles did not experience the same. As seen above, the work of the Spirit may be described in relation to the apostles as a group. For those who are mentioned as individuals, however, the Spirit's work is described in the lives of Peter, Paul, and John.

The Apostle Peter

The book of Acts records Peter being filled with the Spirit (Acts 4:8), speaking on behalf of the Spirit (Acts 5:3, 9), and receiving the Spirit's words (Acts 10:19; 11:12).

Acts 4:8

Peter healed a lame man in the temple gate (Acts 3:1–10), preached to the crowd that gathered as a result (Acts 3:11–26), and was consequently arrested by the Jewish officials (Acts 4:1–4). When he was interrogated by the officials (Acts 4:5–7), "Peter, filled with the Holy Spirit" (Acts 4:8), spoke in defense of his actions (cf. Acts 4:8–22).[132]

The description of Peter as "filled with the Holy Spirit" uses the verb *pimplēmi* for what is translated as "filled." It was explained earlier that Luke's use of the verb *pimplēmi* with the Spirit as the object of filling typically describes a work of the Spirit that brings about a dramatic event (cf. Acts 2:4). The dramatic event in Acts 4:8 would be Peter's Spirit-enabled defense of his message and actions as he stood before the Jewish officials.[133]

Not only does Luke bring attention to this unique filling of the Spirit with his vocabulary, but this instance of the Spirit's work is an example of what Jesus promised to the apostles in the gospels. To use the language of Luke 12:11–12, Jesus could have said to Peter in this situation, "And when they bring you before the synagogues and the rulers and the authorities, do not be anxious about how you should defend yourself or what you should say, for the Holy Spirit will teach you in that very hour what you ought to say" (cf. Matt 10:20; Mark 13:11; Luke 21:15). The Spirit filled Peter to teach him what to say in the moment of his defense.[134]

Acts 5:3, 9

A married couple named Ananias and Sapphira sold some land, and each at different times brought part of the proceeds to the apostles with the intent that this partial gift would be seen as the full sum of the sale (Acts 5:1–11).

---

132. This summary does not exclude the role of John (cf. Acts 3:4, 11; 4:1, 13). It is Peter, however, who spoke to the lame man and took his right hand to raise him up (Acts 3:6–7) and was the spokesman for the two before the officials (Acts 4:8).

133. Bock, *Acts*, 190; Bruce, *The Acts of the Apostles*, 151; Larkin, *Acts*, 73. Pierson points out that this defense is also characterized by "boldness," which later characterized the church's witness as a whole after "they were all filled with the Holy Spirit" as well (Acts 4:31; *Acts of the Holy Spirit*, 37). Acts 4:31 likewise uses the verb *pimplēmi* for the Spirit's filling (see above). The term "boldness" is *parrēsia* in both Acts 4:8 and 4:31. Cf. also Acts 2:29; 4:29; 28:31. The church at large, however, was not standing before authorities to defend the gospel.

134. Bruce, "The Holy Spirit in the Acts of the Apostles," 180; Harvey, *Anointed with Spirit and Power*, 125–26; Turner, "Spirit Endowment In Luke/Acts," 54.

When Ananias did so, Peter asked, "Ananias, why has Satan filled your heart to lie to the Holy Spirit and to keep back for yourself part of the proceeds of the land?" (Acts 5:3). When Sapphira did so, Peter likewise asked, "How is it that you have agreed together to test the Spirit of the Lord?" (Acts 5:9). In both instances, Peter condemned this sin against the Spirit, resulting in the death of each spouse (Acts 5:5, 10).

The activity of the Spirit in both of Peter's questions is described as passive. The couple lied to the Spirit and tested the Spirit (cf. Isa 63:10; Eph 4:30; Heb 10:29). However, it may be inferred that the Spirit responded to this treachery by first revealing to Peter what he would have otherwise not known and then miraculously ending the couple's lives as well.[135] It is natural to assume that, just as these sins were described as being against the Spirit, so also the Spirit responded with an appropriate punishment. The work of the Spirit in these deaths was likely in mind in Luke's summary description that "many signs and wonders were regularly done among the people by the hands of the apostles" (Acts 5:12), which kept the people in the temple at a respectful distance from the apostles (Acts 5:13).[136]

This work of the Spirit finds precedent in one of the visions of Ezekiel. The Spirit "fell upon" Ezekiel during one of his visions (Ezek 11:5; cf. 8:3; 11:1), and he prophesied to twenty-five of Israel's leaders (Ezek 11:1–12). While he was doing so, one of them fell dead before him (Ezek 11:13).

Acts 10:19; 11:12

Peter went to the roof of a housetop to pray and saw the same vision three times (Acts 10:9–16). "While Peter was pondering the vision, the Spirit said to him, 'Behold, three men are looking for you. Rise and go down and accompany them without hesitation, for I have sent them'" (Acts 10:19–20). Peter obeyed, went with them, and preached the gospel to Cornelius, his relatives, and his friends (Acts 10:21–48). Peter later related these events to the apostles in Jerusalem and recalled the Spirit's revelation to him: "the Spirit told me to go with them" (Acts 11:12).

The Spirit spoke to Peter and commanded him to go to Cornelius in order to give him and others the gospel. Peter may be said to have functioned here as a prophet by receiving direct revelation from the Spirit.[137]

---

135. Shepherd, *The Narrative Function of the Holy Spirit*, 172–73.
136. Ibid.
137. Ibid., 200.

The Apostle Paul

The work of the Spirit through the apostle Paul is described numerous times in the book of Acts (Acts 9:17; 13:9; 19:21; 20:22, 23) and in several of his letters (1 Thess 1:5; 1 Cor 2:4; 1 Cor 7:40; 2 Cor 3:6; Rom 15:19; Phil 1:19).

ACTS 9:17

After Saul was blinded by light and instructed by the Lord on his way to Damascus, he was led to a house where a disciple named Ananias was told to go as well in order restore the sight of Saul and give him further instruction (Acts 9:1–16). Ananias did so, laid his hands on Saul, and stated, "Brother Saul, the Lord Jesus who appeared to you on the road by which you came has sent me so that you may regain your sight and be filled with the Holy Spirit" (Acts 9:17).

The verb *pimplēmi* is used to describe how Saul as an individual would "be filled with the Spirit" (Acts 9:17). Though Saul immediately regained his sight, it is not explicitly stated that he was also filled with the Spirit. Nonetheless, as Ananias promised Saul's sight to return and it then did (Acts 9:18), so also it may be inferred that he was filled with the Spirit at this point as well. The dramatic event that resulted from this filling was that "immediately he proclaimed Jesus in the synagogues, saying, 'He is the Son of God.'" (Acts 9:20).[138] This special filling of the Spirit enabled Saul to immediately be an empowered witness of the gospel of Jesus Christ, something quite remarkable for someone who had just previously been persecuting the infant church.[139]

---

138. See the lengthy discussion by George, *Galatians*, 122–25. Both Acts 9:18 and 9:20 continue the narrative with "and immediately" (*kai eutheōs*), suggesting the time of Paul's filling in Acts 9:18 to be continuous with his preaching in the synagogues in Acts 9:20. It is not clear in Acts 9:18–26 where exactly to place Paul's three years in Arabia (Gal 1:17), but whatever the solution may be, it is not incorrect to assume that Paul did not stay at first to preach for some days in the Damascus synagogues before he left for Arabia.

139. Turner recounts the fact that Ananias told Saul that he would regain his sight and be filled with the Spirit and, without any further comment, states, "It seems that Paul's whole mission empowered by the Spirit, not some immediate charisma, is intended" ("Spirit Endowment In Luke/Acts," 55). If this was the case, it would seem unnecessary for Luke to again record that Saul was "filled with the Holy Spirit" in Acts 13:9 (*pimplēmi* is used for "filled"). Though the activity of Paul's preaching in the synagogues does not immediately follow what took place after the laying of Ananias's hands (Paul was baptized and then ate; Acts 9:18–19), it is the next dramatic event to take place within Luke's narrative and is one of the types of events that one would expect to see after a filling of

ACTS 13:9

While in Cyprus, Paul and Barnabas came to the city of Paphos where they were opposed by the magician Elymas in their attempt to give the gospel to the proconsul Sergius Paulus (Acts 13:4–8). In response to this opposition, "Saul, who was also called Paul, filled with the Holy Spirit" (Acts 13:9), looked at Elymas, condemned his sin, and announced that a temporary blindness would be his punishment, which took place immediately thereafter (Acts 13:9–11).

As in Acts 9:17, Luke described Paul as having been "filled" with the Spirit with the verb *pimplēmi*, and a dramatic event was the result.[140] Paul smote his opponent with blindness. This description in Acts 13:9 differs from other fillings of the Spirit in Luke-Acts described with *pimplēmi* in that the primary activity in view was not speech, though speech was obviously involved. Another layer of significance for this miracle is that, along with the change of name (Saul to Paul; Acts 13:9), Paul was shown through this miracle to have a "new status as one invested with authority surpassing that of Satan."[141]

ACTS 19:21; 20:22, 23

Three statements in Acts 19:21, 20:22, and 20:23 may be examined together because they all speak of some work of the Spirit involving Paul and his journey to Jerusalem. Acts 19:21 states, "Paul resolved in the Spirit to pass through Macedonia and Achaia and go to Jerusalem." Similarly, Paul spoke for himself in Acts 20:22 and stated, "I am going to Jerusalem, constrained by the Spirit." In the very next verse (Acts 20:23), Paul describes how the Spirit spoke to him of what would take place in Jerusalem: "the Holy Spirit testifies to me in every city that imprisonment and afflictions await me."

Though some are hesitant to identify whether Acts 19:21 refers to the spirit of Paul or the Spirit of God,[142] Acts 20:23 clearly refers to the Spirit, which some see as evidence enough to conclude that Acts 20:22 refers to the Spirit as well.[143] In turn, the similarity of terminology and function of *tō*

---

the Spirit (cf. Acts 4:8, 31).

140. Cf. Bock, *Acts*, 445; Peterson, *The Acts of the Apostles*, 381.
141. Shepherd, *The Narrative Function of the Holy Spirit*, 212.
142. E.g., Larkin, *Acts*, 279.
143. Bock, *Acts*, 628; Shepherd, *The Narrative Function of the Holy Spirit*, 233.

pneumati in Acts 19:21 and Acts 20:22 lead some to conclude that 19:21 also speaks of the Spirit.[144] Just as Paul was "constrained by the Spirit" to go to Jerusalem in Acts 20:22, so also "Paul resolved in the Spirit to . . . go to Jerusalem" in Acts 19:21.[145] The fact that Paul's journey to Jerusalem has echoes of Christ's earlier resolve to do the same (cf. Luke 9:53; 12:50)[146] and that this journey "is the climax of the narrative of Acts" strengthens this conclusion.[147]

Acts 20:23, however, is dissimilar from Acts 19:21 and 20:22 in that the Spirit is not described as a compelling force upon Paul but as one who directly speaks to Paul about his looming trials.[148] The statement "the Holy Spirit testifies to me" (Acts 20:23) could refer to Paul's reception of revelation from the Spirit or that the Spirit spoke about these matters to Paul through the means of a prophet other than himself, just as the prophet Agabus would do a few verses later (cf. Acts 21:4, 11).[149]

First Thessalonians 1:5

In his opening words of thanks to God for the Thessalonians' conversion (1 Thess 1:2–9), Paul explains how he knew God had chosen the Thessalonians for salvation (1 Thess 1:4): "because our gospel came to you not only in word, but also in power and in the Holy Spirit and with full conviction" (1 Thess 1:5).

Four phrases in 1 Thess 1:5 describe the manner of how Paul and his companions preached the gospel to the Thessalonians ("in word," "in power," "in the Holy Spirit," and "with full conviction").[150] Paul's "not only . . . but also" construction emphasizes that what is described in the latter three phrases bolstered his confidence in God's choice of the Thessalonians more than what is described in the first phrase, that the gospel came to

---

144. Peterson, *The Acts of the Apostles*, 543; Shepherd, *The Narrative Function of the Holy Spirit*, 231.

145. Acts 20:22–23 speaks of Paul being "constrained" (*deō*) by the Spirit to go to Jerusalem where "imprisonment" (*desmos*) awaits. This wordplay may account for Luke's change in terminology from one verse to the next. Cf. Bruce, *The Acts of the Apostles*, 432; Larkin, *Acts*, 295. The NASB reflects this wordplay: "*bound* by the Spirit, I am on my way. . . *bonds* and afflictions await me" (Acts 20:22–23; italics added).

146. Pierson, *Acts of the Holy Spirit*, 124; Polhill, *Acts*, 407.

147. Peterson, *The Acts of the Apostles*, 544.

148. Shepherd, *The Narrative Function of the Holy Spirit*, 233.

149. Bruce, *The Acts of the Apostles*, 432; Larkin, *Acts*, 295.

150. Martin, *1, 2 Thessalonians*, 58.

them "in word."[151] The parallelism of the latter three phrases indicates that "no attempt should be made to understand any element of the clause as subordinate to another."[152] This being the case, that the "gospel came . . . in the Holy Spirit" likely means something in addition to how the gospel came "in power"[153] or "with full conviction."[154] Since Paul is describing the manner of how his company preached the gospel, "in the Holy Spirit" thus describes the empowering source of their preaching.[155]

First Corinthians 2:4

In explaining the nature of true wisdom (1 Cor 1:18–2:5), Paul reminded his readers how he presented this message of wisdom to them: "my speech and my message were not in plausible words of wisdom, but in demonstration of the Spirit and of power, so that your faith might not rest in the wisdom of men but in the power of God" (1 Cor 2:4–5).

Paul did not rely on "plausible words of wisdom" to convince his listeners that the content of his preaching was true (1 Cor 2:4).[156] The "demonstration"[157] of truthfulness to his listeners was by the Spirit whose

---

151. Wanamaker, *The Epistles to the Thessalonians*, 79.

152. Green, *The Letters to the Thessalonians*, 96, suggests that though Paul does not specify exactly how the gospel came "in power," a comparison to Rom 15:18–19 suggests this power was displayed as "the power of signs and wonders" that affirmed the validity his message to his hearers (Rom 15:19; cf. 2 Cor 12:12). See the discussion of Rom 15:18–19 below.

153. Ibid.

154. As with the preceding two phrases, Paul is describing how the gospel came to the Thessalonians. It seems that the conviction here is on the part of Paul and his companions.

155. Fee, *The First and Second Epistles to the Thessalonians*, 35.

156. Lim states that in 1 Cor 2:4, "[H]e appears to be rejecting not human communication in general, but that specific, studied art of persuasive speech as was practiced by orators and rhetoricians of the Graeco-Roman world and by at least some of the Corinthian preachers" ("Not in persuasive words of wisdom," 146). Carson, *The Cross and Christian Ministry*, 39, adds that Paul approves of persuasion (2 Cor 5:11), but not *manipulative* persuasion.

157. Lim, "'Not in persuasive words of wisdom, but in the demonstration of the Spirit and power' (I Cor. 2:4)," 147, defines "demonstration" (*apodeixis*) as ". . . a technical term in rhetoric which means a demonstration or cogent proof of argument from commonly agreed premises."

demonstrative work was an exertion of the power of God (1 Cor 2:4).[158] It was necessary for Paul to preach his message properly so that the Spirit could demonstrate its truthfulness to the Corinthians, and it was necessary for the Corinthians to believe this message for the Spirit to be described as having given such a demonstration. It would seem, then, that the Spirit's "demonstration" in 1 Cor 2:4 involved both the preaching of Paul and the belief of the Corinthians, though the emphasis in context seems to be on the latter. The Spirit worked through both.[159]

Paul's description of the Spirit's work in 1 Cor 2:4–5 involved both his preaching and the belief of the Corinthians. In the language of John 15:26–27, Paul bore witness to Christ, and the Spirit bore witness as well by convincing the Corinthians of his message (cf. John 16:7–11). The Spirit's work in Paul's ministry of proclamation is no different than what Christ promised to the apostles in the Farewell Discourse.

First Corinthians 2:10, 13

Paul continued to explain the nature of true wisdom to the Corinthians by describing its source (1 Cor 2:6–16). Speaking of the content of this wisdom, Paul stated, "these things God has revealed to us through the Spirit" (1 Cor 2:10). He continued, "And we impart this in words not taught by human wisdom but taught by the Spirit" (1 Cor 2:13).

In 1 Cor 2:10, Paul[160] speaks of his reception of revelation through the agency of the Spirit. God is the one who "revealed" (*apokalyptō*) to Paul "these things" and did so "through the Spirit" (1 Cor 2:10). Paul then speaks of the communication of this revelation as taking place by the work of the Spirit.[161] "We impart this in words . . . taught by the Spirit" (1 Cor 2:13). Not only was the content of wisdom revealed to Paul by the Spirit (1 Cor

---

158. Paul's emphasis on his own weakness in 1 Cor 2:3 likely rules out the Spirit's means of convincing the Corinthians through miracles as in Rom 15:18–19 (cf. 2 Cor 12:12). See Fee, *The First Epistle to the Corinthians*, 95. For a survey of suggestions as to what Paul's trembling and weakness may have been, see Garland, *1 Corinthians*, 85–86.

159. Thiselton, *The First Epistle to the Corinthians*, 222.

160. Paul speaks of both himself and the Corinthians in 1 Cor 2:10 ("us") as the ones to have received the wisdom of God, but his reference to himself with the use of the editorial "we" in 1 Cor 2:13 implies that Paul was the one to both receive and communicate the content of God's wisdom by means of the work of the Spirit. Cf. Fee, *The First Epistle to the Corinthian*, 114.

161. Kaiser, Jr., "A Neglected Text in Bibliology Discussions," 315–18.

2:10), but the Spirit continued to work through Paul for the transmission of this revelation as well.[162] Paul was one who led the church as an apostle guided by the Spirit and God's Word, and 1 Cor 2:10 and 2:13 indicate that the Spirit gave him revelation to give to the church as well. What Jesus promised to the other apostles in his Farewell Discourse, Paul experienced as well. The Spirit revealed to Paul truth that further explained the role and person of Jesus Christ (cf. John 16:12–15).

First Corinthians 7:40

Paul ended his instruction on singleness and marriage (1 Cor 7:1–40) by addressing the topic of remarriage for widows (1 Cor 7:39–40). After having given his judgment in the matter, he stated, "And I think that I too have the Spirit of God" (1 Cor 7:40).

Paul's mention of his possession of the Spirit establishes the validity of his instruction concerning widows. It could be that Paul intended this instruction to be seen as having been given to him directly by the Spirit of God (cf. 1 Cor 2:13).[163] One could also infer, however, that Paul is answering the claim by the ascetics that their advice comes from the Spirit. He is simply claiming that he, too, has the Spirit of God.[164]

Second Corinthians 3:6

Paul contrasted the Old and New Covenant (2 Cor 3:1–18) and described himself as one of the "ministers of a new covenant, not of the letter but of the Spirit" (2 Cor 3:6).

Paul's role as a minister of the New Covenant involved the preaching of the gospel (cf. 2 Cor 2:12, 14, 15; 5:18–21),[165] which is said elsewhere to be empowered by the Spirit (cf. 1 Thess 1:5; see above). The focus at hand, however, is that Paul[166] brought a message to others that, if received, would allow them to experience the Spirit's work as promised according to the terms of the New Covenant (cf. Jer 31:31–34). They would be enabled by

---

162. Ibid., 317.
163. Ciampa and Rosner. *The First letter to the Corinthians*, 367.
164. Garland, *1 Corinthians*, 344–45; Thiselton, *The First Epistle to the Corinthians*, 606.
165. Barnett, *The Second Epistle to the Corinthians*, 176; Furnish, *II Corinthians*, 197.
166. Barnett, *The Second Epistle to the Corinthians*, 175. This is likely another use of the "apostolic plural" by Paul with reference to himself.

the Spirit to obey God, something the Old Covenant did not promise to its participants.[167] The mention of the Spirit in this context does not refer to the work of the Spirit through Paul but implies the work of the Spirit in those who believed the gospel.

Romans 15:19

Towards the beginning of Paul's defense as to why he had not yet visited Rome (Rom 15:14–33), Paul described the nature of his ministry to the Gentiles (Rom 15:14–21) and how Christ worked through him "to bring the Gentiles to obedience" (Rom 15:18). Christ's work through him was "by word and deed, by the power of signs and wonders, by the power of the Spirit of God" (Rom 15:18–19).

Multiple issues create difficulty in identifying how exactly Paul assumes the Spirit to exert his power in this context. The phrase "by the power of the Spirit of God" is immediately preceded by two phrases that describe activities that may all be said to be related to the work of the Spirit.[168] Paul also mentions "the power of signs and wonders," suggesting to some that an additional phrase with reference to "power" ("the power of the Spirit of God") must refer to something other than signs and wonders.[169] However, it is not clear that Paul has a particular exertion of the Spirit's power in mind, and the phrase likely refers to his ministry as a whole,[170] which thus implies the Spirit's agency behind all of "what Christ has accomplished through" him.[171]

---

167. Belleville, *2 Corinthians*, 94–95.

168. Schreiner helpfully states, "The dynamic of the Spirit is the means by which Paul achieved all that he did in every area: his speech, his actions, and his signs and wonders" (*Romans*, 768). Schreiner also points out that the meaning of "the power of the Spirit of God" could be identified as the power of God through the preaching of Paul if this verse contained a chiastic structure that parallels "word" with "the power of the Spirit of God" and "deed" with "the power of signs and wonders" in between. However, this structure was likely not Paul's intent. Along this line of thought, see also Moo, *The Epistle to the Romans*, 892–93.

169. Cf. Stott, *The Message of Romans*, 381.

170. Moo, *Romans*, 892–93; Osborne, *Romans*, 390.

171. Cf. Jewett, *Romans*, 911.

Philippians 1:19

In relating his thoughts about his experience in prison (Phil 1:12–26), Paul explained to the Philippians why he had cause to rejoice: "for I know that through your prayers and the help of the Spirit of Jesus Christ this will turn out for my deliverance" (Phil 1:19).

Paul rejoiced that "the help of the Spirit of Jesus Christ" would somehow "turn out for my deliverance" (Phil 1:19). It could be that the genitive phrase "of the Spirit" (*tou pneumatos*) is subjective, indicating that the Spirit helps Paul in some way while he is in prison.[172] More likely, however, "the Spirit" is an objective genitive, himself being "the help" or "provision" (*epichorēgia*) given to Paul who needed to be strengthened during this trying time.[173] Galatians 3:5 supports this understanding of Phil 1:19. There Paul uses *epichorēgeō*, the verbal cognate of *epichorēgia*, and describes God as "he who supplies the Spirit to you" (Gal 3:5).[174] Just as the Spirit himself is the "supply" or "help" in Gal 3:5, so also Phil 1:19 describes the Spirit as being a supply or help as well. What is implied is that the Spirit would give Paul the strength to persevere in prison.

The Apostle John: Revelation 1:10; 4:2; 17:3; 21:10

The apostle John records four times in Revelation that he was "in the Spirit" (Rev 1:10; 4:2; 17:3; 21:10).[175] Though an apostle, the content following each of these references indicates John spoke as a prophet who related apocalyptic visions of the future for the benefit of his readers (cf. Rev 1:3; 22:6–7). His visions and movement therein (cf. Rev 4:1–2; 17:3; 21:10) are analogous to what Ezekiel had experienced long ago (Ezek 3:12, 14; 8:3; 11:1, 24; 37:1; 43:5).[176]

---

172. Hawthorne, *Philippians*, 40–41, suggests that *tou pneumatos* could be either a subjective or objective genitive.

173. Hansen, *The Letter to the Philippians*, 79–80.

174. Ibid. Fee explains that the unique use of the next genitive phrase "of Jesus Christ" (*Iēsou Christou*) indicates "Christ will be glorified in his life or death only as he is filled with the Spirit of Christ himself" (*Paul's Letter to the Philippians*, 134).

175. The Greek phrase is identical in each of these four references (*en pneumati*).

176. Cf. Block, "The Prophet of the Spirit," 33–34.

Groups with Apostles and Other Leaders

The work of the Spirit is described in relation to groups of men that include the apostles and other leaders. These leaders include apostolic delegates (Acts 13:2, 4; 16:6–7) and elders as well (Acts 15:28).

Barnabas and Saul: Acts 13:2, 4

While staying with the church in Antioch which included some prophets and teachers (Acts 13:1), Barnabas and Saul were given a special commission by the Spirit: "While they were worshiping the Lord and fasting, the Holy Spirit said, 'Set apart for me Barnabas and Saul for the work to which I have called them'" (Acts 13:2). After fasting and prayer, the group "sent them off" (Acts 13:3), and "being sent out by the Holy Spirit, they went" (Acts 13:4).

As in instances involving Stephen (Acts 8:29) and Peter (Acts 10:19; 11:12), the Spirit directly speaks in order to give instructions for the purpose of a missionary endeavor. What is dissimilar from these instances involving Stephen and Peter, however, is that Acts 13:1 records the presence of the church and other individuals, "prophets and teachers." For this reason, the general understanding of "the Holy Spirit said" is that this phrase is a shorthand description for the Spirit having spoken through one of the prophets who were present.[177] Just as prophecies were given at Timothy's commission to ministry (1 Tim 1:18; 4:14; see below), so also it seems natural to assume the same took place here for Barnabas and Saul.[178] It could have been that Barnabas and Saul were among the prophets through whom the Spirit spoke in order to send them on their way.[179] However, if a clearer situation informs another that is not as clear, the prophecy by others at the commissioning of Timothy suggests that the Spirit enabled a prophecy by individuals other than Barnabas and Saul when they were sent on their way.

---

177. Bruce, "The Holy Spirit in the Acts of the Apostles," 182; Shepherd, *The Narrative Function of the Holy Spirit*, 210.

178. Fee, *God's Empowering Presence*, 760. Cf. Packer, "Holy Spirit," 319.

179. Bock, *Acts*, 439, apparently takes the list of names as identifying those who are the prophets and teachers.

The Jerusalem Council: Acts 15:28

While in Antioch, Paul and Barnabas debated with some Judeans who argued that circumcision was necessary for salvation (Acts 14:24–15:2). They went to Jerusalem to settle the matter, and the debate arose there as well (Acts 15:3–5). "The apostles and the elders were gathered together to consider this matter" (Acts 15:6; cf. 15:6–21) and wrote a letter to the church in Antioch as a result (Acts 15:22–28). They stated, "For it has seemed good to the Holy Spirit and to us to lay on you no greater burden than these requirements: that you abstain from what has been sacrificed to idols, and from blood, and from what has been strangled, and from sexual immorality" (Acts 15:28–29).

The consensus understanding is that the apostles and elders convened for discussion and were consequently guided by the Spirit to discern what "seemed good to the Holy Spirit" (Acts 15:28).[180] However, closer inspection of the phrase "it seemed good to the Holy Spirit" in the context of Acts 15 suggests that this phrase describes the Spirit as a character who himself discerns what is good in addition to the apostles and the elders. Acts 15:28 yields a clear distinction between the Spirit and the group of apostles and elders ("it seemed good to the Holy Spirit *and* to us"), showing the Spirit to be someone that Shepherd describes as "a direct actor in the decision-making process of the church."[181] The Spirit objectively evidenced his approval of the conversion of the Gentiles by being given to the Gentiles (Acts 15:8–9), confirming the gospel among the Gentiles with signs and wonders (Acts 15:12), and having inspired revelation concerning this matter long before the conversion ever took place (Acts 15:16–18; cf. Amos 9:11–12).[182] It may be correctly inferred that the Spirit actively guided the apostles and elders to correctly deduce that the Spirit approved of the conversion of the Gentiles, but that is not the express thought of the phrase "it seemed good to the Holy Spirit."

This type of description of the Spirit is not foreign to the book of Acts. Earlier, Peter spoke for the apostles before the Jewish officials and stated, "We are witnesses to these things, and so is the Holy Spirit, whom God has given to those who obey him" (Acts 5:32; see above). Just as the apostles pointed to the Spirit's witness of the validity of their message in Acts 5:32,

---

180. McIntosh, "For it seemed good to the Holy Spirit," 131–32. See e.g., Harvey, *Anointed with Spirit and Power*, 181; Inch, *Saga of the Spirit*, 86.

181. Shepherd, *The Narrative Function of the Holy Spirit*, 218.

182. McIntosh, "'For it seemed good to the Holy Spirit' Acts 15:28," 132–33.

so also the apostles and elders noted the Spirit's approval of the Gentiles' conversion in Acts 15:28.

Paul, Silas, and Timothy: Acts 16:6–7

During his second missionary journey, Paul was accompanied by Silas and Timothy (cf. Acts 15:40 16:3–4). While on their journey, "they went through the region of Phrygia and Galatia, having been forbidden by the Holy Spirit to speak the word in Asia" (Acts 16:6). A similar prohibition by the Spirit took place immediately thereafter: "And when they had come up to Mysia, they attempted to go into Bithynia, but the Spirit of Jesus did not allow them" (Acts 16:7). The reason for these prohibitions became apparent when, having reached Troas (Acts 16:8), Paul received a vision in the night of a man in Macedonia "urging him" to come, after which Paul immediately left with his company (Acts 16:9–10).[183]

The Spirit could have revealed these prohibitions to one or all of the company, but the details are simply not given.[184] Paul regularly received revelation as an apostle (cf. Acts 16:9–10), and Silas was a prophet who received the same on occasion as well (cf. Acts 15:32).[185] The Spirit could have revealed his prohibitions to any one of the three. As with Paul and Barnabas in Acts 13:1–4 (cf. Acts 8:29; 10:19–20), the Spirit directed multiple individuals in some way for the purpose of evangelism.

Apostolic Delegates

The Spirit's work is described in the lives of three apostolic delegates—Barnabas, Apollos, and Timothy.

Barnabas: Acts 11:24

The Jerusalem church heard of the conversion of Gentiles in Antioch and sent Barnabas as a result (Acts 11:19–22). He rejoiced in their conversion

---

183. As indicated by Luke's use of "we" in Acts 16:10, Luke apparently joined Paul and the others in Troas and accompanied them to Philippi (16:11–12). See Bruce, *The Acts of the Apostles*, 307–08.
184. Bock, *Acts*, 526–27.
185. Bruce, *The Acts of the Apostles*, 355.

and encouraged them to be faithful to the Lord (Acts 11:23). The reason he did so is given: "for he was a good man, full of the Holy Spirit and of faith" (Acts 11:24).

Luke occasionally describes an individual as "full of the Holy Spirit" to indicate the Spirit as the source of their power (Luke 4:1; see above) or the means of having a vision (Acts 7:55; see below). Typically, however, this phrase describes someone's character (cf. Acts 6:3, 5; see below). Barnabas is identified as "a good man," and the phrase "full of the Holy Spirit and of faith" explains this identity further.[186] The Holy Spirit was the source of his good character,[187] and his faith was evident through his ministry and preaching. He firmly believed in truth and powerfully exhorted others to do the same.[188]

Apollos: Acts 18:25

Acts 18:24–28 records the first mention of Apollos in Acts and describes him as "an eloquent man, competent in the Scriptures" (Acts 18:24). Acts 18:25 goes on to record a description of his preaching: "And being fervent in spirit, he spoke and taught accurately the things concerning Jesus, though he knew only the baptism of John."

The meaning of Apollos "being fervent in spirit" (*zeōn tō pneumati*) is variously understood for multiple reasons. First, "he knew only the baptism of John" (Acts 18:25), which suggests that, like the Ephesian disciples in Acts 19:1–6, he himself did not know of the Spirit's coming and had not yet received the Spirit.[189] However, because the text is silent on the matter of his reception of the Spirit, it could also be assumed that Apollos had already received the Spirit and thus engaged in Spirit-empowered preaching, though, strangely enough, his preaching consisted of an accurate but incomplete knowledge of the gospel.[190] His preaching was all the more effective after receiving further instruction (Acts 18:26–28). Second, the phrase "fervent

---

186. Cf. Peterson, *The Acts of the Apostles*, 355.

187. Larkin, *Acts*, 178.

188. Cf. Peterson, *The Acts of the Apostles*, 355.

189. Bock, *Acts*, 591–92. Larkin understands this absence of the Spirit to indicate Apollos was not even a believer but only something like a modern "nominal cultural Christian" (*Acts*, 271). It would seem that this understanding of Apollos is unnecessary given his zeal for the gospel, whether or not he had yet received the Spirit.

190. Bruce, *The Acts of the Apostles*, 406–07

in spirit" (*tō pneumati zeontes*) in Rom 12:11 could mean "fervent in the Spirit,"[191] and this similarity in language to Acts 18:25 (*zeōn tō pneumati*) could support the description of Apollos as "being fervent in the Spirit" as well.[192] Third, Luke's record of Paul's words in Acts 20:22 is similar to the description of Apollos in Acts 18:25. Paul described himself as being "constrained by the Spirit," which is a combination of *tō pneumati* with a participle (*poreuomai*), similar to the description of Apollos in Acts 18:25 (*zeōn tō pneumati*).

All factors considered, Luke likely records an anomaly that could only take place during a turning point in redemptive history. Though incomplete in his knowledge of the gospel, Apollos assumedly received the Spirit and fervently preached the gospel as a result. He is not described as having received the Spirit or not, but his powerful preaching is described as being zeōn tō pneumati, which likely refers to the Spirit in light of similarities to other passages in Acts (Acts 20:22) and elsewhere in the NT (Rom 12:11). Having been instructed further concerning the details of the gospel (Acts 18:26), his Spirit-empowered preaching was all the more effective (Acts 18:27–28).

Timothy: 2 Timothy 1:7, 14

Timothy was a young man who traveled with Paul (Acts 16:3–4) and was sent by Paul on various missions (e.g., 1 Thess 3:2; 1 Tim 1:3). In one of Paul's letters to Timothy, Paul encouraged Timothy "to fan into flame the gift of God, which is in you through the laying on of my hands, for God gave us a spirit not of fear but of power and love and self-control" (2 Tim 1:6–7). In the same letter, Paul later stated, "By the Holy Spirit who dwells within us, guard the good deposit entrusted to you" (2 Tim 1:14).

It is highly likely that Paul refers to the Spirit and not Timothy's spirit in 2 Tim 1:7,[193] but if this is the case, it is difficult to discern whether or not this work of the Spirit is a work in Timothy specifically for the pur-

---

191. E.g., Moo, *Romans*, 778.

192. Schnabel, *Acts*, 785.

193. If nothing else, the clear reference to the Spirit in 2 Tim 1:14 with the command to "guard the deposit" concludes a section that began with a command to "fan into flame the gift of God" by way of the *pneuma*. The conceptual and terminological links between 1:6–7 and 1:14 form a nice *inclusio* and imply the Spirit is in view in 1:7. Cf. Towner, *The Letters to Timothy and Titus*, 479–80. The mention of Timothy's "gift" and the command to exercise as much with "power and love and self-control" (1 Tim 1:7) are themes that assume the Spirit's work as well (see below).

pose of leadership. Power, love, and self-control may be uniquely displayed through leaders, but these works of the Spirit are common to all Christians as well.[194] Also, Paul appeals to Timothy to "guard the good deposit" on the basis of the Spirit who indwells him, but the Spirit's indwelling, too, is something common to all Christians (cf. Rom 8:9, 11; 1 Cor 6:19).

Though the Spirit indwells believers in general and thus the Christian leaders among them, the context of 2 Tim 1:7 and 1:14 suggests that Paul's descriptions of the Spirit's work are in terms of Timothy's leadership despite this otherwise "shared" terminology.[195] The power, love, and self-control were to be shown through the exercise of Timothy's "gift" (2 Tim 1:6). In Paul's previous letter to Timothy, Timothy was told to "not neglect the gift" he possessed (1 Tim 4:14), which comes immediately after Paul's command to devote himself "to exhortation, teaching" (1 Tim 4:13). The implication is that his gift was to exhort and teach God's Word, which likely carries over to the understanding of "gift" in 2 Tim 1:6.[196]

A work of the Spirit for Timothy as a leader is also implied by his commission to ministry. Paul describes that this gift was "in" (*en*) Timothy in conjunction with "the laying on of my hands" (2 Tim 1:7). This laying of hands was by others as well, and prophecy was given at the same time (1 Tim 4:14; cf. 1 Tim 1:18).[197] This prophecy likely confirmed Timothy

---

194. The Spirit gives power to all Christians (Rom 15:13; Eph 3:16) and to leaders to empower miracles (Rom 15:19) and preaching (1 Thess 1:5; 1 Cor 2:4; cf. Luke 4:14; Acts 1:8; 10:38). Love is the work of the Spirit (Gal 5:22; cf. 1 Cor 13:1–3). Though Paul's word for "self-control" (*sōphronismos*) is used only here in the NT, its cognates and their uses elsewhere indicate he means something similar here (cf. 1 Tim 3:2; Titus 1:8; 2:2, 5, 12). Cf. Knight, *The Pastoral Epistles*, 372. This self-control is the Spirit's fruit translated "self-control" (*enkrateia*) in Gal 5:22–23, suggesting Paul thought of *sōphronismos* as a product of the Spirit as well. Cf. Mounce, *Pastoral Epistles*, 479.

195. Marshall states, "The determining factor is that the qualities here associated with the Spirit are in no way peculiar to leaders, although they are applied here especially to the ability of the leader to speak the gospel without fear" (*A Critical and Exegetical Commentary on the Pastoral Epistles*, 699). Thomas is similar: "The teaching as to the Holy Spirit in these Epistles is concerned almost entirely with the ministry (1 Tim. iv. 1; 2 Tim. i. 6, 7, 14)" (*The Holy Spirit of God*, 27).

196. Fee, *1 and 2 Timothy, Titus*, 108. Interestingly, Huther, "The Pastoral Epistles," 149, ties Timothy's gift not only to teaching and exhortation (cf. 4:13) but also to *kybernēsis* (cf. 1 Cor 12:28; see the discussion on "The Spiritual Gift of Leadership" below). The common term for "gift" in all of these texts is *charisma*. Paul elsewhere refers to exhortation and teaching as "gifts" (Rom 12:6–8), and he sources all "gifts" in the Spirit (1 Cor 12:4; cf. 12:7).

197. See the lengthy "Excursus: Prophecies about Timothy" in Mounce, *Pastoral Epistles*, 70–72. Others would see the events of 1 Tim 4:14 and 2 Tim 1:6 referring to

in his commission to ministry, similar to how Barnabas and Saul were commissioned for their missionary journey in Acts 13:1–4. Paul could thus later use this prophecy as the basis for exhorting Timothy to "wage the good warfare" of upholding sound doctrine in his teaching while leading the church of Ephesus (1 Tim 1:18; cf. 1 Tim 1:3–4). These prophecies indicated that Timothy had been gifted and called for such a purpose.

The Spirit indwelled Timothy and enabled him to minister with power, love, and self-control. Though this indwelling and work of the Spirit are true of all Christians, the focus on the role of the Spirit in Timothy's leadership is implied by Paul's commands to uphold God's Word and his references to Timothy's gift and commission to ministry.

Summary

The Spirit's work through the apostles involved the miraculous from time to time (Acts 5:4–5, 9–10; 13:9–11), but the descriptions of the Spirit's work primarily involved the proclamation and defense of the gospel. The Spirit spoke to and through leaders in the church in order to guide them to where they would proclaim the gospel (Acts 10:19; 11:12; 13:2, 4; 16:6–7), and the Spirit was an internal guide along these lines as well (Acts 19:21; 20:22). With reference to the act of proclamation, the Spirit filled Paul after his conversion to boldly preach (Acts 9:17; cf. 9:20), and Apollos' fervency in preaching came from the Spirit as well (Acts 18:25). Paul identified the Spirit as the empowering source of his preaching (1 Thess 1:5) and noted that the Spirit also bore witness to his listeners to demonstrate the truthfulness of God's Word (1 Cor 2:4–5). As to the manner of proclamation, the indwelling Spirit in Timothy enabled him to teach with courage, love, and self-control (2 Tim 1:6–7, 14). When being persecuted for proclaiming the gospel, the Spirit granted Peter the words to speak when standing before his opposition (Acts 4:8).

Elders: Acts 20:28

While the NT often mentions the Spirit and his work in relation to Jesus, the apostles, and apostolic delegates, the Spirit is mentioned explicitly but once

---

separate events. E.g., see Towner, *The Letters to Timothy and Titus*, 459.

in relation to elders.[198] On his way to Jerusalem, Paul visited the church in Ephesus and spoke to the elders before his departure (Acts 20:17–35). In the midst of his address, he gave the elders this command: "Pay careful attention to yourselves and to all the flock, in which the Holy Spirit has made you overseers, to care for the church of God, which he obtained with his own blood" (Acts 20:28).

Paul identifies the Spirit as the one who "made" (*tithēmi*) or "appointed" (HCSB) the elders "overseers" (*episkopos*)[199] for a specific purpose: "to shepherd" (HCSB) or "to care for the church of God" (Acts 20:28). This unique reference to the Holy Spirit as the one who "made" the elders overseers has been variously explained.[200] The Spirit could have used prophets to prophesy of the giftedness and calling of these elders, similar to the commission of others (cf. Acts 13:1–4; 1 Tim 1:18; 4:14; see above).[201] The Ephesian church may have appointed the elders to their office in some way (cf. Acts 6:1–7),[202] or Paul could have appointed them as elders by choosing them himself or delegating this task to another (cf. Acts 14:23; Titus 1:5).[203] Whichever process was carried out (or perhaps some combination of the above; cf. 1 Tim 4:14; 2 Tim 1:6), the elders' appointment would have been based upon the Spirit's work in their sanctification (cf. 1 Tim 3:1–7; Titus 1:5–9) and spiritual giftedness (cf. 1 Tim 3:2),[204] and Paul simply meant to encourage the elders not by the process of their appointment, but that the Spirit was the one to appoint them.

---

198. This is not to say that that the Spirit's work is not assumed in the many passages describing the nature of salvation, sanctification, and gifting of Christians in general, elders included.

199. While each term has its respective emphasis, this study assumes both *elder* and *overseer* refer to one and the same office (cf. Titus 1:5, 7). See the chapter entitled "Do the Terms 'Elder' and 'Overseer' Represent the Same Office?" in Merkle, *40 Questions About Elders and Deacons*, 76–83.

200. Paul typically identifies God (1 Cor 12:28) or Christ (1 Tim 1:12) as the one who appointed him or others to service, or he does not say at all (1 Tim 2:7; 2 Tim 1:11).

201. Bruce, *The Acts of the Apostles*, 433; Lampe, "'Grievous Wolves' (Acts 20:29)," 257; Larkin, *Acts*, 298.

202. Cf. Polhill, *Acts*, 426–27.

203. Shepherd, *The Narrative Function of the Holy Spirit*, 234–35. Paul spent three years in Ephesus (Acts 20:31), which would have allowed him ample time to train elders before his departure. Acts 14:23 records that Paul had appointed elders elsewhere, suggesting the same practice took place in Ephesus.

204. Cf. Gromacki, *The Holy Spirit*, 161.

It seems another reason Paul referred to the Spirit was to imply the Spirit's continued role in the elders' carrying out of their responsibilities. All in the same clause Paul speaks of the flock "in which the Holy Spirit has made you overseers to care for the church of God."[205] Just as the Spirit had appointed the elders to their office, so also the Spirit had enabled them to carry out the responsibilities of this office.

What is significant to this study is that the Spirit is said to have appointed these men to *shepherd* the flock of God. Just as Joshua was qualified to shepherd Israel because he was "a man in whom is the Spirit" (Num 27:18; cf. 27:17), so also these elders were to shepherd the flock of God because the Spirit had appointed them to do so (Acts 20:28). The similarities of these descriptions of the Spirit's involvement in the leadership of both OT and NT leaders to shepherd suggests that the Spirit's distinctive work in leadership is similar from one testament to the next.

Deacons

Six passages describe the work of the Spirit in deacons. Though deacons do not function as leaders within the church, it is helpful to examine these passages in order to bring out what distinguishes them from elders.[206] One passage describes the Spirit's work in deacons in general (Acts 6:3), and the other five are split between the work of the Spirit in Stephen (Acts 6:5, 10; 7:55) and Philip (Acts 8:29, 39), both of whom were deacons (cf. Acts 6:5).

Deacons in General: Acts 6:3

When the early church grew, so also did the number of widows needing to be fed, Hellenist and Hebrew alike (Acts 6:1). When a complaint came to the apostles that the Hellenist "widows were being neglected in the daily distribution" (Acts 6:1), they discussed the matter and gave the church their

---

205. Unlike most English translations, there is no punctuation or break between the object "overseers" and the infinitive phrase "to care for the church of God" in Acts 20:28 (*hymas to pneuma to hagion etheto episkopous poimainein tēn ekklēsian tou theou*).

206. The term *leader* in this study was initially defined as "anyone who has been formally recognized by God or his people to lead the people of God." This definition does not exclude deacons (or others in general) from being recognized as leaders over the course of time as it becomes apparent that the Spirit's work in them has also enabled them to be leaders. To clarify, leadership is not essential to the *office* of deacon (see Chapter 4).

solution (Acts 6:3–7), which included this command: "Therefore, brothers, pick out from among you seven men of good repute, full of the Spirit and of wisdom, whom we will appoint to this duty" (Acts 6:3).

Acts 6:1–7 is typically understood to describe the origin of the office of deacon in the church.[207] Understanding this passage in this way, Acts 6:3 identified what should be true of deacons, namely, that they were "of good repute, full of the Spirit and of wisdom" (Acts 6:3). That deacons were to be "full of the Spirit" indicated their lives were to be characterized by the work of the Spirit in general.[208] The additional phrase "and of wisdom" indicated the Spirit was also to be manifest in their wisdom in ministering to the needs of the church. This wisdom from the Spirit would enable them to wisely handle the affairs of the church concerning the feeding of widows.[209]

Stephen

Stephen was one of the first deacons, and the Spirit is described to have worked through him in multiple ways (Acts 6:5, 10; 7:55).

Acts 6:5

As described above, Acts 6:1–7 records the origin of the office of deacon. Acts 6:5 records the church's obedience to the apostles' instruction (cf. Acts 6:3) and identifies the seven men who first served in this office: "And what they said pleased the whole gathering, and they chose Stephen, a man full of faith and of the Holy Spirit, and Philip, and Prochorus, and Nicanor, and Timon, and Parmenas, and Nicolaus, a proselyte of Antioch."

Unlike the others, Stephen is described as "a man full of faith and of the Holy Spirit" (Acts 6:5). Apart from order of genitive phrases, Barnabas is described almost exactly the same way in Acts 11:24: "he was a good man, full of the Holy Spirit and of faith." Stephen's life was characterized by

---

207. Merkle, *40 Questions about Elders and Deacons*, 227. Merkle points out that some object to this conclusion because apostles were leading the church and not elders and because the seven are not explicitly identified as "deacons." "Still," he says, "Acts 6 does provide a pattern or paradigm that seems to have been continued in the early church" (Ibid.).

208. Köstenberger, "What Does It Mean to Be Filled with the Spirit," 237. Cf. Bock, *Acts*, 260; Larkin, *Acts*, 101.

209. Peterson, *The Acts of the Apostles*, 233.

the work of the Spirit in general, and his ministry was the result of his firm trust and belief in the Lord even in the face of opposition (cf. Acts 7:1–60).

Acts 6:10

The narrative of Acts 6 continues and records Stephen's miracles (Acts 6:8) and consequent opposition (Acts 6:9). When these opponents "rose up and disputed with Stephen" (Acts 6:9), their efforts were to no avail: "But they could not withstand the wisdom and the Spirit with which he was speaking" (Acts 6:10).

Stephen earlier met the requirement to be a deacon based upon the fact that he was "full of the Spirit and of wisdom" (Acts 6:3). His wisdom would be manifest through his care of the Hellenist widows. Now it was not his works but his speech that was characterized with "the wisdom and the Spirit" (Acts 6:10). This wisdom allowed Stephen to immediately respond to the charges of his opponents and ably defend the gospel.[210]

Though wisdom is typically understood in more general terms, the Spirit's bestowal of wisdom to Stephen in this situation was for the purpose of giving him the words to say in the context of persecution. As seen above, Jesus promised the apostles that the Spirit would teach them what to say when standing before their opposition (Luke 12:12). Jesus later stated this promise again in another way: "I will give you a mouth and wisdom" (Luke 21:15). The Spirit of Christ gave Stephen the wisdom to articulate an impenetrable defense of the gospel.

Acts 7:55

Unable to refute Stephen, his opponents charged him with false accusations in order to place him on trial before the Jewish officials (Acts 6:11–15). Stephen gave his defense and rebuked the Jews (Acts 7:1–53), provoking them to stone him (Acts 7:54–60). Just before his death, "he, full of the Holy Spirit, gazed into heaven and saw the glory of God, and Jesus standing at the right hand of God" (Acts 7:55).

Though the phrase "full of the Holy Spirit" is used by Luke to describe the work of the Spirit in one's character in general (cf. Acts 6:3, 5; 11:24), its

---

210. Cf. Harvey, *Anointed with Spirit and Power*, 129; Peterson, *The Acts of the Apostles*, 240.

use here is to describe Stephen as a prophet who is enabled by the Spirit to have a vision of "the glory of God, and Jesus standing at the right hand of God" (Acts 7:55).[211] Luke's use of *plērēs* ("full of") cannot be limited to the description of character alone.[212]

Philip

Philip was a deacon (Acts 6:5) who met the requirement of being "full of the Spirit" (Acts 6:4). The Spirit's activity in his life is described in other ways as well (Acts 8:29, 39).

Acts 8:29

Philip was directed by an angel to go to a specific road in a desert area, and there he saw an Ethiopian court official traveling along the road (Acts 8:26–28). At this point, the Spirit spoke to Philip: "And the Spirit said to Philip, 'Go over and join this chariot'" (Acts 8:29).

This command from the Spirit to Philip finds parallels in other instances in Acts (Acts 10:19; 13:2) and relates to Philip's role as an evangelist (cf. Acts 21:8). The Spirit commanded him to go to the Ethiopian for the purpose of explaining to him the gospel (Acts 8:35). Philip may be termed as a prophet in the sense that he received direct revelation from the Spirit.[213]

Acts 8:39

After Philip went to the Ethiopian and explained to him the gospel (Acts 8:30–35), the Ethiopian believed and was baptized immediately (Acts 8:36–38). Acts 8:39 records what happens next: "And when they came up out of the water, the Spirit of the Lord carried Philip away, and the eunuch saw him no more, and went on his way rejoicing" (Acts 8:39). Luke does not leave the reader to wonder where Philip went: "Philip found himself at Azotus" (Acts 8:40).

For some, the physical movement of the evangelist Philip in Acts 8:39 is similar to the movement of the apostle John and Ezekiel in their

---

211. Bruce, *The Acts of the Apostles*, 210.
212. Köstenberger, "What Does It Mean to Be Filled with the Spirit," 237.
213. Cf. Bruce, *The Acts of the Apostles*, 226.

respective visions (cf. Ezek 3:12, 14; 8:3; 11:1, 24; 37:1; 43:5; Rev 4:1–2; 17:3; 21:10; see above). The verb "carried" (*harpazō*) is used elsewhere by Luke to refer to physical movement (Acts 23:10),[214] and it may have been that Philip was supernaturally transported away from the eunuch, similar to the transport of Enoch and Elijah in the OT (Gen 5:24 with Heb 11:5; 2 Kgs 2:11–12; cf. esp. 1 Kgs 18:12).[215] However Philip's departure took place, the purpose of the activity of the Spirit is once again to guide an individual to a new location in order to give the gospel (Acts 8:40; cf. 8:29; 10:19–20; 11:12; 13:2, 4; 16:6–7).

Summary

Deacons' lives were to be characterized by the Spirit's work in general and specifically in the Spirit's granting them the necessary wisdom for effectively ministering to the needs of others (Acts 6:3).[216] Stephen and Philip were deacons who experienced this work of the Spirit and additional works of the Spirit as well. The Spirit granted Stephen the words to speak in persecution and a vision before his death (Acts 6:10; 7:55). The Spirit spoke to Philip in guiding him to the Ethiopian (Acts 8:29) and then transported him away (Acts 8:39).

The Spiritual Gift of Leadership

The study thus far has examined the work of the Spirit in specific leaders as it is described in Scripture. This chapter will close not by examining the work of the Spirit in another specific leader but in what is commonly called *the spiritual gift of leadership*.

---

214. The verb *harpazō* is used to describe physical movement of people elsewhere as well (cf. John 6:15; 10:28, 29; 2 Cor 12:2, 3; 1 Thess 4:17; Jude 23; Rev 12:5).

215. Bruce, *The Acts of the Apostles*, 230; Horton, *What the Bible Says about the Holy Spirit*, 52; Shepherd, *The Narrative Function of the Holy Spirit*, 187. In contrast, Peterson claims this was not a miracle but "the Spirit's forceful direction of Philip" (*The Acts of the Apostles*, 297–98).

216. The similarity in character requirements for elders and deacons in 1 Tim 3:1–13 suggests that the requirement for deacons to be of "good repute" (Acts 6:3) could be applied to elders as well. Commenting on Acts 6:3, Peterson, *Acts*, 233, notes that deacons were to be "of good repute" (*martyroumenous*), just as elders were to be "well thought of" (*martyrian*) by outsiders (1 Tim 3:7).

Spiritual Gifts in General

Though this study cannot explore the myriad of issues related to spiritual gifts, it is at least necessary to offer and explain a working definition for the term *spiritual gift*. The closest parallel to the English term *spiritual gift* is found in Rom 1:11 (*charisma pneumatikon*), and its meaning is somewhat ambiguous.[217] What is typically meant by *spiritual gift* stems from terms such as *charisma*[218] and *pneumatikos*[219] and may be defined as some type of Spirit-enabled ministry that a Christian exercises for the benefit of the body of Christ.[220]

Six passages are typically cited as providing incomplete lists of spiritual gifts (Rom 12:6–8; 1 Cor 12:8–10; 12:28; 12:29–30; Eph 4:11; and 1 Pet 4:10–11), and a comprehensive list from these passages yields approximately twenty gifts.[221] Though using different terminology, both 1 Cor 12:28 and

---

217. Moo surveys two options and then tentatively concludes the phrase to mean "an insight or ability, given Paul by the Spirit, that Paul hopes to 'share' with the Romans" (*Romans*, 59–60).

218. The term *charisma* implies a manifestation of the Spirit that is itself an expression of the grace (*charis*) of God. See BDAG, "χάρις," 1079–81. "The *charis* of God manifests itself in various *charismata*: Ro 12:6; Eph 4:7; 1 Pt 4:10" (Ibid., 1080).

219. The term *pneumatikon* implies the agency of the Spirit (*pneuma*) in enabling an individual to carry out a specific ministry. The terms *charisma* and *pneumatikon* overlap in their meaning as they are used interchangeably by Paul (cf. 1 Cor 12:1, 4). See Fee, "Spiritual Gifts," 341 and Thomas, *Understanding Spiritual Gifts*, 19. Both authors discuss why this term refers to spiritual gifts and not spiritual people. The context of 1 Corinthians 12–14 has to do more with the gifts themselves than the people who exercise them. The reason some understand *pneumatikos* to refer to individuals is due to the possibility that its genitive form in 1 Cor 12:1 could be either neuter or masculine in gender. If neuter, Paul speaks of spiritual gifts. If masculine, Paul could be speaking of people who are characterized by spiritual activity ("spirituals" or "spiritual ones"). However, the term's use in 1 Cor 14:1 is clearly neuter, suggesting that it is highly probable that Paul used the term as a neuter in 1 Cor 12:1 as well.

220. This definition excludes the notion that *people* are spiritual gifts (cf. Eph 4:8, 11), though it may be said that the people who are gifts are spiritually gifted according to their role in the church. The confusing conflation of people and ministries as gifts stems from the use of the English term *gift* as a translation for the terms *charisma* (typically found in the "gift lists"; cf. Rom 12:6; 1 Cor 12:4, 30; 1 Pet 4:10) and *doma* (refers to people in Eph 4:8; cf. 4:11). For an excellent discussion on this issue, see Berding's article "Confusing Word and Concept in 'Spiritual Gifts,'" 37–51, or his longer work *What Are Spiritual Gifts?*.

221. One of the reasons for a variation in number is whether or not one assumes the people in Eph 4:11 to have a unique gift related to their office (e.g., apostles possessing the gift of "apostleship"). Cf. Berding, *What Are Spiritual Gifts*, 89–90.

Rom 12:8 identify what is commonly called the spiritual gift of leadership. This gift is examined in the context of each verse below.

First Corinthians 12:28

After demonstrating the need for both unity in the body and a diversity of spiritual gifts (1 Cor 12:12–26; cf. esp. 12:27), Paul closes this matter by stressing again the need for diversity by listing several offices and ministries in the church (1 Cor 12:28–30). One of the ministries identified in 1 Cor 12:28 is "administrating" or "gifts of leadership" (NET Bible).[222]

The term translated "gifts of leadership" is the plural form of *kybernēsis*, which, though only used once in the NT, may be understood to include the notion of guidance according to its use in the OT (Prov 1:5; 11:14; 24:6 LXX).[223] The cognate *kybernētēs* refers to the pilot or helmsman of a ship in both the OT (Prov 23:34; Ezek 27:8, 27, 28 LXX) and NT (Acts 27:11; Rev 18:17), and it may be said that a *kybernētēs* (a helmsman) possesses *kybernēsis* (the ability to guide his vessel on the sea).

In Paul's day, this nautical term was a commonly used image for leadership in the political arena and likely functioned in 1 Cor 12:28 as a metaphor for polity, implying the role of an elder in keeping the unity of the church.[224] The spiritual gift of leadership speaks to the leader's ability to avoid the "rocks and shallows" of division within the church[225] or difficulties in general.[226]

Though Paul speaks of a spiritual gift and does not specify who possesses this gift, multiple reasons suggest that elders are in view. Assuming Rom 12:8 to refer to the spiritual gift of leadership as well (see below), if Rom 12:8 is understood to refer to elders, the gift as listed in 1 Cor 12:28 could refer to elders as well. Also, the juxtaposition of "helps" next to "gifts of leadership" in 1 Cor 12:28 is parallel in concept to the juxtaposition of "one who leads" next to "acts of mercy" in Rom 12:8. Though Paul does not refer to an office that exercises either of these gifts, it could be that he has

---

222. Translations offering a plural term (NASB, NET Bible) reflect the plural use of *kybernēsis* (*kybernēseis*).

223. Cf. Thiselton, *The First Epistle to the Corinthians*, 1021.

224. Mitchell, *Paul and the Rhetoric of Reconciliation*, 163–64.

225. Garland, *1 Corinthians*, 599–600; Thiselton, *The First Epistle to the Corinthians*, 1021.

226. Ciampa and Rosner. *The First letter to the Corinthians*, 614.

elders and deacons in mind, which would be similar to his address to "the overseers and deacons" in Phil 1:1.[227]

Based upon the imagery and background of the term *kybernēsis* and its juxtaposition next to spiritual gifts that could refer to the ministry of deacons, it is plausible to suggest that Paul has elders in mind as those who are uniquely gifted to govern the body of Christ. At the least, it may be said that those who rightfully govern the body are uniquely gifted by the Spirit to do so.

Romans 12:8

Similar to 1 Corinthians 12, Paul exhorts the Romans concerning the matters of unity among the body and having a diversity of spiritual gifts (Rom 12:4–5) and lists what several of these gifts would be (Rom 12:6–8). In giving this list, Paul not only identifies several gifts, but also the manner or means whereby they should be used. All of the gifts were to be exercised, and for "the one who leads, with zeal" (Rom 12:8).

There does not seem to be any apparent structure to Paul's list of seven gifts in Rom 12:6–8,[228] though it is tempting to see the final three gifts as a group in order to conclude that the phrase *ho proistamenos en spoudē* means "the one who gives aid, with zeal" instead of "the one who leads, with zeal."[229] The reason it is tempting to do so is that all three gifts would then refer to some type of service to others.[230] The first of these three refers to giving, the last to meeting the needs of others, and the gift in between could be understood as giving aid to others.[231] At the same time, Paul's use of *prohistēmi* in the phrase *ho proistamenos en spoudē* likely accords with its consistent usage elsewhere.[232] Paul uses *prohistēmi* to refer to those who

---

227. Beyer, "κυβέρνησις," 3:1036. Meyer claims that "most interpreters" (during his time of writing) associate "services of help" with the diaconate and that "most commentators" associate "governments" with elders (he terms them presbyters and bishops; *Critical and Exegetical Hand-book to the Epistles to the Corinthians*, 295). He sees this interpretation as so because their "juxtaposition . . . points to this interpretation" (Ibid.).

228. Schreiner, *Romans*, 660.

229. Dunn, *Romans 9–16*, 735.

230. Ibid., 731. Dunn sees this placement as "almost certainly decisive" for this meaning.

231. It is possible that *prohistēmi* could refer to giving someone aid. See BDAG, "προΐστημι," 870.

232. Despite the fact that he sees a structured list similar to Dunn, Stott, *The Message of Romans*, 328, nonetheless opts for this meaning of *prohistēmi*.

"have charge" over the body (1 Thess 5:12), the overseer who must "manage" his household well (1 Tim 3:4, 5), and the elders who should "rule" well (1 Tim 5:17). Not only do these uses refer to the exercise of leadership, but each of the uses refers to the leadership of an elder. That the leadership should be characterized "with zeal" indicates that this leadership should be carried out eagerly and with diligence, [233] a notion similar to Peter's exhortation to elders to "shepherd . . . eagerly" in 1 Pet 5:2.[234]

It is reasonable to conclude that Paul has elders in mind when referring to the spiritual gift of leadership in Rom 12:8.[235] If this is so, Paul again identifies a spiritual gift that is unique to elders for the purpose of governing the body of Christ. The terminology reflects Paul's descriptions of elders elsewhere (1 Thess 5:12; 1 Tim 3:4, 5; 5:17), and the manner whereby they serve is similar to Peter's exhortation to elders in 1 Pet 5:2. As above with 1 Cor 12:28, it may be said at the least that those who rightfully govern the body are uniquely gifted by the Spirit to do so.[236]

Summary

In both 1 Cor 12:28 and Rom 12:8, leadership is identified as a distinct spiritual gift among a range of gifts that the Spirit may grant to a Christian. There is evidence to suggest that Paul had elders in view when referring to this gift, but whether or not this is so, it may at least be said that those who govern God's people are gifted by the Spirit to do so, which would include those who are elders. The fact that this gift is identified in isolation from others strongly argues that the Spirit's work in the leadership of a leader is distinct from other works of the Spirit.

---

233. Moo, *Romans*, 769; Morris, *The Epistle to the Romans*, 442.

234. The term for "eagerly" is *prothymōs*, which Jobes describes as ". . . a term often used in secular writings to characterize the benefactor of a city who enthusiastically provides time and money for civic duties" (*1 Peter*, 305).

235. Calvin, *Commentaries on the Epistles of Paul the Apostle to the Romans*, 463.

236. Cf. Kruse, *Paul's Letter to the Romans*, 473. Jewett, *Romans*, 753; Moo, *Romans*, 768–69; Osborne, *Romans*, 328; Schreiner, *Romans*, 660. Commentators typically suggest that this gift could refer to elders but could refer to others who lead as well.

Conclusion

The Spirit's work in the leadership of God's people is both similar and different from one testament to the next. In the OT, leaders were enabled by the Spirit to effectively lead Israel's affairs, and in the NT, Jesus was expected to do the same as Israel's Spirit-anointed king (cf. Matt 3:16–17; cf. Ps 2:7; Isa 42:1). Though Jesus announced himself as this king (cf. Matt 12:28), it was made clear that the Spirit's work through Jesus' initial ministry omitted the execution of justice against his enemies (Luke 4:18–21; cf. Isa 61:1–2a) and would be of a gentle nature (Matt 12:18–21; cf. Isa 42:1–4). His initial ministry primarily involved the proclamation of the gospel (Luke 4:14–15, 18–21; cf. Isa 61:1–2a).

After his death and resurrection, Jesus sent the Spirit to his followers to continue the task of proclamation (Acts 2:33) and empowered the witness of the apostles and the church at large (cf. Acts 1:8; 4:31). The Spirit could be described as "the Spirit of Jesus" in that Jesus guided apostles and their delegates through the Spirit on their missionary journeys (Acts 16:6–7). Jesus through the Spirit enabled the ministries of each member of the church (1 Cor 12:4–5) and revealed truth about himself to the apostles as exampled in the book of Revelation (Rev 2:7, 11, 17, 29; 3:6, 13, 22; cf. John 16:12–15).

The description of the Spirit's work through the apostles and their delegates clearly shows an emphasis on the proclamation of the gospel as well. The Spirit guided individuals in a variety of ways to lead them to those who needed gospel (Acts 8:39, 39; 10:19; 11:12; 13:2, 4; 16:6–7; 19:21; 20:22). The Spirit also enabled the act of preaching and tempered its manner as well (Acts 9:17, 20; 18:25; 1 Thess 1:5; 2 Tim 1:6–7, 14). In the context of persecution, the Spirit granted defendants of the gospel the words to say to their opponents (Acts 4:8; 6:10).

In all of the above, though the emphasis is not so much on the Spirit's work in leadership as it is in proclamation, the work of the Spirit in leadership had not vanished. Jesus' entire ministry was characterized by the Spirit (Matt 12:18–21; Luke 4:18–21), and he was also distinct in his leadership as the head of the church who sent the Spirit (Acts 2:33), granted spiritual gifts (1 Cor 12:4–5), and spoke the words of the Spirit (cf. Rev 2:7). The apostles discerned the work of the Spirit and thereby governed the early church (Acts 5:4–5, 9–10; 15:28). Similar to Joshua in the OT (Num 27:17–18), elders were appointed by the Spirit to shepherd and guide the flock of God (Acts 20:28). Though deacons are not leaders who exercise authority in the church, they were appointed to their official ministry on the basis of the Spirit's general work in their lives and granting them wisdom for ministry (Acts 6:3).

The identification of leadership as a spiritual gift is perhaps the most convincing argument that there is a distinct work of the Spirit in biblical leaders. Paul identified this gift in both 1 Cor 12:28 and Rom 12:8, and it may have been that he was thinking of elders as the ones to exercise this gift. Whether or not elders were in view, elders would necessarily possess this gift, and it is likely that the apostles and their delegates also possessed this gift to govern the early church. Moreover, if the Spirit distinctly gifted leaders to lead in the NT, it could be said that this work of the Spirit is similar to what is described of OT leaders as well.[237] The Spirit's work in leadership in the OT was described as the Spirit granting the necessary wisdom to a leader in order for him to lead God's people in carrying out the various purposes of God. In the NT, the Spirit's work in leadership could be described as the Spirit granting the necessary wisdom to a leader in order for him to shepherd God's people in carrying out the task of gospel proclamation. Though the purpose of the Spirit's work in leadership changes from one testament to the next, it may still be said that there is a distinct work of the Spirit in the leadership of biblical leaders.

---

237. This statement would apply only to leaders who are described as being enabled by the Spirit.

4

A Systematized Biblical Theology of Spiritual Leadership

Introduction

THE PREVIOUS TWO CHAPTERS attempted to survey every text that mentioned the Spirit, a leader, and the Spirit's work in the exercise of the leader's leadership. These chapters provided the necessary data for a systematized biblical theology of spiritual leadership.[1] Several themes began to emerge in these two chapters, and the present chapter attempts to grasp these themes and discuss them in a systematic manner.

In creating this theology, the process will be to note clear examples of a theme from its beginning to end and then show how these examples imply the presence of this theme in other leaders discussed as well. In tracing a theme from one leader to the next, issues of continuity and discontinuity will be discussed, and it will be noted when a given theme according to the topic of spiritual leadership seems to be part of a larger theme in Scripture. It will also be discussed as necessary how a theme related to biblical leaders overlaps with God's people in general in order to clarify how the Spirit's work is distinct between the two. Each theme will be discussed in relation to the overarching storyline of Scripture as necessary as well.

Wisdom in Leadership

It may be said that the primary description of how the Spirit enables a leader to lead is to grant a leader the necessary wisdom to carry out the task that God has given him. This wisdom is not so much the perception or communication of wisdom as it is a wisdom that is shown through action in

---

1. For a fuller explanation of a systemized biblical theology, see Köstenberger, "The Challenge of a Systematized Biblical Theology," 445–48.

leadership.[2] This wisdom primarily "focuses on conduct as a consequence of right perception, on proper behavior in everyday life,"[3] and it may be said that this wisdom is also narrowly given for the exercise of leadership.[4]

Wisdom for Leadership in the Old Testament

Several examples bring out an explicit connection between the Spirit and wisdom in the leadership of a leader. Joshua was described as being "full of the spirit of wisdom" (Deut 34:9), which was concluded to be "the Spirit of wisdom" based upon the previous description that Joshua was "a man in whom is the Spirit" (Num 27:18). The Spirit gave Joshua the wisdom necessary to shepherd the flock of Israel and lead the nation in battle (Num 27:17). Isaiah prophesied of the Messiah that "the Spirit of the LORD shall rest upon him, the Spirit of wisdom and understanding" (Isa 11:2). This Spirit would give the Messiah the wisdom necessary to execute perfect justice and bring about worldwide peace (Isa 11:3–5).

Since wisdom clearly involves leading Israel in general as well as specifically in battle, it may be said that other OT leaders enjoyed this wisdom as well, though they are not explicitly stated to possess the Spirit of wisdom as are Joshua and the Messiah. The Spirit granted wisdom to Moses to bear the burden of judging Israel's affairs, a wisdom that was extended to the seventy elders as well (Num 11:17, 25–26; cf. Deut 1:9–18). Wisdom to lead the nation in battle was granted to Othniel (Judg 3:10), Gideon (Judg 6:34), Jephthah (Judg 11:29), Saul (1 Sam 11:6), and David (1 Sam 16:13; cf. 2 Sam 5:10).[5]

---

2. Cf. Schnabel, "Wisdom," 843. Schnabel breaks wisdom in the OT into three categories: *perceiving wisdom, action-related wisdom,* and *communicating wisdom.*

3. Ibid.

4. Ibid. Though Schnabel has defined *action-related wisdom* in this way, he notes that Joseph, David, and Solomon are prototypes of this wisdom. These men are noted in this study for having been given a special measure of wisdom by means of the Spirit (though for Solomon the Spirit is not explicitly mentioned in relation to his wisdom).

5. Perhaps Samson may be said to have been given the wisdom necessary for battling Israel's enemies as well, but this wisdom would have been limited to his individual accomplishments. He led no army and did not command Israel as did the other three judges.

Wisdom for Leadership in Christ

The heads of Israel clearly showed a pattern of overcoming enemies in war as the Spirit gave them the wisdom to do so. Though the Messiah would be enabled by the Spirit to overcome his enemies as well (cf. Isa 11:4; 61:2b), the NT shows that Jesus did not continue this pattern in the record of the Gospels.

As seen in the previous chapter, the Spirit's coming upon Jesus at his baptism was joined with declarations by the Father that identified Jesus as the Messiah and Israel's king. It was natural for Israel to expect that the Messiah upon whom "the Spirit of wisdom" rested (Isa 11:2) would "strike the earth with the rod of his mouth, and with the breath of his lips he shall kill the wicked" (Isa 11:4). He was declared to be the beloved Son (Matt 3:17; cf. Ps 2:7) who the Israelites expected to overcome the wicked kings and rulers of the earth and "break them with a rod of iron and dash them in pieces like a potter's vessel" (Ps 2:9; cf. 2:1–3).

What Israel did not know is what Jesus would reveal during his ministry before his death. His initial ministry was one of proclamation and the execution of justice against God's enemies as something yet to come. At the outset of Jesus' ministry, Jesus claimed to fulfill Isa 61:1–2a, that he had been anointed by the Spirit to herald the good news (Luke 4:18–21). He did not yet claim to fulfill Isa 61:2b, which was to proclaim and execute "the day of vengeance of our God," implying this vengeance was yet to come. Likewise, when the Pharisees sought to kill Jesus, Jesus evaded them, an action which Matthew claimed as a fulfillment of Isa 42:1–4. The Father had put the Spirit on Jesus to proclaim hope to the Gentiles. His ministry would be marked not by retaliation in crushing his enemies but by gentleness until the time came to execute justice (Matt 12:14–21). The wisdom of Jesus would be shown primarily in his articulation of the gospel. His execution of worldwide justice over his enemies is yet to be seen.

Wisdom for Leadership in the New Testament

This shift in how wisdom was expressed continued for leaders after Jesus as well. Jesus would grant them wisdom when they were brought before their adversaries to defend the gospel, which itself is called the "wisdom of God" (1 Cor 2:7; cf. 2:6, 13).[6] Jesus encouraged the apostles by promising them

---

6. Cf. Schnabel, "Wisdom," 846.

wisdom to defend the gospel in the midst of persecution: "I will give you a mouth and wisdom, which none of your adversaries will be able to withstand or contradict" (Luke 21:5). It was seen above that the Spirit would be the agent whereby Jesus would grant this wisdom (Matt 10:20; Mark 13:11; Luke 12:12). Peter was "filled with the Holy Spirit" (Acts 4:8) and exercised this wisdom before the Jewish officials (Acts 4:8–12). Though not an apostle, Stephen was granted this wisdom as well. He defended the gospel to his opponents who "could not withstand the wisdom and the Spirit with which he was speaking" (Acts 6:10).

Wisdom for those who held office in the NT church was not limited to proclamation alone. Wisdom was also expressed through righteous living and the ability to minister to the practical needs of the church. Deacons were to be "of good repute, full of the Spirit and of wisdom" in order to help the widows in the church (Acts 6:3). Stephen was one of these deacons who was "full of faith and of the Holy Spirit" (Acts 6:5; cf. 11:24). The "good repute" necessary for deacons is detailed further in 1 Tim 3:8–13, similar to the character requirements for elders in 1 Tim 3:1–7 and Titus 1:5–9.

The NT also describes the Spirit-given wisdom of Christians in general with language that previously described the wisdom given to OT leaders. Paul echoed Isa 11:2 when he prayed for the Ephesians that God "may give you the Spirit of wisdom" (Eph 1:17). Paul was not praying that his readers would possess the omniscient wisdom of Christ but that they would increase in their understanding of him.[7] The following phrase in Eph 1:18 gives the parallel thought of "having the eyes of your hearts enlightened" to better understand truth that had already been revealed.[8]

What can be seen from the above is that the Spirit grants wisdom to both leaders and believers in general, but the nature of this wisdom is not the same from one situation to the next. Though some may claim that the line between wisdom in general and wisdom for leadership may at times be "distinctly fuzzy,"[9] this distinction may still be made. To clarify, some instances

---

7. Turner, "Spiritual Gifts," 794.

8. Arnold, *Ephesians*, 104–05. Peter also echoed Isa 11:2 when he encouraged his readers that any persecution they faced meant that "the Spirit of glory and of God rests upon you" (1 Pet 4:14). Cf. Michaels, *1 Peter*, 264. Jobes, *1 Peter*, 288, helpfully explains that it seems Peter did not so much mean to explain anything of his readers' wisdom as much as he did to encourage them about what would follow their persecution. Just as the Spirit rested upon Jesus who suffered and was then glorified in his exaltation, so also "the Spirit of glory" rested upon believers who suffered and would be later glorified as well.

9. Turner, "Spiritual Gifts," 791.

of *wisdom in understanding and speech* are clearly revelatory in nature (e.g., Acts 6:10) and distinct from the wisdom that the Spirit grants to Christians in general (e.g., Eph 1:17).[10] Though elders are nowhere told to expect new revelation today, their wisdom in understanding and speech is shown by their giftedness to understand and effectively teach the Scriptures (1 Tim 3:2; cf. Rom 12:7).[11] The *wisdom for godly living* is required to be of an evident and consistent nature for leaders (Acts 6:3; cf. 1 Tim 3:1–13; Titus 1:5–9) who are to be examples for Christians to follow (cf. 1 Pet 5:3). Though Christians should all use *wisdom in serving* one another, this wisdom is more apparent for some, perhaps owing to spiritual giftedness (cf. 1 Pet 4:10–11), which may lead a congregation to give them charge over certain ministries (Acts 6:3) or even the church as a whole (Rom 12:8; 1 Cor 12:28).

Confirmation of Enablement

The description of multiple leaders in this study demonstrates that the Spirit's enablement for leadership was often confirmed to the leader himself or God's people in some way, typically at the outset of their leadership. This confirmation took place through the exercise of miracles, prophecy, some type of anointing, the laying on of hands, or the Spirit's work in leadership and godly living.

Miracles

For several leaders, their Spirit-enabled leadership was confirmed through their exercise of miracles. Moses was described as being enabled by the Spirit in Num 11:17, and it was suggested that his enablement likely began in Exodus 3 when God commissioned Moses to lead Israel out of Egypt. God confirmed to Moses that he would lead Israel by enabling him to see miracles for himself, miracles that he would also perform in the court of Pharaoh. His staff became a serpent and then became a staff again (Exod 4:3–4), and his hand became leprous and was healed (Exod 4:6–7). He did several other miracles in Egypt as well (Exodus 7–14). These miracles confirmed the leadership of Moses in the eyes of Israel and others (cf. Isa 63:11–12).

10. Ibid., 795.
11. Deacons must likewise "hold the mystery of the faith" (1 Tim 3:9), i.e., they understand the gospel and truth revealed in Scripture, but it is not required of deacons to teach. Cf. Mounce, *Pastoral Epistles*, 200.

Joshua's leadership was confirmed in part through a miracle as well.[12] He commanded Israel to pass through the Jordan River, and this crossing was made possible by the waters being miraculously stopped from flowing (Josh 3:7–17). The LORD made clear the purpose of the miracle to Joshua: "Today I will begin to exalt you in the sight of all Israel, that they may know that, as I was with Moses, so I will be with you" (Josh 3:7). Just as Moses' leadership was reaffirmed through crossing the sea (Exod 14:31), so also Joshua' authority was reaffirmed through crossing the Jordan.

In the NT, Jesus' many miracles confirmed his role as the Messiah as well. Peter plainly stated this fact in his message on the day of Pentecost. He spoke of Jesus as "a man attested to you by God with mighty works and wonders and signs that God did through him in your midst" (Acts 2:22). Likewise, Paul stated of apostles that "signs and wonders and mighty works" were "the signs of a true apostle" (2 Cor 12:12). This is not to say that miracles were reserved only for the purpose of confirming a leader's leadership,[13] but it is to say that miracles were sometimes used to do so.

Prophecy

Another confirmation of a leader's Spirit-enabled leadership was a prophecy by the leader at the outset of his leadership. When the LORD placed the Spirit upon the seventy elders, it was recorded that "they prophesied. But they did not continue doing it" (Num 11:25). Two of the elders prophesied in the midst of the camp of Israel as well (Num 11:26). The prophecy of the elders by the tent of meeting would have confirmed to Moses and these elders that God had enabled them by the Spirit to lead. The prophecy of the other two elders would have confirmed to Israel that all of the elders had been enabled to lead as well.

Saul's prophetic confirmation of the Spirit's enablement was similar to the seventy elders. The prophet Samuel promised Saul that three events would take place that would confirm God's choice of him as king, the third of which would be to prophesy with a traveling group of prophets (1 Sam 10:5–6). Before listing out these events, Samuel stated their purpose in this

---

12. As already noted in this study, the primary means of identifying Joshua as a leader was when Moses visibly confirmed to Israel that Joshua would succeed him by placing his hands upon him before the congregation (Deut 34:9; cf. Num 27:19–21).

13. One of the purposes of miracles seen in the previous chapter was to confirm the authenticity of the message of the gospel (Acts 14:3; Heb 2:3–4).

way: "And this shall be the sign to you that the LORD has anointed you to be prince over his heritage" (1 Sam 10:1). Though the people who saw Saul prophesy were unclear as to the meaning of his prophecy, Saul would have understood its meaning, as would the readers of 1 Samuel. Interestingly, Saul prophesied towards the end of his kingship as well (1 Sam 19:24). Though the people who observed this prophecy were again unclear as to the meaning of this prophecy (1 Sam 19:24), it seems this prophecy marked the end of Saul's kingship to the readers of 1 Samuel, just as the previous prophecy confirmed its beginning.

It was noted in the previous chapter of this study that on the day of Pentecost, though others were likely with the apostles in the house where they were staying, the apostles were the primary characters in view (cf. Acts 2:1, 14). The background of leaders and prophecy in the OT finds a parallel to Pentecost in that the apostles (and probably others) gave a type of prophetic utterance by speaking in tongues (Acts 2:1–3). The Spirit had inaugurated a new age, and the believers' speaking in tongues not only announced that Jesus had sent the promised Spirit, but that the apostles were empowered by the Spirit to lead the church as effective witnesses as well. To clarify, the utterance of a prophecy or speaking in tongues does not demand that the individual speaking is a leader, but an individual enabled by the Spirit to lead was occasionally confirmed in his leadership by prophesying at the outset of his leadership.

Anointing

The anointing of a king with oil was occasionally joined with the Spirit's "anointing" or enablement of this king to lead God's people. The prophet Samuel anointed Saul with oil (1 Sam 10:1) and then promised God's Spirit would later "rush upon" him (1 Sam 10:6). Samuel commanded Saul what to do when the Spirit's enablement took place: "do what your hand finds to do, for God is with you" (1 Sam 10:7). For David, the anointing with oil and the Spirit's enablement are more tightly connected. Whereas there was a gap of time between Saul's anointing with oil and his enablement by the Spirit, 1 Sam 16:13 describes both events as taking place together for David: "Then Samuel took the horn of oil and anointed him in the midst of his brothers. And the Spirit of the LORD rushed upon David from that day forward."

In Isaiah's prophecy of the royal prophet, the prophet said of himself, "the Spirit of the LORD God is upon me, because the LORD has anointed me"

(Isa 61:1). There is no reference to anointing with oil, and the similarity of this prophecy to others indicates that the messianic king to come is the one who is in view (cf. Isa 11:1–5; 42:1–7). Jesus stated this prophecy to be fulfilled in himself (Luke 4:18–21; cf. Acts 4:26; 10:38), and his anointing with the Spirit was clearly the Spirit's coming upon him at his baptism (Luke 3:22).

Engelhard notes these two types of anointing in stating that anointing "was viewed as God's act and as the outpouring of the Spirit to equip for service."[14] Sometimes the anointing with oil took place alongside an anointing of the Spirit, but one anointing does not necessarily demand the presence of the other.

Believers in the NT are said to be anointed by the Spirit as well. Paul states that "God . . . has anointed us" (2 Cor 1:21) and then immediately follows this statement with a description of the Spirit as the seal and guarantee for believers that they will be fully redeemed by Christ when he comes again (2 Cor 1:22; cf. Eph 4:30). It is not entirely clear to some whether the meaning of the Spirit's anointing overlaps with the ideas of the Spirit as the seal and guarantee,[15] but Paul does not indicate that believers are anointed by the Spirit in the same way experienced by Christ at his baptism. Harris suggests that, given the function of the Spirit's anointing in the OT, it could be that Paul thought of this anointing as "consecration to divine service."[16]

John gives clearer statements in the NT about a believer's anointing in 1 John 2:20, 27. John states that "you have been anointed by the Holy One, and you all have knowledge" (1 John 2:20). He then states that "the anointing that you have received from him abides in you, and you have no need that anyone should teach you" (1 John 2:27). He states again that "his anointing teaches you about everything" (1 John 2:27). Anointing by the Spirit "teaches" the believer and gives him "knowledge" in the sense that they are illumined by the Spirit to understand spiritual truth in distinction from spiritual error.[17]

---

14. Engelhard, "Anointing," 1:129.

15. Ryrie, *The Holy Spirit*, 176, suggests that Paul could be referring either to himself, himself and the other apostles, or believers in general. If Paul refers only to himself or himself along with the other apostles, Ryrie limits the meaning to their consecration for service. If Paul refers to believers in general, Ryrie would then equate anointing with indwelling and sealing.

16. Harris, *The Second Epistle to the Corinthians*, 206.

17. Cf. Ryrie, *The Holy Spirit*, 177. Akin, *1, 2, 3 John*, 125, sees Jesus' promises of the *Paraclete* in John 14:16–17, 14:26, and 16:13 as related to John's explanation of anointing in 1 John 2:20, 27. As mentioned earlier in this study, the Spirit guided the apostles "into

The OT presents those who are anointed as specially consecrated or enabled by the Spirit to serve God's people in some way. Jesus is God's Anointed like none other, and all believers today are anointed by the Spirit in the sense that they are illumined by the Spirit to discern the truth of the Scriptures. Though this study argues that there is a distinct work of the Spirit in biblical leaders to enable them to carry out their leadership, this language of anointing is only used on occasion in the OT and only with Christ in the NT to describe a Spirit-anointed leader. Elders and those gifted to be leaders today should not expect a special anointing by the Spirit that hastes them into an official capacity to serve as the Spirit did with Saul, David, or Christ. Rather, the NT describes leaders as those whom the Spirit has gifted and appointed to lead.

Laying on of Hands

Another sign of confirmation of the Spirit's enablement was the laying on of hands.[18] In order for Israel to see that Joshua was Moses' successor, the LORD commanded Moses, "Take Joshua the son of Nun, a man in whom is the Spirit, and lay your hand on him" (Num 27:18). This act was to take place before the congregation of Israel (Num 27:19), and the LORD specified its purpose to Moses: "You shall invest him with some of your authority, that all the congregation of the people of Israel may obey" (Num 27:18). This connection between the Spirit, authority, and the laying of hands is repeated in Deut 34:9: "And Joshua the son of Nun was full of the [S]pirit of wisdom, for Moses had laid his hands on him. So the people of Israel obeyed him and did as the LORD had commanded Moses." Joshua was enabled by the Spirit to exercise authority over Israel, and the laying of Moses' hands on Joshua confirmed this enablement to Israel.

The laying on of hands is similar in the NT. The early church often laid hands on someone in order to indicate that the Spirit had enabled a given individual to carry out a specific ministry. Ananias laid his hands upon Saul (not yet Paul) who was consequently filled with the Spirit to preach

---

all the truth" by revealing new truth to them (John 16:13). In a secondary sense, one could say that believers are guided into understanding preexisting truth by the illumination of the Spirit of God.

18. This statement is not meant to limit the laying on of hands only to instances of confirming the leadership of a leader. Hands were laid upon individuals or animals for a variety of purposes in the OT and NT. Cf. Wead, "Hands, Laying on of," *ISBE*, 2:611–12.

the gospel (Acts 9:17, 20). The church in Antioch laid hands on Paul and Barnabas and commissioned them to journey as missionaries according to the Spirit's command (Acts 13:3; cf. 13:1–4). Timothy was commissioned with the laying on of hands by Paul and others to exercise his gift of proclaiming and teaching the gospel (1 Tim 4:14; 2 Tim 1:6). When the early church chose the first deacons who were required to be "full of the Spirit and of wisdom" for their ministry (Acts 6:3), "they prayed and laid their hands on them" (Acts 6:6). In a context delineating guidelines for how the Ephesian church was to choose its elders, Paul commanded Timothy, "Do not be hasty in the laying on of hands" (1 Tim 5:22). If the early church rightly appointed elders to their office, it could be said that the practice of the laying on of hands would have confirmed that the Spirit had gifted them and set them aside for their ministry as elders (Acts 20:28).

The Exercise of Leadership

Sometimes the confirmation of leadership is simply the exercise of the Spirit's work in leadership before one has been officially designated as a leader. The LORD designated Joshua to succeed Moses because he was "a man in whom is the Spirit" (Num 27:18). It was noted earlier that, like Moses, the beginning of the Spirit's enablement in Joshua's leadership is not specified. It could have been that Joshua was enabled by the Spirit to effectively lead Israel's army as early as the victory over the Amalekites in Exod 17:8–13. Whenever his enablement began, Joshua was clearly qualified to follow Moses as the head of Israel because he had already demonstrated the Spirit's enablement in his leadership.

The NT lists several requirements for the church's elders and deacons. The first deacons were to be "of good repute, full of the Spirit and of wisdom" (Acts 6:3). These men would be chosen as deacons based upon the fact that the Spirit's work in their character and wisdom was already present. This "good repute" is detailed further in the requirements for deacons listed in 1 Tim 3:8–13. Should there be any question of the Spirit's work in their character or wisdom, deacons are to "be tested first," and only "then let them serve as deacons if they prove themselves blameless" (1 Tim 3:10). The Spirit's work in character and wisdom should be evident in the life of one who is to be a deacon.

The same may be said of elders. Before being appointed to the office of elder, a man must first meet the character requirements listed in passages such as 1 Tim 3:1–7 and Titus 1:5–9. By doing so, he would show that he is similar to deacons in that he is also "of good repute, full of the Spirit and wisdom" necessary for his ministry (Acts 6:3).

It was suggested in the previous chapter that Paul likely saw the spiritual gift of leadership in Rom 12:8 and 1 Cor 12:28 as exercised by those who were elders, and even if this gift extends beyond those who are (or would be) elders, it may be at least said that elders should possess this spiritual gift. This being the case, a man's exercise of this gift would need to be apparent before he is appointed to the church as an elder. This leadership would be seen in the home (1 Tim 3:4–5), and it would also be seen in the church over time as well.[19] Similar to the instruction to let deacons "be tested first" (1 Tim 3:10), an elder-to-be "must not be a recent convert" (1 Tim 3:6). This requirement primarily alleviates the potential elder from becoming proud of himself by being a new convert whose spiritual aptitude is thought to be worthy of leading the church (1 Tim 3:6). It could also be inferred that this allowance of time would eventually reveal whether or not such a one was capable of leading the church.

It can also be said for elders that the Spirit's work in their leadership was to be apparent in their exercise of teaching God's word. Elders are to be "able to teach" (1 Tim 3:2), and "teaching" is listed by Paul as a spiritual gift (Rom 12:7), a work of the Spirit (1 Cor 12:4, 11, 28). It seems fair to conclude that a potential elder would need to be given opportunity to teach before actually being appointed to an office that had such a requirement. As he showed himself effective in his teaching due to his giftedness to do so, he would be confirmed in one of the requirements necessary to be an elder.

Obedience and Enablement

The relation between the Spirit's enablement of a leader and the leader's obedience is given different emphases from one testament to the next and finds unique expression in the person of Jesus Christ.

---

19. Though deacons are likewise to manage their households well (1 Tim 3:12), it is not stated that they are to also manage the church. Merkle states, "The reason for this omission is most likely due to the fact that deacons are not given a ruling or leading position in the church—that function belongs to the elders" ("The Biblical Qualifications and Responsibilities of Deacons," 10). The ability to manage one's family does not necessarily imply the ability to manage the church as a whole, though it implies the ability to oversee a given ministry within the church (cf. Acts 6:1–7).

Spiritual Leadership

Obedience and Enablement in the Old Testament

Moses was the first head of Israel said to be enabled by the Spirit and was a prophet like none other (cf. Deut 34:10–12). Despite his prominence in biblical history, he was not perfect. The Lord commanded Moses to speak to the rock at Meribah so the Lord could show himself powerful by opening the rock to give Israel water. Unfortunately, Moses struck the rock out of anger and was refused admittance to the Promised Land as his punishment (Num 20:8, 12). Joshua failed the Lord on at least one occasion as well. The Gibeonites deceived Joshua and Israel by claiming to be from far away. Joshua and Israel's leaders "did not ask counsel from the Lord" but believed the Gibeonites and made a covenant with them (Josh 9:14–15). As a result, the Gibeonites were allowed to live in the Promised Land with Israel (Josh 9:16–21). In both of these instances, these failures were inconsistent with the otherwise faithful leadership of Moses and Joshua. It was said for neither of these men that the Spirit departed from them as a result of their disobedience.

Upon entrance into the period of the judges, however, the Spirit's enablement is given to leaders whose lives were not generally characterized by faithfulness to the Lord. As discussed previously, Judg 3:7–11 gives the first of several "hero stories" which follow the formula of Judg 2:11–19 to show the progress of sin in both the lives of Israel's judges and Israel as a whole.[20] By the end of the book of judges, the author characterizes the period of the judges in this way: "In those days there was no king in Israel. Everyone did what was right in his own eyes" (Judg 21:15; cf. 17:6; 18:1; 19:1). Of the four judges who were enabled by the Spirit, Othniel is not noted for any act of unfaithfulness (cf. Judg 3:7–11), but the other three are. Gideon created an idol that Israel worshiped (Judg 8:27); Jepththah sacrificed his daughter (Judg 11:30–31, 34–35, 39); and Samson was disobedient (Judg 14:9; 16:17), immoral (Judg 14:1; 16:1), and vengeful (Judg 14:19; 15:3–5;

---

20. As discussed in Chapter 2, if Judg 2:18 implies that all judges were enabled by the Spirit to deliver Israel, the explicit mention of the Spirit's enablement of Othniel in Judg 3:7–11 was for the purpose of identifying the first and expected enablement of Israel's judges. For Gideon, Jephthah, and Samson, however, it could have been necessary to remind the reader that the Spirit had indeed enabled these leaders because their disobedience could have implied the absence of such an enablement. At the same time, it was also suggested that the mention of the Spirit in their leadership was the narrator's means of distinguishing these individuals a leaders, just as he had used other means to do so for other leaders. Whichever the case may be, Gideon, Jephthah, and Samson were clearly disobedient to the Lord in significant ways.

16:28–30). Not only do their acts of disobedience increase in intensity, but Judg 16:20 clearly implied the Spirit departed from Samson.

A question that arises is whether or not these three leaders (especially Samson) abused their leadership and sinned while being enabled by the Spirit. Comparing Scripture with Scripture, it is theologically contradictory to claim the work of the Spirit to be employed in an act of sin. The Spirit is the Spirit of perfect holiness and cannot be engaged in sin in any way because the Spirit is God who cannot sin (Hab 1:13; Acts 5:3–4). A better explanation of the connection between these judges' disobedience and their enablement by the Spirit is not difficult to suggest. The significant sins of Gideon and Jephthah came *after* their enablement to lead Israel into victory. For Samson, however, his disobedience and enablement are often placed side-by-side. It could be said that the circumstances whereby Samson found opportunity to attack Israel's enemies were brought about by his sinful actions, something allowed but not caused by the Lord. Thereafter, the Spirit's enablement of Samson to overcome his enemies was not to allow Samson to carry out his personal vengeance, but for the Lord to overcome the enemies of Israel. Judges 13:25 suggests that the Spirit moved Samson to be righteously angry by the presence of Israel's enemies before his enablement took place, and his Spirit-enabled attack upon the Lord's enemies could have been carried out with pure motives, despite the means that brought the conflict about.

However one explains the connection between Samson's disobedience and enablement by the Spirit, it is clear that he eventually lost the enablement by the Spirit due to his persistent disobedience (Judg 16:20). Saul, the first of Israel's kings, was repeatedly disobedient and experienced this same phenomenon (1 Sam 16:14; cf. 18:12). King David likewise sinned by committing adultery and murder, but though he feared the loss of the Spirit's enablement as a result, it seems his request for the Spirit's continued enablement was granted in light of his repentance (Ps 51:11). David's request implicitly acknowledged the necessity of faithful obedience to the Lord for this enablement to continue. He referred to the "Holy Spirit," implying the necessity for the practice of holiness by the one enabled by the Spirit.

Obedience and Enablement in the Person of Jesus Christ

This theme continues with Isaiah's prophecies of a perfectly obedient king to come. "The Spirit of the Lord" was to "rest upon" this king, and the

Spirit was also described as "the Spirit of... the fear of the LORD" (Isa 11:2). This fear would characterize his entire reign: "And his delight shall be in the fear of the LORD" (Isa 11:3). As seen in the previous chapter, the NT identified this king to be Jesus. As both the Son of God and God the Son his obedience was perfect, and it was no surprise that the Father granted him the Spirit "without measure" (John 3:34).

It was also pointed out previously that Isaiah's prophecies of the coming king came during the reign of the good king Hezekiah. As good a king as Hezekiah was, Isaiah gave Israel hope for a perfect king. In light of the present study, it could be said that the sins of all of the previous heads of Israel were recorded to show that, despite their enablement by the Spirit, they could not perfectly lead God's people. This record provides a backdrop that allows the prophecies of Isaiah and the record of their fulfillment in Christ to stand out all the more.

Obedience and Enablement in the New Testament Church

In the NT church, the requirement for the obedience of the leaders of God's people is heightened. Whereas God exercised a great deal of patience in the OT with Spirit-enabled leaders who committed significant sins, some of their sins would clearly disqualify elders or deacons from holding their offices.[21] To clarify, the NT does not suggest that a leader could lose his enablement or spiritual giftedness by the Spirit to lead or serve in some way. Rather, the NT has requirements for these leaders that necessitate forbidding or removing a leader from office if a given individual does not meet these requirements (1 Tim 3:1–13; cf. 5:19–20). Whereas disobedience could bring about the loss of a leader's enablement by the Spirit in the OT, disobedience by an elder or deacon in the NT church would bring about the loss of his office and thus the opportunity to exercise his giftedness to others in an official capacity. The NT does not state that disobedience by a leader results in the loss of the spiritual gift of leadership.

---

21. An example of this fact would be that David committed adultery with Bathsheba (2 Sam 11:1–5) and could not have been said to have faithfully been "the husband of one wife" (1 Tim 3:2).

Duration of Enablement

There is no strict pattern from one leader to the next as to the duration or frequency of the Spirit's enablement for leadership.

Moses

Moses experienced a continuous enablement by the Spirit to lead Israel.[22] It was discussed previously that though the beginning of his enablement is not specified, there is good reason to see this beginning in Exodus 3–4. Moses was granted the ability to perform miracles as a confirmation to himself that God had chosen him to be Israel's leader (Ex 4:1–9). He then performed these miracles and more in Egypt. By the time the Spirit is mentioned with connection to Moses in Numbers 11, the Spirit is said to be "on" Moses (Num 11:17). Moses had apparently been enabled by the Spirit to lead Israel for some time. There seems to be no reason to suggest that he lost this enablement at any point during his leadership.

Joshua

Joshua was similarly enabled by the Spirit. Like Moses, the beginning of his enablement by the Spirit is not specified. Before he was the head of Israel, God pointed out to Moses that Joshua would be his successor because he was "a man in whom is the Spirit" (Num 27:18). As with Moses, there seems to be no reason to suggest that he lost this enablement during his leadership.

Judges and Saul

The duration of enablement for the four judges and King Saul could be described as intermittent or occasional. The Spirit came upon Othniel (Judg 3:10), Gideon (Judg 6:34), and Jephthah (Judg 11:29) at the times when they were to lead Israel to victory in battle. The experience of Samson in particular brings out the occasional nature of the Spirit's enablement in that the Spirit was repeatedly described to move within him or come upon him for some purpose (Judg 13:25; 14:6, 19; 15:14). The Spirit likewise came

---

22. The term *continuous* is meant to communicate the ongoing nature of the Spirit's enablement in contrast to something *continual* which takes place on occasion.

upon Saul multiple times for the purpose of prophecy (1 Sam 10:10; 19:23) and leading Israel in battle (1 Sam 11:6). What was implied for Samson was explicitly described for Saul, namely, that their persistent disobedience resulted in the departure of the Spirit and his enablement (Judg 16:20; 1 Sam 16:14). Othniel, Gideon, and Jephthah experienced the Spirit's enablement for a time. For Samson and Saul, they experienced a similar enablement, and their disobedience eventually denied them the opportunity experience the Spirit's enablement further.

David

The Spirit "rushed upon" King David as with Saul (1 Sam 16:13; cf. 11:6), but for David it is said that "the Spirit of the LORD rushed upon David *from that day forward*" (1 Sam 16:13; italics added). The phrase "from that day forward" seems to imply a continuous enablement similar to that of Moses and Joshua. The general descriptions of his success as a leader seem to confirm the continuous nature of his enablement (e.g., 2 Sam 5:10).[23]

Jesus, the Prophesied King of Isaiah

The Spirit-enabled king of Isaiah's prophecies is described as one whose enablement by the Spirit would be continuous as well. It was said that the Spirit would "rest upon him," implying an enablement the entire duration of his leadership (Isa 11:2). The Spirit would be "upon him" to bring justice to the earth (Isa 42:1; cf. 42:1–4) and be "upon" him to proclaim good news to all (Isa 61:1; cf. 61:1–2a). Jesus was clearly this king, and the Spirit came upon him and would remain upon him to continuously enable his ministry thereafter (Luke 3:22; Acts 10:38).

Apostles and Their Delegates

The Spirit's enablement of apostles and their delegates was of a more multifaceted nature than that of the Spirit's enablement of leaders prior to Jesus.

---

23. For the possibility of something other than a continuous enablement, see Hamilton, "God with Men in the Prophets and the Writings," 184. Because of the similarity in language describing Saul, Hamilton states, "This could mean that the Spirit was continually upon David, or it could mean that the Spirit continued to 'rush to' him and inspire him at significant moments."

The duration of the Spirit's work through a given apostle depended upon the nature of the specific work taking place. As discussed previously, there would be moments when an apostle would stand before the authorities to answer for his witness of Christ and the Spirit would grant him the words to speak in such a situation. This enablement likely took place during the life of Jesus when Jesus commissioned the apostles to preach to the cities of Israel (Matt 10:20; cf. 10:5–8). This enablement certainly took place after the Spirit was sent at Pentecost as shown in the example of the apostle Peter (Acts 4:8). Stephen was not an apostle, but he experienced this enablement as well (Acts 6:10). The description and circumstances of such an enablement by the Spirit naturally implies that this work of the Spirit was not continuously taking place.

It was also discussed that singular, dramatic events would take place when an apostle or others were "filled with" or "full of" the Spirit on a given occasion. Though some of these events were common to others (cf. Acts 2:4; 4:31), some of these events were not. As already mentioned, the Spirit filled Peter and Stephen to grant the words to say when they were standing before their opponents (Acts 4:8; 6:10). When filled with the Spirit, Paul immediately began to preach the gospel after his conversion (Acts 9:17; cf. 9:20), and he was later filled to smite Elymas with blindness (Acts 13:9; cf. 13:11).

Elders, Deacons, and the Spiritual Gift of Leadership

Concerning elders, deacons, and those gifted by the Spirit to lead, the duration of the Spirit's work is continuous as well. Elders would begin to exercise the gift of leadership to some degree before their appointment to office (cf. Rom 12:8; 1 Cor 12:28), and deacons would likewise exercise their wisdom in ministering to others before their appointment as well (cf. Acts 6:3). To clarify, it is not said that deacons were gifted to lead but that they possessed the wisdom necessary for their ministry.[24] In both cases, their Spirit-enabled ministry would function as a confirmation that they should minister in an official capacity. Their ministry would not begin as the result of this appointment but rather continue in an official capacity.

---

24. Again, as noted in the previous chapter, deacons (or others in general) are not excluded from being recognized as leaders over the course of time as it becomes apparent that the Spirit's work in them has also enabled them to be leaders. To clarify, leadership is not essential to the *office* of deacon.

Another work of the Spirit that would be continuous for elders and deacons was the Spirit's work in their character and lives. This work of the Spirit is universal among all Christians in the church, and it is required of elders and deacons that this work would have been evident and consistent enough for them to be appointed to minister in an official capacity (1 Tim 3:1–13).

Leaders and Prophecy

As seen above, one connection between leaders and prophecy is that some leaders prophesied by the Spirit at the outset of their leadership to confirm that the Spirit had enabled them to lead God's people. This confirmation of leadership was true of the seventy elders and Saul whose experience was somewhat parallel to the apostles on the Day of Pentecost. A more prominent connection between leaders and prophecy is that many leaders did not just prophesy once but were prophets in addition to being leaders.

Moses

Moses referred to himself as a prophet when speaking of a prophet to come after him. He stated, "The LORD your God will raise up for you *a prophet like me* from among you" (Deut 18:15; italics added). He repeated this identification by quoting what the LORD said to him: "I will raise up for them *a prophet like you* from among their brothers" (Deut 18:18; italics added). It was said after Moses' death that "there has not arisen *a prophet* since in Israel *like Moses*" (Deut 34:10; italics added).

David

King David is identified as a prophet as well. Referring to Ps 16:8–11, Peter stated of David, "Being therefore a prophet . . . he foresaw and spoke about the resurrection of the Christ" (Acts 2:30–31). David wrote this prophecy as one of the men who "spoke from God as they were carried along by the Holy Spirit" to write Scripture (2 Pet 1:20–21). In several instances, David is identified in the NT as the author of several other psalms as well,[25] and

---

25. See Matt 22:43 with Ps 110:1 (pars. Mark 12:36; Luke 20:42); Acts 1:16, 20 with Ps 69:25 and Ps 109:8; Acts 2:25–28 with Ps 16:8–11; Acts 2:34 with Ps 110:1; Rom 11:9 with Ps 69:22–23; Heb 4:7; cf. Ps 95:7.

for some of these instances, it is said that David did so by means of the agency of the Spirit. Jesus introduced his quotation of Ps 110:1 as having come from "David, in the Spirit" (Matt 22:43; cf. Mark 12:36; Luke 20:42). Hebrews 3:7 introduces a quotation of Ps 95:7–11 with the phrase "as the Holy Spirit says," and Heb 4:7 introduces a quotation of Ps 95:7 as what God was "saying through David." David was clearly inspired by the Spirit as a prophet to write Scripture. As he himself said, "The Spirit of the LORD speaks by me; his word is on my tongue" (2 Sam 23:2).

Jesus: the Prophesied Prophet

The prophesied king of Isaiah was also a prophet whose words were quoted beforehand by Isaiah: "The Spirit of the LORD God is upon me . . . to bring good news . . . to proclaim liberty . . . to proclaim the year of the LORD's favor" (Isa 61:1–2). Jesus identified himself as this prophet by claiming to fulfill these words (Luke 4:18–21).[26] Jesus indirectly referred to himself as a prophet on multiple occasions (Matt 13:57; 21:46; Mark 6:4; Luke 13:33; John 4:44), and the Gospels record numerous instances of the people's identification of Jesus as a prophet as well (Matt 21:11; Luke 7:16; John 4:19; 9:17). In two instances recorded by John, the people saw Jesus as "the Prophet" (John 6:14; 7:40), that is, the prophet whose coming was foretold by Moses long ago (Deut 18:15, 18).[27] Peter likewise identified Jesus as this prophet in Acts 3:22–26.[28] Though Jesus is obviously much more than a prophet, he was a prophet.

The Apostles and Their Delegates

The apostles and some of their delegates could be said to be prophets as well. As seen in the previous chapter, apostles were prophets in that they received revelation from the Spirit that would deepen their knowledge about Christ (John 16:12–15). This fact did not mean that they were to be equated with prophets (cf. Eph 3:5), but that as apostles, they would reveal truth to the church that had not previously been given (cf. Rev 1:10; 4:2; 17:3; 21:10). Apostles and their delegates could also be said to be prophets in that

---

26. Dunn, *Pneumatology*, 330.
27. Ibid.
28. Ibid., 335.

the Spirit revealed information to them or through them for the purpose of guiding their missionary endeavors (Acts 8:29; 10:19; 13:2, 4; 16:6–7).

Elders and Deacons

When it comes to elders and deacons, the connection between leaders and prophecy fades away. As seen above, the Spirit gave the deacon Stephen the wisdom of speech necessary to defend the gospel before his opponents (Acts 6:10) and enabled him to have a vision of the risen Christ moments before his death (Acts 7:55). The Spirit spoke to the deacon Philip to guide him to the Ethiopian court official (Acts 8:29). These experiences allow Stephen and Philip to be identified as prophets in addition to their roles as deacons.

Though Stephen and Philip were deacons, their prophetic experiences were unique and not to be expected by other deacons. It could be said that elders were not to expect these prophetic experiences as well. When Paul wrote to Timothy in Ephesus, his requirements for both elders and deacons did not include the requirement of being a prophet in addition to whichever office they would have held (cf. 1 Tim 3:1–13). Other major passages containing the requirements for elders and deacons are likewise silent concerning the role of prophecy (cf. Acts 6:3; Titus 1:5–9; 1 Peter 5:1–4). This is not to say that elders and deacons in the early church never functioned as prophets in addition to their official roles, but it is to say that it was not expected for elders and deacons to also be prophets.

With reference to the proclamation of the revelation of God, it should be clarified that elders bear a similarity to leaders who were also prophets, but this similarity does not imply an exact parallel. Just as Moses and others were both leaders of God's people and prophets who revealed to God's people what God had revealed to them, elders are leaders of God's people who are expected to teach and exhort according to what God has already revealed in Scripture. The difference between leaders who were prophets and elders who are not is that elders speak according to what God has already spoken in the Scriptures. To clarify further, elders were to be "able to teach" the Scriptures (1 Tim 3:1), and this teaching is only possible through the Spirit's enablement to do so (cf. Rom 12:6–7; 1 Cor 12:28). For one to teach what is previously revealed in Scripture to all and for one to communicate what the Spirit has directly said to him as an individual both involve the work of the Spirit, but the Spirit's work is not exactly the same in both instances.

Prophets and Leadership

What would help to clarify further the distinction between the Spirit's work in prophecy and the Spirit's work in leadership is an examination of Joseph and Daniel. These men did not lead God's people as the heads of Israel, but they were prophets who led in a foreign context and were providentially used to benefit God's people.[29] What will be seen by studying these men is that a leader who is also a prophet is not exactly the same things as a prophet who is also a leader, though there are parallels between the two. Likewise, the work of the Spirit in prophecy is not exactly the same as the work of the Spirit in leadership. They are distinct from one another.

Joseph

Joseph successfully interpreted the dreams of the Pharaoh's baker and cupbearer while in prison (Gen 40:1–22). Before giving the interpretations, Joseph asserted to Pharaoh's officials that "interpretations belong to God" (Gen 40:8).[30] Similarly, Joseph later interpreted two of Pharaoh's dreams (Gen 41:14–36), and before hearing the dreams recounted, Joseph declared, "It is not in me; God will give Pharaoh a favorable answer" (Gen 41:16). After Joseph successfully interpreted the dreams, Pharaoh asked of Joseph, "Can we find a man like this, in whom is the Spirit of God?" (Gen 41:38). With reference to Joseph's ability to interpret dreams, Pharaoh acknowledged, "God has shown you all this" (Gen 41:39).

Pharaoh's reference to "the Spirit of God" stemmed from his pagan perspective, which has led some translations to translate the phrase *rûaḥ ʾĕlōhîm* as "the divine spirit" (NASB) or "the spirit of the God" (NIV). The assumption is that Pharaoh in his pagan perspective could not have knowledgeably spoken of the Spirit of God. However, it is plausible to suggest that Pharaoh's words could refer to the Spirit of God in one of two ways. The first is that Pharaoh actually did speak of the Spirit of God in a

---

29. There were other prophets who were involved in Israel's national affairs as well. Deborah was a prophetess who functioned as one of Israel's judges (Judg 4:5). Samuel was a prophet and was one of Israel's judges as well (1 Sam 3:20; 7:6). Elisha was likewise a prophet who had dealings with the Israel's affairs (2 Kings 8:7–15; 9:1–13; 13:14–19). However, as will be seen, the terminology describing Joseph and Daniel makes them particularly helpful to this study.

30. The assertion came by means of a rhetorical question. The full question states, "Do not interpretations belong to God?" (Gen 40:8).

knowledgeable way because Joseph had previously explained to Pharaoh that the interpretation of dreams belonged to God (Gen 41:16). Pharaoh was thus duly informed to echo this claim (Gen 41:39).[31] It would not have been inappropriate for Pharaoh to attribute Joseph's interpretation to the Spirit of his God as well. A second way to suggest that Pharaoh's words referred to the Spirit of God is that, whatever Pharaoh's understanding of the Spirit may have been, Moses recorded his words, knowing his readers would associate the phrase *rûaḥ ʾĕlōhîm* with the meaning it had in its first use in Gen 1:2, "the Spirit of God."[32] Either way, the phrase may be understood by the reader (and perhaps by Pharaoh) to refer to the Spirit of God.[33] Even if all the above arguments are cast aside, it would seem theologically incomplete to leave the Spirit's role aside in explaining how Joseph came about the rightful interpretation of Pharaoh's dreams.

Joseph's role with Pharaoh at this point was primarily that of a prophet. However, Pharaoh assumed that the Spirit's wisdom and discernment granted to Joseph to interpret his dreams would be used in administrating the affairs of Egypt as well (Gen 41:39–40; cf. 41:33–36).[34] If this assumption by Pharaoh was meant by Moses to be assumed by the readers of this narrative as well, there seems to be some overlap between the Spirit's role in prophecy and leadership. Both the interpretation of dreams and the exercise of leadership could be described as taking place by the exercise of wisdom and discernment that have been granted to an individual by the Spirit of God. However, it does not follow that the two are exactly the same. Joseph's prophetic moments were occasional, but his wise and discerning leadership was of a more consistent nature.

Concerning Joseph's role as a leader, it could be concluded that the Spirit's work through his leadership was previously described in other biblical

---

31. Hildebrandt, *An Old Testament Theology of the Spirit of God*, 22, 106; Firth, "The Spirit and Leadership," 261–63. Cf. Cole, *He Who Gives Life*, 118, who notes that Genesis uses the phrase "the Spirit of God" but twice (cf. Gen 1:2). This fact could suggest that, since this phrase exists so far only in Gen 1:2 as a clear reference to the Spirit of God, a reader would assume this reference to refer to the same.

32. Howell, *Servants of the Servant*, 3. Howell suggests a *sensus plenior* could be possible with Pharaoh unintentionally identifying the Spirit.

33. Harvey, *Anointed with Spirit and Power*, 15, notes the use of this phrase elsewhere in the OT clearly refers to the Spirit of God (1 Sam 10:10; 11:6; 2 Chr 15:1; 24:20.)

34. Pharaoh stated to Joseph, "Since God has shown you all this, there is none so discerning and wise as you are" (Gen 41:39).

texts.³⁵ Joseph succeeded and prospered as the overseer of Potiphar's house because "the LORD was with him" (Gen 39:2). "The LORD was with him" again to prosper his leadership over the prison (Gen 39:23; cf. 39:21). This "with" language is used later in the OT to describe the Spirit's work through some of the leaders examined in this study. It was concluded that the Spirit's work through a leader's leadership could be assumed with the phrase "the LORD was with him" if the Spirit was explicitly described to have been at work through his leadership as well (cf. Judg 14:19 and 15:14 with 16:20; 1 Sam 16:13–14 with 18:12). If Gen 41:38–39 describes Joseph as interpreting dreams and having the ability to rule Egypt through the wisdom and discernment of the Spirit, then it could be concluded that "the LORD was with him" by enabling him with the Spirit to effectively administrate the affairs of Potiphar's house and the prison as well (Gen 39:2; cf. 39:3, 21, 23).

This brief look at Joseph helpfully clarifies the difference between the Spirit's work in the exercise of leadership and the Spirit's work in prophecy. Both may be described as the wisdom of God, but Joseph did not administrate his affairs according to moment-by-moment revelation from the Spirit of God. Whereas the work of the Spirit through his leadership was nonrevelatory and continuous, the revelatory work of the Spirit involved in the interpretation of dreams was granted on occasion.

Daniel

The description of the Spirit in the life and leadership of Daniel is similar to Joseph. The Spirit's work through Daniel for the purpose of prophecy is described in multiple ways, and the Spirit's work in Daniel's leadership may be implied by the use of the term *rûaḥ* on at least one occasion.

Daniel 4:8–9

King Nebuchadnezzar had a dream (cf. Dan 4:4–18) and called for Daniel to interpret the dream because he was one "in whom is a spirit of the holy gods" (*rûaḥ-ʾĕlāhîn qaddîšîn bēh*; Dan 4:8, 9). The reason Nebuchadnezzar

---

35. E.g., Hildebrandt states, "[I]t was the presence of the *rûaḥ ʾĕlōhîm* that gave Joseph not only the skill to interpret dreams but also his great wisdom and administrative ability.... [H]e uses his influence to settle the people of God in the ideal land of Goshen and to provide for their physical needs" (*An Old Testament Theology of the Spirit of God*, 106).

knew Daniel could interpret his dream and thus described him in this way was because Daniel had done this for him on a previous occasion (cf. Dan 2:1–49). Daniel stated of himself that "God gave them [Daniel and his three companions] learning and skill in all literature and wisdom, and Daniel had understanding in all visions and dreams" (Dan 1:17). When the interpretation of Nebuchadnezzar's first dream was revealed to Daniel (cf. Dan 2:19), Daniel said of God, "he gives wisdom to the wise, and knowledge to those who have understanding" (Dan 2:21). His closing words of praise to God (cf. Dan 2:20–23) clearly identify wisdom in this instance with direct revelation from God: "you have given me wisdom and might, and have now made known to me what we asked of you, for you have made known to us the king's matter" (Dan 2:23; cf. 2:30). What Daniel attributed to God and his wisdom was attributed by Nebuchadnezzar to "the spirit of the holy gods."[36]

Similar to Pharaoh's description of Joseph (cf. Gen 41:38), Nebuchadnezzar's title for the source of Daniel' interpretation could be taken to refer to "the Spirit of the holy God" and not merely "a spirit of the holy gods."[37] As with the original readers of Genesis, it is reasonable to assume that the original readers of Daniel would have identified the *rûaḥ* as the source of Daniel's dream-interpretation to be the Spirit of God. Moreover, whereas Pharaoh simply heard of the Hebrew God from Joseph (cf. Gen 41:16, 25), the title "the spirit of the holy gods" in Dan 4:8, 9 is found within Daniel's record of the words of Nebuchadnezzar after his experience of being humbled by God (cf. Dan 4:4, 34–37). Nebuchadnezzar could thus be said to have knowledgeably spoken of "the Spirit of the holy God" that was in Daniel.

Daniel 5:11, 14

Daniel still served in the courts of Babylon under Nebuchadnezzar's son Belshazzar. When Belshazzar saw a hand write a message on a wall that neither he nor his wise men could read (Dan 5:5–9), the queen told him that Daniel would know the meaning because he was one "in whom is a spirit of

---

36. Hildebrandt, *An Old Testament Theology of the Spirit of God*, 143–44. Nebuchadnezzar had heard Daniel speak of his God in relating the dream and its interpretation (Dan 2:28–29, 37, 44–45) and recognized Daniel's God as distinct from other so-called gods (Dan 2:47).

37. Howell sees this as "the polytheistic king's way of describing Daniel's unparalleled, supernatural ability to unlock the interpretation of these mysterious dreams" (*Servants of the Servant*, 116).

the holy gods" (Dan 5:11). When brought before the king, Belshazzar stated to Daniel, "I have heard of you that the spirit of the gods is in you" (Dan 5:14).

It was seen in the discussion of Dan 4:8–9 above that Daniel attributed to God and his wisdom what Nebuchadnezzar could have knowledgeably attributed to the Spirit of the holy God. At the least, the readers of Daniel would have associated this title with the Spirit of God. Though it is unlikely that Belshazzar or the queen understood their use of this title in the same way in Dan 5:11 and 5:14, the readers of Daniel would likely have associated this title with its previous meaning, and it may have been that this associated meaning was exactly what Daniel intended for his readers to assume.

Just as the Spirit was explained to be the one who granted wisdom to interpret the dreams of Nebuchadnezzar, so also did the queen claim Daniel possessed "light and understanding and wisdom like the wisdom of the gods" to interpret the writing for Belshazzar (Dan 5:11). The queen said again to Belshazzar that "an excellent spirit, knowledge, and understanding to interpret dreams, explain riddles, and solve problems were found in this Daniel" (Dan 5:12).[38]

Daniel 6:3

The four references to the Spirit's role in the life of Daniel thus far are clearly prophetic in nature (Dan 4:8, 9; 5:11, 14). God revealed to Daniel the meanings of dreams and a message that he would have otherwise not known. A final description of Daniel in Dan 6:3 uses the term *rûaḥ* with reference to the source of Daniel's leadership, and it may be that this description alludes to the Spirit's enablement as the source of Daniel's exceptional ability to lead.

Now serving under King Darius, Daniel was appointed to be one of three high officials who oversaw 120 satraps who administrated the affairs of Babylon (Dan 6:1–2). Not only did Darius assume Daniel to be a highly capable leader, but Daniel then "became distinguished above all the other high officials and satraps, because an excellent spirit was in him. And the king planned to set him over the whole kingdom" (Dan 6:3).

In the context of describing his leadership, it was said of Daniel that "an excellent spirit was in him" (Dan 6:3). This phrase (*rûaḥ yattîrāʾ*) is nearly identical to one of the phrases that the queen used to describe Daniel to Belshazzar. She claimed that "an excellent spirit" (*rûaḥ yattîrâ*) and other qualities "were found in this Daniel," which qualified him to decipher for

---

38. Cf. Block, "The View from the Top," 189–90.

Belshazzar the meaning of the writing on the wall (Dan 5:12). This description came immediately after she identified Daniel as one "in whom is the spirit of the holy gods" (Dan 5:11). Though Dan 6:3 does not directly refer to the Spirit as being involved in the leadership of Daniel, the use of *rûaḥ* to refer to the source of Daniel's excellent leadership echoes the terminology of Dan 5:12, which overlaps with the terminology of a reference to the Spirit of God in Dan 5:11. In an indirect manner, Dan 6:3 may identify the Spirit of God as the source of Daniel's leadership.[39]

Summary

Four references in Daniel describe the Spirit's role in Daniel's prophetic ability to receive revelation from God to interpret dreams and handwriting on a wall: Dan 4:8, 9; 5:11, 14. Daniel 6:3 then identifies "an excellent spirit" as the source of Daniel's exceptional leadership. The shared terminology between all of these passages suggests that Dan 6:3 could allude to the Spirit of God as the source of Daniel's ability to lead. Whereas the Spirit would occasionally reveal to Daniel the wisdom necessary for interpretation, the Spirit gave Daniel the wisdom for leadership for what seems to be the entirety of his career in Babylon (cf. Dan 1:17; 6:3).

Leadership, Authority, and the Word of God

Another theme to note involves the relationship between the leader's exercise of authority and the Word of God. At the outset of this study, the term *biblical leader* was defined as anyone formally recognized by God or his people to lead the people of God, and the term *leadership* was defined as any activity of a biblical leader that is an exercise of his authority over the people of God. Keeping these definitions in mind, what is significant in this study is that there is an obvious shift from one testament to the next concerning how authority is exercised in relationship to the Word of God in passages that refer to leaders and the Spirit.

---

39. Ibid., 198.

Leadership, Authority, and the Word of God in the Old Testament

There were several passages in the OT that were found to describe a leader, the Spirit, and the Spirit's work in the exercise of leadership. The Spirit's enablement in these passages was to give the necessary wisdom to a leader in order for him to lead God's people in carrying out the various purposes of God. These purposes were typically limited to Israel's military and civil affairs. The relation of this leadership to the Word of Word was that these leaders typically led as God had specifically commanded them[40] or according to what God had previously revealed in Scripture.[41] Their leadership could at times include the instruction or delivery of the Word of God, but their leadership typically involved the application of what God had already said.

Leadership, Authority, and the Word of God in the New Testament

In the NT, this study demonstrated that when a passage referred to the Spirit's work through a NT leader, many of these passages involved the Spirit's work to enable a leader to proclaim the Word of God.[42] Many passages are indirectly related to this theme in that they describe the work of the Spirit as guiding NT leaders to people for the purpose of proclaiming God's Word as well.[43] Having reviewed these facts, the shift between the testaments of how the Spirit and leadership relates to God's Word is not difficult to see. When the Spirit is specifically mentioned, OT leaders were typically seen to exercise authority over Israel by obeying or applying what God had previously revealed. In the NT, however, the exercise of authority took place through the proclamation of God's Word. (Again, this statement applies to passages that specifically refer to the Spirit.) This is not to say that NT leaders did not apply God's Word to the civil affairs of God's people,

---

40. E.g., Moses led Israel according to what God spoke to him in Exodus 3–4, but he obviously did not have the inscripturated form of Exodus 3–4 as his guide.

41. E.g., David charged his son Solomon to lead according to what God had written in the Law of Moses (1 Kgs 2:3).

42. See, e.g., Luke 24:49; John 14:16–17, 26; 15:26–27; 16:12–15; Acts 1:8; 4:8; 9:17; 2 Tim 1:6–7.

43. See Acts 8:29, 39; 10:19; 11:12; 13:2, 4; 16:6–7. Cf. Acts cf. 19:21; 20:22, 23.

but it is to say that there is an emphasis on the proclamation of God's Word when Scripture explicitly mentions the Spirit and NT leaders.

This shift in the emphasis of the Spirit's work in leaders is especially clear in the person of Jesus Christ. He was anointed by the Spirit as Israel's king (Matt 3:16–17; cf. Ps 2:7) and thus expected to lead the nation and even the world (cf. Isa 11:1–5; 42:1–4), but he himself emphasized his role in proclamation and implied that the execution of justice would be in time to come (cf. Luke 4:18–21 with Isa 62:1–2). After his ascension into heaven, he sent the Spirit to empower his followers to continue proclaiming salvation through him (Acts 2:33; cf. 1:8).

Though it may seem in the NT that the Spirit's role in leadership has been set aside for the purpose of proclamation, it should be remembered that the proclamation of God's Word can itself be an exercise of authority and was a required function of NT leaders. Jesus was unique in that he himself was the Word (John 1:1) and perfectly revealed the words of the Father as the one who was given the Spirit without measure (John 3:34). The Spirit's work through the apostles was to reveal the words of Christ and speak on his behalf, and they thus saw their words as belonging to him (e.g., 1 Cor 14:37; cf. John 16:12–15).[44] In turn, apostolic delegates derived their authority from the apostles and spoke on their behalf (1 Cor 4:17; 1 Thess 3:2).[45] Likewise, an elder exercises authority over God's people by teaching authoritatively from Scripture (cf. 1 Tim 3:2; Titus 1:9).[46]

Given the fact that teaching and leadership are listed as separate spiritual gifts (Rom 12:7, 8; cf. 1 Cor 12:28, 29), it cannot be said that these works of the Spirit are one and the same. However, these spiritual gifts obviously overlap in that elders who are gifted to lead must also be gifted to teach. Teaching is an exercise of authority because it involves authoritatively speaking what God has already said. Leadership is also an exercise of authority because it involves the application of what God has said with respect to the oversight of the church.

The Spirit and Jesus Christ

This study has surveyed a number of passages that have yielded numerous connections between the Spirit and Jesus and his role as a leader. Though

---

44. McDonald, "Authority," 1:452.
45. Cf. Ellis, "Coworkers, Paul and His," 187–88.
46. Merkle, *40 Questions about Elders and Deacons*, 96.

much more could be said of the Spirit's relationship to Jesus, this section attempts to correlate the themes in this study below.

The Spirit, Jesus, and Leadership

Jesus' enablement by the Spirit in the exercise of his leadership could be described according to Jesus' roles as Israel's king and head of the church.

The Spirit and Jesus as Israel's King

The heads of Israel often led as enabled by the Spirit of God. This statement is true of Moses, Joshua, the four judges, Saul, and David. All of the leadership they carried out in the Spirit would be overshadowed by Israel's king to come. Isaiah saw a king whose superlative enablement by the Spirit was like no other head of Israel (cf. Isa 11:2–4), and the NT identified this king as Jesus (Luke 3:22; Acts 10:38). It was seen earlier that Jesus' entire ministry was characterized by the Spirit (cf. Matt 12:18–21; Luke 4:18–21), and it is no surprise to see that the Spirit-enabled activities of previous leaders were seen in Jesus' life as well. Like Moses and Joshua (Num 27:18; Isa 63:11), Jesus came to be Israel's shepherd (Matt 2:6; cf. Mic 5:2). Like Joshua (Deut 34:9), he would exercise wisdom in his role (Isa 11:2). Like Joshua, the judges, Saul, and David (Num 27:21; Judg 3:10; 6:34; 11:29; 1 Sam 11:6–7; 16:13; cf. 2 Sam 5:10), he would battle the enemies of God (Isa 11:2–5). Though Jesus has not executed his enemies yet, he will in time to come (Isa 11:4; cf. Heb 10:12–13).

The Spirit and Jesus as Head of the Church

The relationship between the Spirit and Jesus is also seen in various ways in his role as the head of the church. Jesus poured out the Spirit on his followers to empower them as his witnesses (Acts 2:33; cf. Luke 24:49; Acts 1:5, 8). He is occasionally described as guiding the apostles and their delegates to their destinations by means of the work of the Spirit (Acts 16:6–7). He grants spiritual gifts through the Spirit to enable each of God's people to serve one another in various ways (1 Cor 12:5–6), and the Spirit he sent long ago still functions as a witness to the truth about him today (John 15:26–27).

Spiritual Leadership

The Spirit and Jesus as Leader of Leaders

One of the spiritual gifts given by Christ is the spiritual gift of leadership (Rom 12:8; 1 Cor 12:28; cf. 12:4–5). As head of the church, he leads the church through the Spirit in part by imparting to some the spiritual gift of leadership.

The Spirit, Jesus, and Prophecy

The Spirit's prophetic role in the ministry of Jesus took place in two different ways. He was a prophet, and he would reveal truth through the apostles and prophets as well.

The Spirit and Jesus as Prophet

Some leaders prophesied on occasion (the seventy elders, Saul), and other leaders were described as leaders who were also prophets (Moses, David). Jesus was the Prophet like no other (John 6:14; 7:40; cf. Deut 18:15, 18) who revealed the Father without measure (John 3:34). His anointing by the Spirit signified his role as both prophet and king (Luke 4:18–21; cf. Isa 61:1–2b).

The Spirit and Jesus as Revealer of Truth

Besides being a prophet himself, Jesus revealed truth through the Spirit to the NT apostles and prophets (John 16:12–15; cf. Eph 3:5). It was seen that the apostle John was an example of this phenomenon in Revelation 2–3. What Jesus said to John could also be considered as the words of the Spirit (Rev 2:7, 11, 17, 29; 3:6, 13, 22).

Just as Jesus granted the truth of Scripture through the Spirit, so also he granted some the words to speak in the context of persecution. Christ through the Spirit granted members of the early church the words to speak to ably defend the gospel at the point of persecution (Mark 13:11; Luke 21:5; cf. Acts 4:8; 6:10).

The Spirit, Jesus, and Truth

The Spirit's work through Jesus enabled him to be a prophet and to reveal truth to the apostles and prophets as well. It is also true that the truth revealed concerned the person of Jesus himself. Jesus promised that the Spirit would "bear witness about me" (John 15:26) and stated that the Spirit would "take what is mine and declare it to you" (John 16:14). The truth revealed by the Spirit was the truth about Jesus that Jesus gave to be revealed.

Conclusion

This chapter has attempted to correlate the major themes that emerged from the previous two chapters. By doing so, greater clarity was given to the thesis of this study, namely, that there is a distinct work of the Spirit that takes place in the exercise of leadership by the leaders of God's people. Several points may be made in light of the preceding discussion.

First, this chapter clarified that the term *wisdom* is used in a variety of contexts, and the wisdom granted by the Spirit in one situation is not necessarily the same granted in another. Wisdom could involve the Spirit's work in revelation (Gen 41:38–39; Dan 4:8–9; cf. 2:21), the Spirit's work involved in godly living (Acts 6:3; cf. 1 Tim 3:1–13), or the Spirit's work involved in serving others (Acts 6:3). The OT described leaders as being given the Spirit of wisdom for leading God's people (Deut 34:9; Isa 11:2), and it could be said the spiritual gift of leadership assumes this wisdom as well.

Second, this chapter clarified that the Spirit's work in confirming a leader could simply be the Spirit's work in leadership and sometimes an additional work of the Spirit as well. Leaders enabled by the Spirit were at times confirmed through the Spirit's work in miracles (Exod 4:1–9; Josh 3:7; Acts 2:22; 2 Cor 12:12) or prophecy (Num 11:25–26; 1 Sam 10:10). Anointing with oil could symbolize an anointing with the Spirit (1 Sam 16:13), and the laying on of hands could communicate that the Spirit's work had set apart a leader for God's people (Num 27:18; Deut 34:9; 2 Tim 1:6). The Spirit's work in wisdom for ministry and godly living was required for one to become a deacon (Acts 6:3; cf. 1 Tim 3:8–13), and the same may be said for elders (cf. 1 Tim 3:1–7; Titus 1:5–9). Elders would be confirmed through the Spirit's work in teaching and leading (Rom 12:8; 1 Cor 12:28; cf. Rom 12:7; 1 Tim 3:2, 4–5).

Third, it was seen that obedience and the work of the Spirit in leadership were closely related throughout the Bible. Though God gave OT leaders standards for godly living (cf. Deut 17:14–20), there were no stipulations that promised or denied an enablement by the Spirit. However, it was seen in the lives of Samson (Judg 16:20) and Saul (1 Sam 16:14) and the words of David (Ps 51:11) that the Spirit's enablement could end in the case of persistent or significant sin. The Spirit's work in Jesus was to fear the LORD like no other (Isa 11:2–3), and the Spirit's work in godly living was necessary for elders and deacons to minister according to their offices (Acts 6:3; 1 Tim 3:1–13; Titus 1:5–9).

Fourth, it became apparent that the Spirit's enablement in leadership could be of either a continuous or continual nature. The enablement for some leaders was concluded to be continuous (Moses, Joshua, David, Jesus), and the enablement for others was clearly given on occasion for the task at hand (the judges, Saul). For an elder, the gift of spiritual leadership would be observed over the course of time (cf. 1 Tim 3:6), and the church would eventually appoint and set aside such a one to be an elder to continue to exercise this existing work of the Spirit (cf. Acts 20:28).

Fifth, a study of Joseph and Daniel further clarified that the Spirit's work in prophecy is not the same as the Spirit's work in leadership. Both involve the work of the Spirit and may be described as involving wisdom, but it was seen above that wisdom in revelation and wisdom in leadership are not necessarily one and the same.

Sixth, it was clarified that the emphasis of the Spirit's work in OT leaders differs from the emphasis of the work of the Spirit in NT leaders. OT leaders typically exercised authority according to what God had previously revealed, and NT leaders typically exercised authority by teaching or proclaiming what God had previously revealed. Though both teaching and leadership are spiritual gifts, they are not the same. However, elders are required to possess both of these gifts in leading the people of God.

Finally, this chapter presented a survey of the work of the Spirit in Jesus that showed him to be a leader unlike any other leader in this study. He was to be the king of Israel (Isa 11:2–5), and he is also the head of the church who through the Spirit grants the spiritual gift of leadership (1 Cor 12:5–6, 28). He was the expected Prophet to come (John 6:14; 7:40; cf. Deut 18:15, 18) and revealed the truth through others (John 16:12–15; cf. Rev 2:7). The truth he gave through the Spirit was his truth, the truth about himself (John 15:26; 16:1).

In conclusion, this chapter has strengthened the thesis of this study in several ways. The Spirit's work in leadership was reaffirmed as distinct from the Spirit's work in miracles, prophecy, and godly living. This distinction may be drawn from the OT, and the NT makes this distinction clear by the fact that leadership is identified as a distinct spiritual gift. The Spirit's work in leadership was present in select leaders in the OT and was either of a continuous or occasional nature. The Spirit's work in leadership for NT leaders such as elders is granted by Jesus Christ whose experience of the Spirit is distinct from all other leaders.

5

Biblical Theology and Spiritual Leadership in the Church

Introduction

THIS STUDY HAS DEMONSTRATED that a biblical theology of the role of the Spirit in the leadership of God's people demonstrates a distinct work of the Spirit in biblical leaders. Leaders in the OT were given the Spirit to enable their effective leadership over Israel's military and civil affairs. The OT anticipated this work of the Spirit in Jesus, and the NT presented the work of the Spirit as characterizing Jesus' ministry as a whole. The record of the Spirit's work in the apostles and their delegates did not so much concern the activity of leadership in administrative affairs as it did the proclamation of the gospel. However, what could be inferred of the Spirit's work in their leadership would be made clear of elders and leaders in the church in general. Paul identified leadership as a distinct spiritual gift and likely had elders in view as the ones who exercised this gift. It was concluded that the spiritual gift of leadership was likely true of the apostles and their delegates and that this work was similar to the work of the Spirit in OT leaders.

This chapter will review the work of the Spirit in leaders as it has been presented in this study in order to illustrate and inform how the Spirit's work may be seen through the ministry of leaders in the church today. This chapter will close by giving a portrait of a spiritual leader. To borrow the words of Paul and apply them to the study at hand, "these things" recorded of the Spirit and leaders in the Bible "took place as examples for us" as leaders today (1 Cor 10:6). "They were written down for our instruction, on whom the end of ages has come" (1 Cor 10:11).[1]

---

1. Though the immediate context of 1 Cor 10:6, 11 refers to the sins of Israel that the Corinthians were to avoid (cf. 1 Cor 10:7–10), Paul's use of examples from the OT to instruct the Corinthians demonstrates the principle that the OT in general informs and illustrates the faith and practice of God's people today (cf. Rom 4:23; 15:4; 2 Tim 3:16).

Elders and Deacons

The starting point for this chapter will be to review the roles of the elder and deacon as they have been described in this study. This review will not provide a comprehensive picture of what it means for one to be an elder or a deacon, but it will provide details of how the Spirit is explicitly said to work through elders and deacons in order to see if their ministries are similar to others who are described as leaders in this study. If there are similarities between their roles, the description of the Spirit's work in previous leaders may helpfully illustrate and inform how the Spirit works through leaders today.

Elders

This study has demonstrated that an elder or one who leads in the church is one to whom the Spirit grants the necessary wisdom for leadership (Rom 12:8; 1 Cor 12:28). This leadership must be exercised with zeal (Rom 12:8) and involves maintaining unity among God's people in face of the many issues that could divide them (1 Cor 12:28). The Spirit also grants to elders the ability to teach (1 Tim 3:2; cf. Rom 12:7). As with all Christians, the Spirit gives elders the wisdom for godly living, and it is required of elders that their godliness in character be of a consistent and obvious nature (1 Tim 3:1–7; Titus 1:5–9; cf. Acts 6:3). When all of these descriptions are true of a man who is appointed as an elder of a church, it could be said that the Holy Spirit made such a one an overseer to shepherd the flock of God (Acts 20:28).

Deacons

As with elders, the Spirit's wisdom to deacons in godly living is to be of an obvious and consistent nature (Acts 6:3; 1 Tim 3:8–13). The Spirit's wisdom to deacons is also seen through their effective service to the practical needs of the church (Acts 6:3). Though deacons are required to hold to the gospel and truth of Scripture (1 Tim 3:9), deacons are unlike elders in that they are not required to teach (cf. 1 Tim 3:2). Though deacons are appointed to serve in particular ministries (cf. Acts 6:3), they are not required to manage the church as a whole (cf. 1 Tim 3:4–5, 12). According to how the term *biblical leader* has been defined in this study, deacons are not to be identified as leaders. They have not been formally recognized by God or his people

---

For a fuller discussion of this principle, see Grudem, *Systematic Theology*, 93–95.

to lead the people of God, though they are excellent examples of ministry and character.

How a Biblical Theology of the Role of the Spirit in the Leadership of God's People Demonstrates a Distinct Work of the Spirit in Biblical Leaders

With this review of elders and deacons in hand, this section will briefly review the Spirit's work in the leaders of this study. This review will roughly follow the order that these leaders were previously discussed in this study. Some of the leaders will be grouped together according to how they inform or illustrate a common theme, and a review of the leadership of Joseph and Daniel will be given as well. A brief section will follow each leader's review to suggest how the Spirit's work through a given leader may illustrate and inform the Spirit's work through leaders of God's people today.

Moses and the Seventy Elders

Moses was enabled by the Spirit to do what the Spirit enabled the seventy elders to do as well: "bear the burden of the people" (Num 11:17). The context of Numbers 11 involved Moses receiving complaints from the Israelites, forcing him to admit to the LORD, "I am not able to carry all this people alone; the burden is too heavy for me" (Num 11:14). It was also noted that Moses' language describing his role as one carrying the burden of Israel was also used to describe judging the civil affairs of Israel (Deut 1:9–18). Putting these texts together, it seems that the presence of complaints in addition to the regular leadership over the affairs of Israel gave Moses cause for grief (cf. Num 11:15).

Romans 12:8 instructs "the one who leads" to lead "with zeal" (Rom 12:8), that is, with an eager and diligent manner. Moses clearly lost his zeal to lead in the midst of Israel's complaints. In addition to admitting his inability to meet Israel's demands, Moses also requested that the LORD would end his life (Num 11:15). The LORD's solution was not to limit the burden or end his life but to provide seventy other leaders who were enabled by the Spirit to lead (Num 11:25–26). Elders can learn from Moses' experience and see that the Spirit's enablement in leadership does not mean that one should lead alone. The presence of conflict in addition to a leader's regular responsibilities can drive a man to despair. Similar to the LORD's enablement of the seventy elders, a plurality of elders is helpful and was typical of the early church (cf. Acts 14:23; Titus 1:5).

Joshua

God identified Joshua as "a man in whom is the Spirit" (Num 27:18) in response to Moses' prayer that God would give Israel a military leader, a man "who shall go out before them and come in before them, who shall lead them out and bring them in" (Num 27:17). Moses' prayer also included the request that God would not leave Israel "as sheep that have no shepherd" (Num 27:17). Joshua was to be Israel's leader in battle and a shepherd for the people. With these roles in mind, Deut 34:9 further described Joshua as being "full of the Spirit of wisdom" (author's translation) to lead Israel as Moses before him (cf. Deut 34:9b).

The task of elders in the church is obviously not to lead God's people in physical warfare. However, the examination of Joshua yields the theme of the leader's role as shepherd. Though much more could be said of this theme,[2] it may at least be pointed out that the shepherd is a common metaphor for leaders throughout the Bible.[3] Moses implied his role as a shepherd (Num 27:17–18) and was described as Israel's shepherd by others as well (Ps 77:20; Isa 63:11; Hos 12:13).[4] David shepherded Israel with care and compassion (cf. Ps 78:70–72).[5] Jesus is the Chief Shepherd who gave his life for the sheep (cf. Zech 13:7; Matt 26:31; John 10:11) and continues to be their shepherd (Heb 13:20; 1 Pet 2:25; 5:4; cf. Mic 5:4; Matt 2:6). He will divide his sheep from the goats in time to come (Ezek 34:23; cf. 34:16, 17, 22;

---

2. For a solid work on this subject, see Laniak, *Shepherds after My own Heart*.

3. It should be noted that numerous references describe God as shepherd or use the language of shepherding to describe his relationship to his people: Gen 48:15; 49:24; PS 23:1; 28:9; 80:1; Ecc 12:11; Isa 40:11; Ezek; 34:15, 17, 22, 31; Mic 7:14; et al. Cf. Laniak, *Shepherds after My own Heart*, 110.

4. Ibid., 88. In Ps 77:20, the psalmist states to God, "You led your people like a flock by the hand of Moses and Aaron." Isaiah 63:11–12 speaks of multiple "shepherds of his flock" and implies Moses' role as a shepherd by noting his specific role in leading Israel through the sea. The verb "guarded" (*šmr*) in Hos 12:13 that describes the activity of Moses is the same verb used in reference to Jacob having "guarded" sheep in Hosea 12:12. Laniak notes that *šmr* is used elsewhere with reference to shepherding as well (Gen 30:31; 1 Sam 17:20).

5. Ibid., 108. David is pictured as Israel's shepherd immediately after the description of his days of "following the nursing ewes" (Ps 78:71a; cf. 78:71b).

Matt 25:32). Peter was to feed and tend the flock of God (John 21:15–17), even to the point of death (John 21:18–19).[6] Paul reminded the Ephesians elders they were appointed by the Spirit to shepherd (Acts 20:28). Paul uses *shepherds* as a title for elders (Eph 4:11), and Peter commanded elders to "shepherd the flock of God" in a manner worthy of their calling (1 Pet 5:2; cf. 5:2–3).

A couple of paragraphs about the leader as shepherd hardly introduces this theme. For the moment, however, it can be seen that the Spirit's enablement of the elder to function as shepherd may be seen in multiple ways. Shepherding involves care and compassion for God's people, serving them sacrificially, and feeding God's people with Scripture. From what Peter says explicitly concerning the manner of how elders were to shepherd, they were to lead willingly, eagerly, and by example (1 Pet 5:2–3).

The Judges, Saul, and David

Othniel, Gideon, and Jephthah were enabled by the Spirit to lead Israel's armies in battle (Judg 3:10; 6:34; 11:29). As a result, Gideon overcame his timid nature (cf. Judg 6:15), and Jephthah was a leader despite the circumstances of being the son of a prostitute (cf. Judg 11:1). The Spirit moved Samson to be distressed at Israel's oppression (Judg 13:25), and Samson's enablement with strength was unique (Judg 14:6, 19; 15:14). His persistent sin led to the loss of the Spirit (cf. Judg 16:20).

Though Saul was Israel's first king, his enablement by the Spirit was similar to the judges before him. Though he was naturally a coward (cf. 1 Sam 9:21; 10:21–22; 15:17), the Spirit enabled him to rally Israel's soldiers and courageously lead them to victory in battle (1 Sam 11:6–7). Unfortunately, like Samson before him, Saul's persistent disobedience led to the loss of the Spirit's enablement (1 Sam 16:14).

David's kingship was generally characterized by his enablement by the Spirit. When he was anointed with oil, "the Spirit of the LORD rushed upon David *from that day forward*" (1 Sam 16:13; italics added). Statements that the LORD was "with" David implied the Spirit's enablement in David's leadership in battle (1 Sam 18:12, 14; 2 Sam 5:10; 7:9). Though David committed significant sin by sleeping with Bathsheba and murdering her husband

---

6. Ibid., 222. Cf. Köstenberger, *John*, 598–99. Jesus' command to Peter ("Follow me"; John 21:19) comes after his description of how Peter would die, likely by crucifixion.

(2 Sam 12:8–9), David repented and requested the continued enablement of the Spirit (Ps 51:11).

Though it could probably be said of all of Israel's Spirit-enabled leaders that they had the courage for battle (cf. Josh 1:6, 7, 18; 10:25), the Spirit's role in giving courage is especially clear in the examples of Gideon and Saul. Both were of a timid nature, and the Spirit's enablement gave them courage to rally their troops and lead them to victory in battle. It could be said that the courage given by the Spirit in physical warfare against God's enemies is the same courage necessary for battling their heresies as well.[7] In supporting his command to Timothy to teach God's Word (2 Tim 1:6; cf. 1 Tim 4:13–14) to a church once plagued with false teachers (1 Tim 1:3–4; cf. Acts 20:28–31), Paul explained, "for God gave us a Spirit not of fear but of power" (2 Tim 1:7; author's translation). The contrast between fear and power implies that the Spirit's work in Timothy's teaching included giving Timothy the courage to teach in the face of opposition. Though Timothy was not an elder, an elder's role is also to teach (1 Tim 3:2), sometimes in the face of opposition (cf. Acts 20:28–31). The Spirit not only enables elders to teach but to do so with courage and power.

Both elders and deacons can learn from the judges, Saul, and David concerning the topic of obedience. Samson and Saul both lost the Spirit's enablement for their persistent disobedience, and David feared his loss of the Spirit in light of his disobedience as well (cf. Ps 51:11). However, David's repentance assumedly granted him the continuation of the Spirit's work, though there were consequences for his sin. Elders and deacons are nowhere described as possibly losing the Spirit's work in light of disobedience, but they may lose their ministries by failing to live up to the requirements for their character as officers in the church (Acts 6:3; 1 Tim 3:1–13; Titus 1:5–9). Even if they sin, they can learn from David that no one is beyond repentance and being shown the mercy of God. At the same time, the presence of repentance does not guarantee one can maintain his position as an officer in the church. Even when there is repentance and restoration, some sins may demand an officer step down from his position within the church.

---

7. This statement is not intended to imply that Israel's enemies were not spiritual enemies as well.

Spiritual Leadership

Joseph and Daniel

Joseph and Daniel were prophets who also served as leaders and examples for elders today. Both gave the interpretations of dreams to foreign rulers who consequently placed them in positions of leadership (Gen 41:38–40; Dan 2:47–48). These foreign leaders assumed Joseph and Daniel's revelatory wisdom in the interpretation of dreams meant they would also have the wisdom in leadership necessary to manage the affairs of their kingdoms.

Other descriptions of Joseph and Daniel implied the Spirit's role in their leadership as well. Before Joseph served under Pharaoh, he prospered as the administrator over Potiphar's house and the prison because "the LORD was with him" (Gen 39:2, 23; cf. 39:21). As demonstrated in this study, the description of the LORD being "with" a leader could imply the Spirit's role in their leadership (cf. 1 Sam 18:12; Acts 10:38). After multiple direct and indirect references to the Spirit of God in Daniel (Dan 4:8, 9; cf. 5:11, 14), it was suggested that the description of Daniel having "an excellent spirit" (Dan 6:3) indirectly pointed to the Spirit as the source of his wisdom in leadership (cf. Dan 5:11–12).

The Spirit's work in the leadership of Joseph and Daniel is similar to the ministry of elders who oversee the people of God and the resources of the church (Rom 12:8; 1 Tim 3:5; 5:17).[8] Assuming the spiritual gift of leadership exercised by elders is similar to the Spirit's work through the leadership of Joseph and Daniel, these two men show that the Spirit's work in leadership can been shown in even the highest levels of capacity. Except for the one who gave them their charge, entire kingdoms were under their domain (Gen 41:40; Dan 6:3).

Another lesson to learn from Joseph and Daniel is that the Spirit's work in leadership may not always be exercised directly among the people of God or in the midst of the church. One who possesses the spiritual gift of leadership may show this gift in a secular environment. However, it should be remembered that the exercise of leadership as a spiritual gift somehow benefits the body of Christ (cf. 1 Cor 12:7). It could be more easily said

---

8. It was pointed out above that the word *prohistēmi* is used to describe the management that both elders and deacons exercise in their homes (1 Tim 3:4, 12). This word is also used to describe the "rule" of elders (1 Tim 5:17) and the spiritual gift of leadership (Rom 12:8). It should be remembered that deacons are to have the necessary wisdom to oversee particular ministries as well (Acts 6:3; cf. 1 Tim 3:12). Though deacons are not given the responsibility of ruling or overseeing the church, the requirement that they manage their homes well suggests that they evidence some degree of oversight over the ministries placed in their care.

that many who are not elders often exercise the spiritual gift of leadership as they lead parachurch ministries or other Christian organizations. Their exercise of this gift would seem all the more likely if such individuals were able to teach God's Word as well (cf. 1 Tim 3:2).

Jesus

The Spirit's role in the leadership of Jesus was prophesied by Isaiah, recorded in the Gospels and Acts, and described in the letters as well. Some passages imply the Spirit's role in his ministry as a whole (cf. Matt 12:18–21; Luke 4:18–21), and other passages are more specific. The Spirit rested upon Jesus at his baptism (Matt 3:16; et al) to enable him to lead with wisdom, understanding, counsel, might, knowledge, and the fear of the LORD (Isa 11:2). This cluster of qualities would allow him to faithfully lead with perfect righteousness and justice for the sake of the meek and poor of the earth (Isa 11:2–5). His initial ministry recorded in the Gospels was of a more gentle nature (Isa 42:1–4; Matt 12:15–21), and one of his primary tasks was to proclaim the good news of salvation (Isa 61:1–2a; Luke 4:14–15, 18–21). He will execute perfect justice against his enemies when he comes again (cf. Isa 61:2b with Luke 4:19). Until then, he has sent the Spirit to embolden the witness of the church (Acts 2:33; cf. 4:31) and witness with the church by convicting the lost of their sin (cf. John 15:25–26; 16:7). His ministry through the Spirit enables each member of his church to serve in particular ways (1 Cor 12:4–5), including the ministry of elders (1 Cor 12:28). He also led the early church by guiding the proclamation of the gospel (Acts 16:6–7) and giving revelation about himself (John 16:12–15; cf. Rev 2:7).

An examination of the Spirit's work through Jesus does not merely provide illustrations for God's people today but informs them as to his active role in their lives as well. He is the living head of the church who sent the Spirit at Pentecost (Acts 2:33) and actively guided his witnesses at times to where and to whom they would give the gospel (Acts 16:6–7). Though there seems to be no reason to expect this guidance today, he still presently enables each member in carrying out their ministries for the sake of serving one another (1 Cor 12:4–5). His role to elders includes his ministry through the Spirit of giving the spiritual gift of leadership (1 Cor 12:28). It could be said that he gives to deacons their ability to effectively serve in their capacity as well.[9]

---

9. This fact is clearly established in 1 Cor 12:4–5, but it was also discussed earlier

It was also noted that there is a secondary sense in which the *Paraclete* promises given to the apostles apply to the church today. When a Christian is a witness of the truth of Christ to others, the Spirit still bears witness to the hearers by convicting them "concerning sin and righteousness and judgment" (John 16:7). In this way, both the Christian and Spirit bear witness to the gospel of Jesus Christ (John 15:26–27). These truths give peace to Christians in general (cf. John 14:27) and to elders who regularly teach God's Word as well. If an elder is faithfully teaching the Word of God, he can rest assured that the Spirit will function as a witness with his teaching to yield spiritual fruit according to the gracious plan of God.

The Spirit's work in Jesus' ministry is illustrative as well. In one sense, Jesus' entire ministry was characterized by the Spirit (cf. Matt 12:18–21; Luke 4:18–21), and this study would have no end in describing Jesus as an example to all (cf. John 21:25). However, a few thoughts may be offered according to some of the passages examined in this study. The Spirit gave Jesus a perfect balance between boldness and gentleness in teaching. He was bold to teach and demonstrate the truth (Matt 12:9–13; Luke 4:14–15), but he was quick to leave a situation in order to avoid unnecessary conflict (Matt 12:14–21; cf. Isa 42:1–4). It should also be noted that behind this example is the underlying theme of Jesus' delay of final justice against his enemies until he comes again (Isa 61:1–2a; Luke 4:18–21). Putting these passages together, Jesus' example for elders today is to faithfully teach God's Word in a bold yet gentle manner. Even when conflict arises as the result of the proclamation of God's Word, an elder must continue to show a gentle character (cf. 1 Tim 3:3). This gentleness must even be shown when responding to opposition (cf. 2 Tim 2:24–25). If persecution comes an elder's way, he can know that Christ will eventually come again and execute justice on his behalf.

Apostles and Their Delegates

The description of the Spirit's work in the apostles and their delegates primarily involved the proclamation of the gospel. Given their role as leaders in the church, it was safely inferred that apostles and their delegates possessed the spiritual gift of leadership as well. Though examples of their leadership could be helpful to inform and illustrate the role of an elder, this study offered no passages that mentioned the apostles or their delegates

---

that 1 Cor 12:28 and Rom 12:8 may have implied the roles of deacons as well.

and the Spirit with reference to their leadership.[10] However, it was clarified that the teaching of the Word of God by a leader is an exercise of authority among God's people, and an elder must be able to teach (1 Tim 3:2; Titus 1:9). The description of the Spirit's work in the teaching of the apostles and their delegates informs and illustrates for elders how the Spirit should be at work when he teaches Scripture and thereby exercises authority among the people of God.

Just as Paul pointed to the Spirit as the empowering source of his preaching (1 Thess 1:5), an elder should realize that his ability to teach comes from the Spirit as well (cf. Rom 12:7). Just as the apostles were emboldened by the Spirit to be witnesses of the gospel (Luke 24:49; Acts 1:8), an elder should be bold when proclaiming Scripture as well. Like Barnabas, his effective teaching must be tied to a life characterized by the Spirit and a firm trust in the Lord (Acts 11:23-24; cf. 1 Tim 3:1-7). Like Apollos, his teaching should be fervent and marked with zeal (Acts 18:25; cf. Rom 12:8, 11; 1 Pet 5:2). Like Timothy, he should defend and proclaim God's Word with courage, love, and self-control (2 Tim 1:7, 14).

Apart from his own role in the activity of his teaching, an elder can take comfort in the fact that Spirit works within his listeners as well. The Spirit takes God's Word as it is taught and demonstrates its truth to those who hear (1 Cor 2:4-5). It may similarly be said that the Spirit convinces the listeners concerning their sin, righteousness, and judgment (John 16:8-11) so that a response of obedience to God may take place (Acts 5:32). As the elder bears witness to the truth about Christ, so also will the Spirit bear witness to the truth (John 15:26-27).

Summary

The description of the Spirit's work in OT and NT leaders is a rich source of data that informs and illustrates the roles of elders and those who are spiritually gifted to lead. Their examples of wisdom in service and obedience are helpful to deacons as well.

---

10. To clarify, it was pointed out that the Spirit did work through these leaders in several ways that, though related to their leadership, were works of a more extraordinary nature. The Spirit gave revelation to the apostles (John 16:12-15; cf. Eph 3:5; Rev 2:7), and they were also given the words to say on occasion when defending the gospel (Matt 10:20; Mark 13:11; Luke 12:12; cf. Acts 4:8). They were directed by the Spirit as to where and to whom to give the gospel (Acts 10:19; 11:12; 16:6-7), and Peter and Paul performed miracles of judgment through the Spirit's work as well (Acts 5:4-11; 13:9-11).

The spiritual gift of leadership is clearly a distinct work of the Spirit in biblical leaders, and this work is illustrated by some of the heads of Israel and the leaders of the early church. Jesus' experience of the Spirit is distinct from all other leaders, but he is nonetheless the perfect example for all who lead God's people. The spiritual gift of leadership is granted to those who function as elders and others who use this gift for the good of the people of God.

A Biblical Portrait of a Spiritual Leader

Numerous passages list requirements for those who lead the people of God (e.g., Deut 17:14–20; 1 Tim 3:1–7; Titus 1:5–9; 1 Pet 5:2–3). As seen above, there is much to be learned from the biblical narratives of leaders as well. The following section is far from complete in that it is limited to what has been said in this study. At the same time, it may at least be said with confidence that each characteristic below is a work of the Spirit that should be true of every leader of God's people today. These characteristics have been categorized according to the Spirit's work that should be true of a spiritual leader in his ministry in general, in the exercise of his leadership, and in his role as a teacher.

The Leader's Ministry in General

In his ministry in general, the leader must be a man of character and gentle and loving with others. He must be focused on the Great Commission as well.

A Man of Character

A spiritual leader must be a man of character. He is full of the Spirit in that he lives obediently to God's Word in a consistent and obvious manner (1 Tim 3:1–7; Titus 1:5–9; cf. Acts 6:3; 1 Tim 3:8–13). A pattern of disobedience or even a single instance of disobedience of a great degree could keep a man from leadership or necessitate his removal from his role (1 Sam 13:13–14). He delights to fear the LORD (Isa 11:2–3), and this character will affect his role as a teacher (Acts 11:23–24).

Gentle with Others

A spiritual leader is gentle. His manner of interaction with others is pictured as the ability to handle a candle without snuffing its smoldering wick and to not snap a reed that is ready to break (Matt 12:20; cf. Isa 42:3). He firmly upholds God's Word in the midst of opposition (Matt 12:9–14), but he refuses to engage in needless controversy or use his authority to harshly demand his way (Matt 12:15–16; cf. 12:17–21; 1 Tim 3:3).

Loving Toward Others

A spiritual leader shows love to others. He is motivated by love as he uses his spiritual gifts of leadership and teaching for the good of the people of God (1 Cor 12:7; 2 Tim 1:6–7).

Focused on the Great Commission

A spiritual leader is focused on the Great Commission. This commission is to lead and equip God's people in proclaiming the gospel of Jesus Christ (Acts 1:8; cf. 4:31). For the spiritual leader, he takes his stand in the front line of declaring the gospel and showing an example for others to do the same (Acts 18:25).

The Leader's Exercise of Leadership

In the exercise of his leadership, the leader bears and shares the burdens of others. He is a shepherd who maintains unity and manages God's people with zeal.

A Bearer of Burdens

A spiritual leader bears the burdens of God's people. He makes difficult decisions on a regular basis and continues to do so in the midst of complaint (Num 11:17; cf. Deut 1:9–18). He realizes that his giftedness does not demand that he make these decisions alone (Num 11:14).

Spiritual Leadership

A Sharer of Burdens

A spiritual leader shares the burdens of God's people. When faced with overwhelming challenges, he prays to God for help and gladly delegates opportunities to minister (Num 11:14). He realizes that he is not the only means of leading the people of God (Num 11:25–26).

A Shepherd

A spiritual leader is a shepherd. He cares for his sheep as a shepherd would gently and compassionately care for his lambs (Num 27:17; Ps 78:70–72). He shepherds with care and leads his people as a willing and eager example (1 Pet 5:2–3).

Maintains Unity among God's People

A spiritual leader maintains unity among God's people. He is wise to discern when friction and fracture are taking place and carefully tends to relational problems without division taking place (1 Cor 12:28).

Leads God's People with Zeal

A spiritual leader leads God's people with zeal. He is not reluctant to carry out his ministry, and he is not lazy in studying God's Word. He is enthusiastic and excited to lead God's people in carrying out God's will (Rom 12:8; 1 Pet 5:2).

The Leader as a Teacher

A leader must be a passionate teacher who is dependent on the Spirit for results.

Able to Teach

A spiritual leader is able to teach. He is spiritually gifted to effectively communicate God's Word to others (1 Tim 3:2; cf. Rom 12:7). This ability is seen through his regular instruction of God's Word and his refutation of error (Titus 1:9).

Passionate in His Teaching

A spiritual leader is passionate in his teaching. This passion is seen in his fervency when declaring God's Word in general (Acts 18:25) and in his boldness to declare God's Word to the lost (Acts 1:8). When faced with opposition, he exercises self-control and courageously upholds the gospel of Christ (2 Tim 1:6–7, 14).

Dependent upon the Spirit for Results

A spiritual leader is dependent upon the Spirit for results. He faithfully witnesses to the truth and leaves the internal demonstration of this truth to the Spirit (1 Cor 2:4–5). He faithfully explains sin, righteousness, and judgment, and he leaves it to the Spirit to convince (John 16:8–11). He knows that it is the Spirit who will take God's Word and bring a response of obedience to the faith (Acts 5:32).

Conclusion

This chapter has used the foregoing study to illustrate and inform how the Spirit may be seen to work through elders and leaders today. This chapter began with a review of the Spirit's work in the ministry of elders and deacons. It was clarified that a deacon is not to function as a leader within the church, and an elder leads the church through the exercise of the spiritual gift of leadership.

The Spirit's work in the leaders of this study was then reviewed in order to inform and illustrate how the Spirit may work through leaders today. The Spirit's manifold work through previous leaders may be seen by the Spirit giving the leader what is necessary to lead God's people: the ability to bear the burden of God's people (Num 11:17); wisdom to shepherd (Num 27:17–18; Deut 34:9; cf. Acts 20:28); courage for spiritual warfare (Judg 6:34; 1 Sam 11:6–7; cf. 2 Tim 1:6–7); wisdom in godly living (Ps 51:11; cf. Acts 6:3; 1 Tim 3:1–13); the ability to lead those who are not God's people (cf. Gen 41:38–40; Dan 6:3); enablement from Christ who heads the church and grants the gift of leadership (1 Cor 12:4–5, 28); gentleness and boldness in proclamation (Matt 12:14–21; cf. 1 Tim 3:3); and the ability to effectively and powerfully preach (1 Thess 1:5; 2 Tim 1:7, 14).

These works of the Spirit and others examined in this study were then condensed into a biblical portrait of a spiritual leader. The Spirit's work should be evident in the leader's life in general, in his exercise of leadership, and in his ministry of teaching.

6

Conclusion

THIS STUDY HAS ARGUED in various ways that a biblical theology of the role of the Spirit in the leadership of God's people demonstrates a distinct work of the Spirit in biblical leaders.

A study of the OT demonstrated that the Spirit worked through multiple leaders by enabling their effective leadership over God's people. These leaders were Moses, Joshua, the four judges, Saul, and David. Isaiah prophesied of a king to come whose experience of the Spirit would distinguish him from all other leaders. Based upon the examination of these leaders, it was concluded that the Spirit's work in leadership could be described as the Spirit giving these leaders the wisdom necessary to carry out their respective tasks in leadership over God's people.

This study of the Spirit's work in OT leaders helped to clarify that these leaders sometimes experienced additional works of the Spirit that *confirmed* the Spirit's work in leadership, but that these works were *something other* than the Spirit's work in leadership. These works included miracles and prophecy, and an examination of the leadership of Joseph and Daniel further clarified that wisdom in prophecy was revelatory in nature and was of not the same exact nature as the wisdom necessary for leadership.

The study of the Spirit's work in OT leaders also showed from the leadership of Samson, Saul, and David that the Spirit's enablement was exercised in obedience to the LORD and that obedience to some degree was necessary for this enablement to continue. However, the failures of these leaders also showed that the Spirit's work in leadership did not necessarily mean that a given leader would be consistent in his obedience or refrain from significant sins.

A study of the NT demonstrated that the work of the Spirit in leadership was not emphasized in the leadership of Jesus, the apostles, or their delegates. What was recorded of the Spirit's work through these leaders primarily involved the proclamation of the gospel. However, it was pointed out Jesus' ministry as a whole (leadership included) involved the work of the Spirit, and that it could be plausibly inferred that the Spirit's work in leadership was granted to the apostles and their delegates as well. For these leaders and others, it was noted that their activity in teaching God's Word was an exercise of their authority.

A study of the NT also showed that the Spirit appointed elders to shepherd the flock of God (Acts 20:28), but the means or process whereby the Spirit did so were not immediately stated. However, Paul likely had elders in mind when he spoke of the spiritual gift of leadership in both Rom 12:8 and 1 Cor 12:28. The words used for this gift indicated that the Spirit's work in the leadership of elders (or others gifted to lead) involved managing the church (*prohistēmi*) and maintaining unity among God's people (*kybernēsis*). The fact that leadership was identified as a distinct spiritual gift provides the strongest argument that there is a distinct work of the Spirit in biblical leaders. The Spirit's work in elders and other leaders today is illustrated and informed by the work of the Spirit in the other leaders of this study.

It was clarified that deacons were to be full of the Spirit in that they displayed the Spirit's wisdom in their ministry and godly living. However, though they are like elders in that they are officers in the church, they are not required to teach or lead. This fact implies that they are not formally to function as leaders over the church as a whole.

A biblical theology of the role of the Spirit in the leadership of God's people demonstrates a distinct work of the Spirit in biblical leaders. This work was identified as the spiritual gift of leadership, and examples of men throughout the Bible illustrate and inform the nature of this work. May Isaiah's words to God concerning this work in leaders of old be words that are true of this work in leaders today: "So you led your people to make for yourself a glorious name" (Isa 63:14).

Bibliography

Akin, Daniel L. *1, 2, 3 John*. New American Commentary 38. Nashville, TN: Broadman & Holman, 2001.
Alden, Robert L. "Ecstasy and the Prophets." *Bulletin of the Evangelical Theological Society* 9 (1966) 149–56.
Allen, David L. *Hebrews*. New American Commentary 35. Nashville, TN: Broadman & Holman, 2010.
Aloisi, John "The Paraclete's Ministry of Conviction: Another Look at John 16:8–11." *Journal of the Evangelical Theology Society* 47 (2004) 55–69.
Anderson, Francis I. and A. Dean Forbes. *The Vocabulary of the Old Testament*. 1989. Reprint, Rome: Editrice Pontificio Istituto Biblico, 1992.
Armerding, Carl E. "Judges." In *New Dictionary of Biblical Theology*, edited by T. Desmond Alexander, Brian S. Rosner, D. A. Carson, and Graeme Goldsworthy, 171–76. Downers Grove, IL: InterVarsity, 2000.
Arnold, Clinton E. *Ephesians*. Exegetical Commentary on the New Testament 10. Grand Rapids, MI: Zondervan, 2010.
Assis, Eliyahu. *Self-interest or Communal Interest: An Ideology of Leadership in the Gideon, Abimelech, and Jephthah Narratives (Judges 6–12)*. Boston, MA: Brill, 2005.
Averbeck, Richard E. "Breath, Wind, Spirit and the Holy Spirit in the Old Testament." In *Presence, Power and Promise: The Role of the Spirit of God in the Old Testament*, edited by David G. Firth and Paul D. Wegner, 25–37. Downers Grove, IL: IVP Academic, 2011.
Balla, Peter. "Challenges to Biblical Theology." In *New Dictionary of Biblical Theology*, edited by T. Desmond Alexander, Brian S. Rosner, D. A. Carson, and Graeme Goldsworthy, 20–27. Downers Grove, IL: InterVarsity, 2000.
Barentsen, Jack. "Restoration and Its Blessing: A Theological Analysis of Psalms 51 and 32." *Grace Theological Journal* 5 (Fall 1984) 247–70.
Barnett, Paul W. "Apostle." In *Dictionary of Paul and His Letters*, edited by Gerald F. Hawthorne, Ralph P. Martin, and Daniel G. Reid, 45–50. Downers Grove, IL: InterVarsity, 1993.
———. *The Second Epistles to the Corinthians*. New International Commentary on the New Testament. Grand Rapids, MI: Eerdmans, 1997.
Barrett, C. K. *The Acts of the Apostles*. 2 vols. Edinburgh: T&T Clark, 1994.
Bateman, Herbert W., IV. *Three Central Issues in Contemporary Dispensationalism*. Grand Rapids, MI: Kregel, 1999.
Baxter, Ronald E. *Gifts of the Spirit*. Grand Rapids, MI: Kregel, 1983.

BIBLIOGRAPHY

Beale, G. K. *The Book of Revelation: A Commentary on the Greek Text*. New International Greek Testament Commentary. Grand Rapids, MI: Eerdmans, 1999.

Beale, G. K. and D. A. Carson. *Commentary on the New Testament Use of the Old Testament*. Grand Rapids, MI: Baker Academic, 2007.

Beasley-Murray, George R. *John*. Word Biblical Commentary 36. Dallas, TX: Word, 2002.

Beckwith, Roger T. "The Canon of Scripture." In *New Dictionary of Biblical Theology*, edited by T. Desmond Alexander, Brian S. Rosner, D. A. Carson, and Graeme Goldsworthy, 27–34. Downers Grove, IL: InterVarsity, 2000.

———. *Elders in Every City: The Origin and Role of the Ordained Ministry*. Carlisle: Paternoster, 2004.

Belleville, Linda L. *2 Corinthians*. IVP New Testament Commentary. Downers Grove, IL: InterVarsity, 1995.

Bennema, Cornelis. "The Giving of the Spirit in John 19–20: Another Round." In *The Spirit and Christ in the New Testament & Christian Theology*, edited by I. Howard Marshall, Volker Rabens, and Cornelis Bennema, 86–104. Grand Rapids, MI: Eerdmans, 2012.

Benson, Alphonsus. *The Spirit of God in the Didactic Books of the Old Testament*. Washington, D. C.: The Catholic University of America Press, 1949.

Berding, Kenneth. "Confusing Word and Concept in 'Spiritual Gifts': Have We Forgotten James Barr's Exhortations?" *Journal of the Evangelical Theology Society* 43 (2000) 37–51.

———. *What Are Spiritual Gifts? Rethinking the Conventional View*. Grand Rapids, MI: Kregel, 2006.

Betz, Otto. *Der Paraklet: Fürsprecher im Häretischen Spätjudentum, im Johannesevangelium und in Neu Gefundenen Gnostischen Schriften*. Leiden: E. J. Brill, 1963.

Blackaby, Henry and Richard Blackaby. *Spiritual Leadership: Moving People on to God's Agenda*. Nashville, TN: Broadman & Holman, 2001.

Blenkinsopp, Joseph. *Isaiah*. 3 vols. Anchor Bible 19–19B. New York: Doubleday, 2000–2003.

———. *Sage, Priest, Prophet: Religious and Intellectual Leadership in Ancient Israel*. Louisville, KY: Westminster John Knox, 1996.

Block, Daniel I. "Empowered by the Spirit of God: The Holy Spirit in the Histographic Writings of the Old Testament." *Southern Baptist Journal of Theology* 1 (Spring 1997) 42–61.

———. *Judges, Ruth*. New American Commentary 6. Nashville, TN: Broadman & Holman, 1999.

———. "The Prophet of the Spirit: The Use of RWH[set dot below H] in the Book of Ezekiel." *Journal of the Evangelical Theological Society* 32 (1989) 27–49.

———. "The View from the Top: The Holy Spirit and the Prophets." In *Presence, Power and Promise: The Role of the Spirit of God in the Old Testament*, edited by David G. Firth and Paul D. Wegner, 175–207. Downers Grove, IL: IVP Academic, 2011.

Blomberg, Craig L. "Gifts of Holy Spirit." In *Evangelical Dictionary of Biblical Theology*, edited by Walter A. Elwell, 348–51. Grand Rapids, MI: Baker, 1996.

———. *Matthew*. New American Commentary 22. Nashville, TN: Broadman & Holman, 1992.

———. "The Unity and Diversity of Scripture." In *New Dictionary of Biblical Theology*, edited by T. Desmond Alexander, Brian S. Rosner, D. A. Carson, and Graeme Goldsworthy, 64–72. Downers Grove, IL: InterVarsity, 2000.

BIBLIOGRAPHY

Bock, Darrell L. *Acts.* Baker Exegetical Commentary on the New Testament. Grand Rapids, MI: Baker, 2007.

———. *Jesus according to Scripture: Restoring the Portrait from the Gospels.* Grand Rapids, MI: Baker Academic, 2002.

———. *Luke 1:1–9:50.* Baker Exegetical Commentary on the New Testament 3A. Grand Rapids, MI: Baker, 1996.

———. *Luke 9:51–24:53.* Baker Exegetical Commentary on the New Testament 3B. Grand Rapids, MI: Baker, 1996.

Borchert, Gerald L. *John 1–11.* New American Commentary 25A. Nashville, TN: Broadman & Holman, 1996.

———. *John 12–21.* New American Commentary 25B. Nashville, TN: Broadman & Holman, 2002.

Bowe, Barbara E. "Spiritual Gifts." In *Eerdmans Dictionary of the Bible*, edited by David Noel Freedman, Allen C. Myers, and Astrid B. Beck, 1249. Grand Rapids, MI: Eerdmans, 2000.

Brand, Chad. "Spiritual Gifts." In *Holman Illustrated Bible Dictionary*, edited by Chad Brand, Charles Draper, Archie England, Steve Bond, E. Ray Clendenen, Trent C. Butler, and Bill Latta, 1528–31. Nashville, TN: Holman Bible Publishers, 2003.

Bredfeldt, Gary J. *Great Leader, Great Teacher: Recovering the Biblical Vision for Leadership.* Chicago, IL: Moody, 2006.

Brown, Raymond E. "Diverse Views of the Spirit in the New Testament." *Worship* 77 (May 1983) 225–36.

———. *The Gospel According to John, XIII–XXI.* Anchor Bible 29. New York: Doubleday, 1970.

Bruce, F. F. *1 and 2 Thessalonians.* Waco, TX: Word, 1982.

———. *The Gospel of John: Introduction, Exposition, and Notes.* Grand Rapids, MI: Eerdmans, 1983.

———. *The Acts of the Apostles: The Greek Text with Introduction and Commentary.* 3d ed. Grand Rapids, MI: Eerdmans, 1990.

———. "The Holy Spirit in the Acts of the Apostles." *Interpretation* (1973) 166–183.

Brunner, Emil. *Vom Werk Desk Heilegn Geistes.* Zürich: Zwingli-Verlag Zürich, 1934.

Buchanan, James. *The Office and Work of the Holy Spirit.* New York: Robert Carter, 1847.

Büchsel, Friedrich. *Der Geist Gottes im Neuen Testament.* Gütersloh: Druck und Verlag von T. Bertelsmann, 1926.

Bullinger, E. W. *Word Studies on the Holy Spirit.* Grand Rapids, MI: Kregel, 1979.

Burgess, Stanley M. *The Holy Spirit: Ancient Christian Traditions.* Peabody, MS: Hendrickson, 1984.

———. *The Holy Spirit: Easter Christian Traditions.* Peabody, MS: Hendrickson, 1989.

———. *The Holy Spirit: Medieval Roman Catholic and Reformation Traditions.* Peabody, MS: Hendrickson, 1997.

Calvin, John. *Commentaries on the Epistles of Paul the Apostle to the Romans.* Translated by John Owen. Grand Rapids, MI: Eerdmans, 1948.

Canada, David. *Spiritual Leadership in the Small Membership Church.* Nashville, TN: Abingdon, 2005.

Carson, D. A. *The Cross and Christian Ministry: Leadership Lessons from 1 Corinthians.* Grand Rapids, MI: Baker, 1993.

———. *The Gospel According to John.* Pillar New Testament Commentary. Grand Rapids, MI: Eerdmans, 1991.

———. *Showing the Spirit: A Theological Exposition of 1 Corinthians 12-14*. Grand Rapids, MI: Baker, 1987.

———. "Systematic Theology and Biblical Theology." In *New Dictionary of Biblical Theology*, edited by T. Desmond Alexander, Brian S. Rosner, D. A. Carson, and Graeme Goldsworthy, 89–104. Downers Grove, IL: InterVarsity, 2000.

———. "When Is Spirituality Spiritual? Reflections on Some Problems of Definition." *Journal of the Evangelical Theology Society* 37 (1994) 381–94.

Carter, Charles W. *The Person and Ministry of the Holy Spirit: A Wesleyan Perspective*. Grand Rapids, MI: Baker, 1974.

Childs, Brevard S. *Isaiah*. Louisville, KY: Westminster John Knox, 2001.

Chisholm, Jr., Robert B. "The 'Spirit of the Lord' in 2 Kings 2:16." In *Presence, Power and Promise: The Role of the Spirit of God in the Old Testament*, edited by David G. Firth and Paul D. Wegner, 306–20. Downers Grove, IL: IVP Academic, 2011.

Chisholm, Jr., Robert B. "The Christological Fulfillment of Isaiah's Servant Songs." *Bibliotheca Sacra* 163 (October-December 2006) 387–404.

Cho, David Yonggi. *Spiritual Leadership for the New Millennium*. Seoul, Korea: Seoul Logos, 2002.

Cho, Youngmo. *Spirit and Kingdom in the Writings of Paul: An Attempt to Reconcile these Concepts*. Waynesboro, GA: Paternoster, 2005.

Ciampa, Roy E. and Brian S. Rosner. *The First letter to the Corinthians*. Pillar New Testament Commentary. Grand Rapids, MI: Eerdmans, 2010.

Clarke, Andrew D. *Called to Serve: A Pauline Theology of Leadership*. Edinburgh: T & T Clark, 2008.

———. "Leadership." In *New Dictionary of Biblical Theology*, edited by T. Desmond Alexander, Brian S. Rosner, D. A. Carson, and Graeme Goldsworthy, 636–40. Downers Grove, IL: InterVarsity, 2000.

Cockerill, Gareth Lee. *The Epistle to the Hebrews*. New International Commentary on the New Testament. Grand Rapids, MI: Eerdmans, 2012.

Cole, Graham A. *He Who Gives Life: The Doctrine of the Holy Spirit*. Wheaton, IL: Crossway, 2007.

Combs, William W. "The Biblical Role of the Evangelist." *Detroit Baptist Seminary Journal* 7 (2002) 23–48.

Compton, R. Bruce. "1 Corinthians 13:8-13 and the Cessation of Miraculous Gifts." *Detroit Baptist Seminary Journal* 9 (2004) 97–144.

Conzelmann Hans. *Acts of the Apostles*. Hermeneia. Minneapolis, MN: Fortress, 1987.

Copan, Victor. *Saint Paul as Spiritual Director: An Analysis of the Concept of the Imitation of Paul with Implications and Applications to the Practice of Spiritual Direction*. Paternoster Biblical Monographs. Milton Keynes: Paternoster, 2007.

Cotton, Roger. 2001. Numbers 11 and Doing a Pentecostal, Biblical Theology of Church Leadership. Faculty Working Paper, 2001, Assemblies of God Theological Seminary. http://www.agts.edu/faculty/faculty_publications/articles/cotton_numbers_11.pdf.

———. "The Pentecostal Significance of Numbers 11." *The Journal of Pentecostal Theology* 10 (October 2001) 3–10. http://www.agts.edu/faculty/faculty_publications/articles/cotton_nu11.pdf.

Csövek, Tamas. *Three Seasons of Charismatic Leadership: A Literary-Critical and Theological Interpretation of the Narrative of Saul, David and Solomon*. Milton Keynes, UK: Regnum, 2006.

Cumming, James Elder. *Through the Eternal Spirit*. Chicago, IL: Fleming H. Revell, 1896.

BIBLIOGRAPHY

Davids, Peter H. *The First Epistle of Peter*. New International Commentary on the New Testament. Grand Rapids, MI: Eerdmans, 1990.

De Kock, Wynand J. "Empowerment Through Engagement—Pentecostal Power for a Pentecostal Task." *Ex Auditu* 12 (1996) 136–146.

Deere, Jack. *Surprised by the Power of the Spirit*. Grand Rapids, MI: Zondervan, 1993.

Dever, Mark. *Nine Marks of a Healthy Church*. Wheaton, IL: Crossway, 2000.

Dodd, C. H. *The Interpretation of the Fourth Gospel*. New York: Cambridge University Press, 1953. Reprint, Gateshead: Athenaeum Press, 1995.

Dorman, Ted M. "Holy Spirit, History, Hermeneutics and Theology: Toward an Evangelical/Catholic Consensus." *Journal of the Evangelical Theology Society* 41 (1998) 427–38.

Du Rand, Jan A. "'. . . Let Him Hear What the Spirit Says . . .': the Functional Role and Theological Meaning of the Spirit in the Book of Revelation." *Ex Auditu* 12 (1996) 43–58.

Duffield, Guy P., and Nathaniel M. Van Cleave. *Foundations of Pentecostal Theology*. Los Angeles: L.I.F.E. Bible College, 1983.

Dumbrell, William J. "Spirit and Kingdom of God in the Old Testament." *Reformed Theological Review* 33 (January–April 1974) 1–10.

Dunlop, Jamie. "Deacons: Shock-Absorbers and Servants." *9Marks Journal* (May–June 2010) 5–7.

Dunn, James D. G. "Spirit, Holy Spirit." In *New Bible Dictionary*, edited by D. R. W. Wood and I. Howard Marshall, 1125–29. Downers Grove, IL: InterVarsity, 1996.

———. *Pneumatology*. Vol. 2 in *The Christ and the Spirit*. Grand Rapids, MI: Eerdmans, 1998.

———. *Romans 9–16*. Word Biblical Commentary 38. Nashville, TN: Thomas Nelson, 1988.

Dunnett, Walter M. "Scholarship and Spirituality." *Journal of the Evangelical Theology Society* 31 (1988) 1–7.

Easley, Kendell H. "The Pauline Usage of *Pneumati* as a Reference to the Spirit of God." *Journal of the Evangelical Theology Society* 27 (1984) 299–313.

Edgar, Thomas R. *Miraculous Gifts: Are They For Today?* Eugene, OR: Wipf and Stock, 1983.

———. *Satisfied by the Promise of the Spirit*. Grand Rapids, MI: Kregel, 1996.

Edwards, James R. "The Baptism of Jesus According to the Gospel of Mark." *Journal of the Evangelical Theology Society* 34 (1991) 43–57.

———. "The Servant of the Lord and the Gospel of Mark." *Southern Baptist Journal of Theology* 8 (Fall 2004) 36–49.

Elbert, Paul. "Calvin and the Spiritual Gifts." *Journal of the Evangelical Theology Society* 22 (1979) 235–56.

Ellis, Earle E. "Coworkers, Paul and His." In *Dictionary of Paul and His Letters*, edited by Gerald F. Hawthorne, Ralph P. Martin, and Daniel G. Reid, 183–88. Downers Grove, IL: InterVarsity, 1993.

Elwell, Walter A., and Philip Wesley Comfort. "Spiritual Gifts." In *Tyndale Bible Dictionary*, edited by Walter A. Elwell and Philip Wesley Comfort, 1222–23. Wheaton, IL: Tyndale, 2001.

Engelhard, David H. "Anointing." In *ISBE* 1:129. Grand Rapids, MI: Eerdmans, 1988.

Erickson, Millard J. *Christian Theology*. 2nd ed. Grand Rapids, MI: Baker, 1998.

BIBLIOGRAPHY

Erickson, Richard J. "The Jailing of John and the Baptism of Jesus." *Journal of the Evangelical Theology Society* 36 (1993) 455–66.

Estes, Daniel J. "Spirit and Psalmist in Psalm 51." In *Presence, Power and Promise: The Role of the Spirit of God in the Old Testament*, edited by David G. Firth and Paul D. Wegner, 122–34. Downers Grove, IL: IVP Academic, 2011.

Evans, Craig A. "How Are the Apostles Judged? A Note on 1 Corinthians 3:10–15." *Journal of the Evangelical Theology Society* 27 (1984) 149–50.

———. "New Testament Use of the Old Testament." Pages 72–80 in *New Dictionary of Biblical Theology*. Edited by T. Desmond Alexander, Brian S. Rosner, D. A. Carson, and Graeme Goldsworthy. Downers Grove, IL: InterVarsity, 2000.

Fee, Gordon D. *1 and 2 Timothy, Titus*. New International Biblical Commentary 13. Peabody, MS: Hendrickson, 1988.

———. "Gifts of the Spirit." Pages 339–47 in *Dictionary of Paul and His Letters*. Edited by Gerald F. Hawthorne, Ralph P. Martin, and Daniel G. Reid. Downers Grove, IL: InterVarsity, 1993.

———. *God's Empowering Presence: The Holy Spirit in the Letters of Paul*. Peabody, MS: Hendrickson, 1994.

———. *Paul's Letter to the Philippians*. New International Commentary on the New Testament. Grand Rapids, MI: Eerdmans, 1995.

———. *The First and Second Epistles to the Thessalonians*. New International Commentary on the New Testament. Grand Rapids, MI: Eerdmans, 2009.

———. *The First Epistle to the Corinthians*. New International Commentary on the New Testament. Grand Rapids, MI: Eerdmans, 1987.

Feinberg, John S., ed. *Continuity and Discontinuity (Essays in Honor of S. Lewis Johnson, Jr.) Perspectives on the Relationship Between the Old and New Testaments*. Wheaton, IL: Crossway, 1988.

Ferguson, Sinclair. *The Holy Spirit*. Downers Grove, IL: InterVarsity, 1997.

Ficek, Jerome L. "The Doctrine of the Holy Spirit in Contemporary Thought." *Bulletin of the Evangelical Theology Society* 3 (1960) 70–75.

Firor, Warfield M. "Fulfillment of Promise: The Holy Spirit and the Christian Life." *Interpretation* (July 1953) 299–314.

Firth, David G. "Is Saul Also Among the Prophets? Saul's Prophecy in 1 Samuel 19:23." In *Presence, Power and Promise: The Role of the Spirit of God in the Old Testament*, edited by David G. Firth and Paul D. Wegner, 294–305. Downers Grove, IL: IVP Academic, 2011.

———. "The Spirit and Leadership: Testimony, Empowerment and Purpose." In *Presence, Power and Promise: The Role of the Spirit of God in the Old Testament*, edited by David G. Firth and Paul D. Wegner, 259–80. Downers Grove, IL: IVP Academic, 2011.

Fitzmyer, Joseph A. *Romans*. The Anchor Bible 33. New York: Doubleday, 1993.

———. *The Gospel According to Luke X–XXIV*. Anchor Bible 28A. New York: Doubleday, 1985.

Fleming, Daniel E. "Anointing." In *Dictionary of the Old Testament: Historical Books*, edited by Bill T. Arnold and Hugh G. M. Williamson, 32–36. Downers Grove, IL: InterVarsity, 2005.

France, R. T. *The Gospel of Mark*. Grand Rapids, MI: Eerdmans, 2002.

———. *The Gospel of Matthew*. New International Commentary on the New Testament. Grand Rapids, MI: Eerdmans, 2007.

———. "Servant of the Lord." Pages 1092–94 in *New Bible Dictionary*. 2d ed. Edited by D. R. W. Wood and I. Howard Marshall. Downers Grove, IL: InterVarsity, 1982.

———. "The Servant Of The Lord In The Teaching Of Jesus." *Tyndale Bulletin* 19 (1968) 26–52.

Fredericks, Gary. "Rethinking the Role of the Holy Spirit in the Lives of Old Testament Believers." *Trinity Journal* 9 (Spring 1988) 81–104.

Furnish, Victor Paul. *II Corinthians*. Anchor Bible 32A. New York: Doubleday, 1984.

Gaffin, Jr., Richard B. "'Life-Giving Spirit': Probing the Center of Paul's Pneumatology." *Journal of the Evangelical Theology Society* 41 (1998) 573–89.

Gaffin, Richard B. *Perspectives on Pentecost*. Phillipsburg, N. J.: P&R, 1979.

Gangel, Kenneth O. "Biblical Theology of Leadership." *Christian Education Journal* 12 (1991) 13–31.

Garland, David E. "The Christian's Posture Toward Marriage and Celibacy: 1 Corinthians 7." *Review and Expositor* 80 (1983) 351–60.

———. *1 Corinthians*. Baker Exegetical Commentary on the New Testament. Grand Rapids, MI: Baker Academic, 2003.

———. *2 Corinthians*. New American Commentary 29. Broadman & Holman, 1999.

Gaventa, Beverly Roberts. "Pentecost and Trinity." *Interpretation* 66 (January 2012) 5–15.

Geldenhuys, . *The Gospel of Luke*. New International Commentary on the New Testament. Grand Rapids, MI: Eerdmans, 1968.

Geoffrion, Timothy C. *The Spirit-Led Leader: Nine Leadership Practices and Soul Principles*. Herndon, VA: The Alban Institute, 2005.

George, Timothy. *Galatians*. New American Commentary 30. Nashville, TN: Broadman & Holman, 1994.

Gipe, William. "Between Text & Sermon: Numbers 11:24–30." *Interpretation* 56 (2002) 196–98.

Goldberg, Louis. "Preaching with Power the Word 'Correctly Handled' to Transform Man and His World." *Journal of the Evangelical Theology Society* 15 (1972) 3–17.

Goldingay, John. "Was the Holy Spirit Active in Old Testament Times? What Was New About the Christian Experience of God?" *Ex Auditu* 12 (1996) 14–28.

Goldsworthy, Graham. "Relationship of Old Testament and New Testament." Pages 81–89 in *New Dictionary of Biblical Theology*. Edited by T. Desmond Alexander, Brian S. Rosner, D. A. Carson, and Graeme Goldsworthy. Downers Grove, IL: InterVarsity, 2000.

Graham, Stephen R. "'Thus Saith the Lord': Biblical Hermeneutics in the Early Pentecostal Movement." *Ex Auditu* 12 (1996) 121–135.

Green, Gene L. *The Letters to the Thessalonians*. Pillar New Testament Commentary. Grand Rapids; Eerdmans, 2002.

Green, Joel B. *1 Peter*. Grand Rapids, MI: Eerdmans, 2007.

———. *The Gospel of Luke*. New International Commentary on the New Testament. Grand Rapids, MI: Eerdmans, 1997.

Green, Michael. *I Believe in the Holy Spirit*. Rev. ed. Grand Rapids, MI: Eerdmans, 2004.

Grenz, Stanley J. "The Holy Spirit: Divine Love Guiding Us Home." *Ex Auditu* 12 (1996) 1–13.

Grindel, John. "Matthew 12,18–21." *Catholic Bible Quarterly* 29 (1967) 110–15.

Gromacki, Robert. *The Holy Spirit*. Nashville, TN: Word, 1999.

Grogan, Geoffrey W. "Isaiah." In *Proverbs-Isaiah*, Expositor's Bible Commentary 6, edited by Tremper Longman III and David E. Garland, 433–863. Grand Rapids, MI: Zondervan, 2008.

———. "Prophecy—Yes, But Teaching—No: Paul's Consistent Advocacy of Women's Participation without Governing Authority." *Journal of the Evangelical Theology Society* 30 (1987) 11–23.

———. *Systematic Theology*. Grand Rapids, MI: Zondervan, 1994.

———. *The Gift of Prophecy in the New Testament and Today*. Westchester, IL: Crossway, 1988.

Gundry, Robert H. *Matthew*. Grand Rapids, MI: Eerdmans, 1982.

Hafemann, Scott. "The 'Temple of the Spirit' as the Inaugural Fulfillment of the New Covenant within the Corinthian Correspondence." *Ex Auditu* 12 (1996) 29–42.

Hagner, Donald A. *Matthew 1–13*. Word Biblical Commentary 33A. Dallas, TX: Word, 1998.

Hailey, Homer. *A Commentary on Isaiah with Emphasis on the Messianic Hope*. Grand Rapids, MI: Baker, 1985.

Hamilton, Jr., James M. "God with Men in the Prophets and the Writings: an Examination of the Nature of God's Presence." *Scottish Bulletin of Evangelical Theology* 23.2 (2005) 166–193.

———. "God with Men in the Torah." *Westminster Theological Journal* 65 (2003) 113–33.

———. "Old Covenant Believers and the Indwelling Spirit: A Survey of the Spectrum of Opinion." *Trinity Journal* 24 (Spring 2003) 37–54.

———. *God's Indwelling Presence: The Holy Spirit in the Old and New Testaments*. Nashville, TN: Broadman, 2006.

Hansen, G. Walter. *The Letter to the Philippians*. Pillar New Testament Commentary. Grand Rapids, MI: Eerdmans, 2009.

Haroutunian, Joseph. "Spirit, Holy Spirit, Spiritism." *Ex Auditu* 12 (1996) 59–75.

Harris, Murray J. *The Second Epistle to the Corinthians: A Commentary on the Greek Text*. New International Greek Testament Commentary. Grand Rapids; Eerdmans, 2005.

Harvey, John D. *Anointed with Spirit and Power: The Holy Spirit's Empowering Presence*. Phillipsburg, NJ: P&R Publishing, 2008.

Hawthorne, Gerald F. *Ephesians*. Word Biblical Commentary 43. Waco, TX: Word, 1983.

———. *The Presence and the Power: The Significance of the Spirit in the Life and Ministry of Jesus*. Dallas, TX: Word, 1991.

———. *The Significance of the Spirit in the Life of Christ*. MA thesis, Wheaton College, 1954.

———. "Timothy." In of *ISBE* 1:857–58. Grand Rapids, MI: Eerdmans, 1988.

Hawthorne, Gerald F. *Philippians*. Word Biblical Commentary 43. Dallas, TX: Word, 2004.

Hendry, George S. *The Holy Spirit in Christian Theology*. Philadelphia: Westminster, 1956.

Henebury Paul Martin. "The Holy Spirit in the Old Testament." *Conservative Theological Journal* 9 (December 2005) 351–69.

Hess, Richard S. "Bezalel and Oholiab: Spirit and Creativity." In *Presence, Power and Promise: The Role of the Spirit of God in the Old Testament*, edited by David G. Firth and Paul D. Wegner, 161–74. Downers Grove, IL: IVP Academic, 2011.

———. "Joshua." In *New Dictionary of Biblical Theology*, edited by T. Desmond Alexander, Brian S. Rosner, D. A. Carson, and Graeme Goldsworthy, 165–71. Downers Grove, IL: InterVarsity, 2000.

Hildebrandt, Wilf. *An Old Testament Theology of the Spirit of God.* Peabody, MS: Hendrickson, 1995.

Hinson, E. Glenn. *Spiritual Preparation for Christian Leadership.* Nashville, TN: Upper Room, 1999.

Hoehner, Harold W. "Can a Woman Be a Pastor-Teacher?" *Journal of the Evangelical Theology Society* 50 (2007) 761–71.

———. *Ephesians: An Exegetical Commentary.* Grand Rapids, MI: Baker Academic, 2002.

Horne, Charles M. "The Power of Paul's Preaching." *Bulletin of the Evangelical Theological Society* 8 (1965) 111–16.

Horton, Stanley M. *What the Bible Says about the Holy Spirit.* Springfield, MO: Gospel Publishing House, 1976.

House, Paul R. *1, 2 Kings.* New American Commentary 8. Nashville, TN: Broadman & Holman, 1995.

Howard, David M. "The Transfer of Power from Saul to David in 1 Sam 16:13-14." *Journal of the Evangelical Theology Society* 32 (1989) 473–83.

Howell, Jr., Don N. *Servants of the Servant: A Biblical Theology of Leadership.* Eugene, OR: Wipf & Stock, 2003.

Hughes, Kent. *Disciplines of a Godly Man.* Wheaton, IL: Crossway, 1991.

Hughes, Paul E. "Moses." In *New Dictionary of Biblical Theology*, edited by T. Desmond Alexander, Brian S. Rosner, D. A. Carson, and Graeme Goldsworthy, 668–73. Downers Grove, IL: InterVarsity, 2000.

Hughes, Philip Edgcumbe. *A Commentary on the Epistle to the Hebrews.* Grand Rapids, MI: Eerdmans, 1977.

Huther, John E. and Göttlieb Lünemann. *Critical and Exegetical Hand-book to the Epistle to the Epistles to Timothy and Titus and to the Hebrews.* Translated by David Hunter. New York: Funk & Wagnalls, 1885.

Hybels, Bill. *Courageous Leadership.* Grand Rapids, MI: Zondervan, 2002.

Inch, Morris A. *Saga of the Spirit: A Biblical, Systematic, and Historical Theology of the Holy Spirit.* Grand Rapids, MI: Baker, 1985.

Ingold, John. "A Deacon on a Deacon's Reward." *9Marks Journal* (May–June 2010) 25–27.

Jackson, Don. "Luke and Paul: A Theology of One Spirit from Two Perspectives." *Journal of the Evangelical Theological Society* 32 (September 1989) 335–43.

Jewett, Robert. *Romans.* Hermeneia. Minneapolis, MN: Fortress, 2007.

Jobes, Karen H. *1 Peter.* Baker Exegetical Commentary on the New Testament. Grand Rapids, MI: Baker Academic, 2005.

Johnson, Benjamin J. M. "What Type of Son Is Samson? Reading Judges 13 as a Biblical Type-Scene." *Journal of the Evangelical Theology Society* 53 (2010) 269–86.

Johnson, Dennis E. "Jesus Against the Idols: The Use of Isaianic Servant Songs in the Missiology of Acts." *Westminster Theological Journal* 52 (1990) 343–53.

Johnston, Robert K. "God in the Midst of Life: The spirit and Spirit." *Ex Auditu* 12 (1996) 76–93.

Kaiser, Jr., Walter C. "A Neglected Text in Bibliology Discussions: 1 Corinthians. 2:6–16," *Westminster Theological Journal* 43 (1981) 301–19.

———. "The Old Promise and the New Covenant: Jeremiah 31:31–34." *Journal of the Evangelical Theology Society* 15 (1972) 11–23.

———, Peter H. Davids, F. F. Bruce, and Manfred T. Brauch. *Hard Sayings of the Bible.* Downers Grove, IL: InterVarsity, 1996.

BIBLIOGRAPHY

Keener, Craig S. *Gift Giver: The Holy Spirit for Today*. Grand Rapids, MI: Baker Academic, 2001.

———. *A Commentary on the Gospel of Matthew*. Grand Rapids, MI: Eerdmans, 1999.

———. *The Gospel of John*. 2 vols. Peabody, MS: Hendrickson, 2003.

———. *A Commentary on the Gospel of Matthew*. Grand Rapids, MI: Eerdmans, 1999.

Kenadjian, C. Glenn. "Is the Doctrine That God Is Spirit an Incoherent Concept?" *Journal of the Evangelical Theology Society* 31 (1988) 191-202.

Kistemaker, Simon J. *Exposition of the First Epistle to the Corinthians*. New Testament Commentary 18. Grand Rapids, MI: Baker, 1993.

Kline, Meredith G. *Images of the Spirit*. Grand Rapids, MI: Baker, 1980.

Klink III, Edward W. and Darian R. Lockett. *Understanding Biblical Theology: A Comparison of Theory and Practice*. Grand Rapids, MI: Zondervan, 2012.

Knight, George W. *The Pastoral Epistles: A Commentary on the Greek Text*. New International Greek Testament Commentary. Grand Rapids; Eerdmans, 1992.

Koester, Craig R. *Hebrews*. Anchor Bible 36. New York: Doubleday, 2001.

Konsmo, Erik. *The Pauline Metaphors of the Holy Spirit: The Intangible Presence in the Life of the Christian*. Studies in Biblical Literature 130. New York: Peter Lang, 2010.

Köstenberger, Andreas J. "1-2 Timothy, Titus." In *Ephesians-Philemon*. Vol. 12 of the Expositor's Bible Commentary: 2d ed., edited by David E. Garland and Tremper Longman III, 487-625. Grand Rapids, MI: Zondervan, 2006.

———. *A Theology of John's Gospel and Letters*. Grand Rapids, MI: Zondervan, 2009.

———. *Excellence*. Wheaton, IL: Crossway, 2011.

———. *John*. Baker Exegetical Commentary on the New Testament. Grand Rapids, MI: Baker, 2004.

———. "Mission." Pages 663-68 in *New Dictionary of Biblical Theology*. Edited by T. Desmond Alexander, Brian S. Rosner, D. A. Carson, and Graeme Goldsworthy. Downers Grove, IL: InterVarsity, 2000.

———. *The Missions of Jesus and the Disciples according to the Fourth Gospel*. Grand Rapids, MI: Eerdmans, 1998.

———. "The Challenge of a Systematized Biblical Theology: Missiological Insights from the Gospel of John." *Missiology* 23 (1995) 445-64.

———. "The Present and Future of Biblical Theology." *Themelios* 37 (2012) 445-64.

——— and Peter T. Obrien. *Salvation to the Ends of the Earth*. New Studies in Biblical Theology 11. Downers Grove, IL: Intervarsity, 2001.

———. "What Does It Mean to Be Filled with the Spirit? A Biblical Investigation." *Journal of the Evangelical Theological Society* 40 (June 1997) 229-40.

——— and Richard D. Patterson. *Biblical Interpretation: Exploring the Hermeneutical Triad of History, Literature, and Theology*. Grand Rapids, MI: Kregel, 2011.

Kruse, Colin G. *Paul's Letter to the Romans*. Pillar New Testament Commentary. Grand Rapids, MI: Eerdmans, 2012.

Kuyper, Abraham. *The Work of the Holy Spirit*. New York: Funk & Wagnalls, 1900.

Kydd, Ronald A. N. *Charismatic Gifts in the Early Church*. Peabody, MS: Hendrickson, 1984.

Lampe, G. W. H. "'Grievous Wolves' (Acts 20:29)," In *Christ and Spirit in the New Testament*, edited by Barnabas Lindars and Stephen S. Smalley, 253-68. London: Cambridge University Press, 1973.

Larkin, Jr., William J. *Acts*. InterVarsity Press New Testament Commentary 5. Downers Grove, IL: InterVarsity, 1995.

Land, Steven J. "Be Filled with the Spirit: the Nature and Evidence of Spiritual Fulness." *Ex Auditu* 12 (1996) 108–120.
Lane, William L. *Hebrews 1–8*. Word Biblical Commentary 47A. Dallas, TX: Word, 1991.
Laniak, Timothy S. *Shepherds after My own Heart: Pastoral Traditions and Leadership in the Bible*. New Studies in Biblical Theology 20. Downers Grove, IL: InterVarsity, 2006.
Leeper, Gregory J. "The Nature of the Pentecostal Gift with Special Reference to Numbers 11 and Acts 2." *Asian Journal of Pentecostal Studies* 6 (2003) 23–38.
Lenski, R. C. H. *The Interpretation of St. Luke's Gospel*. Minneapolis, MI: Augsburg, 1946.
———. *The Interpretation of St. Paul's First and Second Epistle to the Corinthians*. Columbus, Ohio: Wartburg, 1946.
Levison, John R. "The Spirit, Simeon, and the Songs of the Servant." In *The Spirit and Christ in the New Testament & Christian Theology*, edited by I. Howard Marshall, Volker Rabens, and Cornelis Bennema, 18–34. Grand Rapids, MI: Eerdmans, 2012.
Lewis, Edwin. "God With Man: The Biblical Doctrine of the Holy Spirit." *Interpretation* (July 1953) 281–298.
Lim, Timothy H. "'Not in persuasive words of wisdom, but in the demonstration of the Spirit and power' (I Cor. 2:4)." *Novum Testamentum* 29 (1987) 137–49.
Lincoln, Andrew T. *Ephesians*. Word Biblical Commentary 42. Nashville, TN: Thomas Nelson, 1990.
Lingenfelter, Sherwood G. *Leading Cross-Culturally, Covenant Relationships for Effective Christian Leadership*. Grand Rapids, MI: Baker Academic, 2008.
Longman, Tremper III and David E. Garland, eds. *Ephesians—Philemon*. The Expositor's Bible Commentary 12. 2d ed. Grand Rapids, MI: Zondervan, 2006.
Luz, Ulrich. *Matthew 8–20*. Hermeneia. Minneapolis, MN: Fortress, 2001.
MacArthur, John F. *Charismatic Chaos*. Grand Rapids, MI: Zondervan, 1992.
———. *The Power of Integrity: Building a Life without Compromise*. Wheaton, IL: Crossway, 1997.
Mare, W. Harold. "Prophet and Teacher in the New Testament Period." *Bulletin of the Evangelical Theological Society* 9 (1966) 139–48.
Marlow, Hilary. "The Spirit of Yahweh in Isaiah 11:1–9," In *Presence, Power and Promise: The Role of the Spirit of God in the Old Testament*, edited by David G. Firth and Paul D. Wegner, 220–33. Downers Grove, IL: IVP Academic, 2011.
Marshall, I. Howard. *The Gospel of Luke: A Commentary on the Greek Text*. New International Greek Testament Commentary. Exeter: Paternoster Press, 1978.
———. *A Critical and Exegetical Commentary on the Pastoral Epistles*. International Critical Commentary. T&T Clark: Edinburgh, 1999.
Martin, D. Michael. *1, 2 Thessalonians*. New American Commentary 33. Nashville, TN: Broadman & Holman, 2002.
Mayhue, Richard L. "Authentic Spiritual Leadership." *Master's Seminary Journal* 22 (2011) 213–224.
McCabe, Robert V. "Were Old Testament Believers Indwelt by the Spirit?" *Detroit Baptist Seminary Journal* 9 (2004) 215–64.
McCune, Kevin L. "Theocratic Anointing in the Old Testament." ThM thesis, Grace Theological Seminary, 1984.
McCune, Rolland. *A Systematic Theology of Biblical Christianity, Volume 2: The Doctrines of Man, Sin, Christ, and the Holy Spirit*. Allen Park, MI: Detroit Baptist Theological Seminary, 2009.

McDonald, Hugh D. "Authority." In *The Zondervan Encyclopedia of the Bible*, edited by Moisés Silva and Merril C. Tenney, 1:451–52. Grand Rapids, MI: Zondervan, 2009.

McHugh, John F. *John 1–4*. The International Critical Commentary. New York: T&T Clark, 2009.

McIntosh, John. "'For it seemed good to the Holy Spirit' Acts 15:28. How did the members of the Jerusalem Council *know* this?" *Reformed Theological Review* 61 (2002) 131–47.

McNeal, Reggie. *Practicing Greatness: 7 Disciplines of Extraordinary Spiritual Leaders*. San Francisco, CA: Jossey-Bass, 2006.

———. *A Work of Heart: Understanding How God Shapes Spiritual Leaders*. San Francisco, CA: Jossey-Bass, 2000.

Menzies, William W. "The Holy Spirit in Christian Theology." *Perspectives on Evangelical Theology: Papers from the thirtieth annual meeting of the Evangelical Theological Society*, edited by Kenneth S. Kantzer and Stanley N. Gundry, 67–79. Grand Rapids, MI: Baker, 1979.

Merkle, Ben. *40 Questions About Elders and Deacons*. Grand Rapids, MI: Kregel, 2007.

———. "Must We Use the Titles 'Elder' and 'Deacon'?" *9Marks Journal* (May–June 2010) 12–13.

———. "The Biblical Qualifications and Responsibilities of Deacons," *9Marks Journal* (May–June 2010) 8–11.

———. *The Elder and Overseer: One Office in the Early Church*. New York: Peter Lang, 2003.

Merrill, Eugene, H. "The Samson Saga and Spiritual Leadership." In *Presence, Power and Promise: The Role of the Spirit of God in the Old Testament*, edited by David G. Firth and Paul D. Wegner, 281–93. Downers Grove, IL: IVP Academic, 2011.

Meyer, Heinrich August Wilhelm. *Critical and Exegetical Hand-book to the Epistles to the Corinthians*. New York: Funk & Wagnalls, 1884.

Mitchell, Margaret M. *Paul and the Rhetoric of Reconciliation: An Exegetical Investigation of the Language and Composition of 1 Corinthians*. Louisville, KY: Westminster/John Knox, 1991.

Michaels, J. Ramsey. *1 Peter*. Word Biblical Commentary 49. Waco, TX: Word, 1988.

Montague, George T. *The Holy Spirit: Growth of a Biblical Tradition*. New York: Paulist, 1976.

Moo, Douglas J. *The Epistle to the Romans*. New International Commentary on the New Testament. Grand Rapids, MI: Eerdmans, 1996.

Morgan, G. Campbell. *The Spirit of God*. New York: Fleming H. Revell, 1900.

Morris, Leon. *The Epistle to the Romans*. Pillar New Testament Commentary. Grand Rapids, MI: Eerdmans, 1988.

———. *The Gospel According to Matthew*. Pillar New Testament Commentary. Grand Rapids, MI: Eerdmans, 1992.

Motyer, J. Alec. *Isaiah*. Tyndale Old Testament Commentaries 18. Downers Grove, IL: InterVarsity, 1999.

Mounce, Robert H. *Romans*. New American Commentary 27. Nashville, TN: Broadman & Holman, 1995.

Mounce, William D. *Pastoral Epistles*. Word Biblical Commentary 46. Dallas, TX: Word, 2000.

Nelson, Peter K. *Leadership and Discipleship: A Study of Luke 22:24–30*. Atlanta: Scholars Press, 1994.

Newton, Phil A. *Elders in Congregational Life: Rediscovering the Biblical Model for Church Leadership.* Grand Rapids, MI: Kregel, 2005.

———. "Moving From a Deacon-Led to an Elder-Led Church." *9Marks Journal* (May–June 2010) 19–21.

Neve, Richard. "Realized Eschatology in Psalm 51." *Expository Times* (1969) 264–66.

Neyrey, J. H. "The Thematic Use of Isaiah 42, 1–4 in Matthew 12." *Biblica* 63 (1982) 457–73.

Niehaus, Jeffrey J. "Joshua and Ancient Near Eastern Warfare." *Journal of the Evangelical Theology Society* 31 (1988) 37–50.

Nolland, John. *Luke 1:9–20.* Word Biblical Commentary 35. Dallas, TX: Word, 1989.

———. *The Gospel of Matthew.* Grand Rapids, MI: Eerdmans, 2005.

Nuttall, Geoffrey F. "Spirit of Power and Love: The Biblical Doctrine of the Holy Spirit" *Interpretation* (January 1950) 24–35.

Oke, C. Clare. "Paul's Method Not a Demonstration but an Exhibition of the Spirit." *The Expository Times* 67 (1955) 35–36.

Osborne, Grant R. *Romans.* Downers Grove, IL: InterVarsity, 2004.

Oswalt, John. *The Book of Isaiah: Chapters 1–39.* New International Commentary on the Old Testament. Grand Rapids, MI: Eerdmans, 1986.

———. *The Book of Isaiah: Chapters 40–66.* New International Commentary on the Old Testament. Grand Rapids, MI: Eerdmans, 1998.

Owen, John. *The Holy Spirit.* Carlisle, PA: Banner of Truth Trust, 1998.

Packer, J. I. "Holy Spirit." Pages 316–19 in *New Dictionary of Theology.* Edited by Sinclair B. Ferguson, and J. I. Packer. Downers Grove, IL: InterVarsity, 1988.

———. *Keep in Step with the Spirit.* Leicester, England: Inter-Varsity, 1984.

Palmer, Edwin. *The Holy Spirit: His Person and Ministry.* Phillipsburg, NJ: P&R, 1985.

Pierson, A. T. *The Acts of the Holy Spirit.* New York: Fleming H. Revell, 1895.

Pervo, Richard I. *Acts.* Hermeneia. Minneapolis, MN: Fortress, 2009.

Peterson, David G. *The Acts of the Apostles.* Pillar New Testament Commentary. Grand Rapids, MI: Eerdmans, 2009.

Peterson, David G. *Possessed by God: A New Testament Theology of Sanctification and Holiness.* New Studies in Biblical Theology 1. Downers Grove: InterVarsity, 2001.

———. *The Acts of the Apostles.* Pillar New Testament Commentary. Grand Rapids, MI: Eerdmans, 2009.

Pettegrew, Larry D. "The New Covenant." *The Master's Seminary Journal* (Fall 1999) 251–70.

———. *The New Covenant Ministry of the Holy Spirit.* Revised ed. Grand Rapids, MI: Kregel, 2001.

Pinnock, Clark. "The Role of the Spirit in Interpretation." *Journal of the Evangelical Theology Society* 36 (1993) 491–97.

Polhill, John B. *Acts.* New American Commentary 26. Nashville, TN: Broadman & Holman, 1995.

Poythress, Vern S. "Linguistic and Sociological Analyses of Modern Tongues-Speaking: Their Contributions and Limitations." *Westminster Theological Journal* 42 (1980) 367–88.

———. "Modern Spiritual Gifts as Analogous to Apostolic Gifts: Affirming Extraordinary Works of the Spirit within Cessationist Theology." *Journal of the Evangelical Theological Society* 41 (1996) 71–101.

BIBLIOGRAPHY

———. "The Nature of Corinthian Glossolalia: Possible Options." *Westminster Theological Journal* 40 (1977) 130–35.

Preiss, Théo. *Das Innere Zeugnis des heiligen Geistes. Heft 21. Theologische Studien: Eine Schriftenreihe herausgegeben von Karl Barth.* Zürich: Evangelischer Verlag U. G., 1947.

———. "The Inner Witness of the Holy Spirit: The Doctrine of the Holy Spirit and Scripture." *Interpretation* (July 1953) 259–280.

Pretlove, John. "John 20:22—Help from Dry Bones?" *Criswell Theological Review* 3 (2005) 93–101.

Preus, Robert. "The Doctrine of Revelation in Contemporary Theology." *Bulletin of the Evangelical Theological Society* 9 (1966) 111–23.

Pritchard, Ray. *Names of the Holy Spirit.* Chicago, IL: Moody, 1995.

Putnam, W. G. "Spiritual Gifts." In *New Bible Dictionary*, 3rd ed, edited by D. R. W. Wood and I. Howard Marshall, 1130–31. Downers Grove, IL: InterVarsity, 1996.

Radmacher, Earl D. *The Nature of the Church.* Portland, OR: Western Baptist Press, 1972.

Ramm, Bernard. *Rapping about the Spirit.* Waco, TX: Word, 1974.

Rea, John. *The Holy Spirit in the Bible: All the Major Passages about the Spirit: A Commentary.* Lake Mary, FL: Creation House, 1990.

Richards, George W. "Spirit-Filled: 'And they were all fuled with the Holy Spirit'—ACTS 2:4 'Be filled with the Holy Spirit'—EPHESIANS 5:18." *Interpretation* (January 1950) 36–39.

Robeck, Cecil M. Jr. "Knowledge, Gift of Knowledge." In *Dictionary of Paul and His Letters*, edited by Gerald F. Hawthorne, Ralph P. Martin, and Daniel G. Reid, 526–28. Downers Grove, IL: InterVarsity, 1993.

Rosner, Brian S. "Biblical Theology." In *New Dictionary of Biblical Theology*, edited by T. Desmond Alexander, Brian S. Rosner, D. A. Carson, and Graeme Goldsworthy, 3–11. Downers Grove, IL: InterVarsity, 2000.

Russell, Walt. "The Anointing with the Holy Spirit in Luke-Acts." *Trinity Journal* 7 (Spring 1986) 47–63.

Ruether, Rosemary and Eleanor McLaughlin, eds. *Women of Spirit: Female Leadership in the Jewish and Christian Traditions.* New York: Simon and Schuster, 1979.

Ryrie, Charles C. *Dispensationalism.* 2d ed. Chicago, IL: Moody, 1995.

———. *The Holy Spirit.* Chicago, IL: Moody, 1997.

Sanders, Oswald. *Spiritual Leadership.* Chicago, IL: Moody, 1994.

Satterthwaite, Philip E. "Biblical History." In *New Dictionary of Biblical Theology*, edited by T. Desmond Alexander, Brian S. Rosner, D. A. Carson, and Graeme Goldsworthy, 43–51. Downers Grove, IL: InterVarsity, 2000.

Saucy, Mark R. "The Role of the Spirit in the Social Ethics of the Kingdom." *Journal of the Evangelical Theology Society* 54 (March 2011) 89–108.

Schlütz, Karl. *Isaias 11, 2 (Die Sieben Gaben des Hl. Geistes) In Den Ersten Vier Christlichen Jahrhunderten.* Münster: Verlag der Aschendorffschen Verlagsbuchhandlugh, 1932.

Schmucker, Matt. "How to Separate Deacon Work from Elder Work." *9Marks Journal* (May–June 2010) 22–24.

———. "The Committee-Free, Task-Specific Deacon." *9Marks Journal* (May–June 2010) 15–17.

Schnabel, Eckhard J. *Acts.* Exegetical Commentary on the New Testament. Grand Rapids, MI: Zondervan, 2012.

———. "Scripture." In *New Dictionary of Biblical Theology*, edited by T. Desmond Alexander, Brian S. Rosner, D. A. Carson, and Graeme Goldsworthy, 34–42. Downers Grove, IL: InterVarsity, 2000.

———. "Wisdom." In *New Dictionary of Biblical Theology*, edited by T. Desmond Alexander, Brian S. Rosner, D. A. Carson, and Graeme Goldsworthy, 843–48. Downers Grove, IL: InterVarsity, 2000.

Schreiner, Thomas R. *Paul, Apostle of God's Glory in Christ*. Downers Grove, IL: InterVarsity, 2001.

———. *Romans*. Baker Exegetical Commentary on the New Testament 6. Grand Rapids, MI: Baker, 1998.

Schuele, Andreas. "The Spirit of YHWH and the Aura of Divine Presence." *Interpretation* 66 (January 2012) 16–28.

Schüngell-Straumann, Helen. *Rûaḥ bewegt die Welt: Gottes schöpferische Lebenskraft in der Krisenzeit des Exils*. Stuttgarter Bibelstudien 151. Stuttgart: Verlag Katholisches Bibelwerk GmbH, 1992.

Schweizer, Eduard. *The Holy Spirit*. Translated by Kreuz Verlag Stuttgart. Philadelphia: Fortress, 1980.

Schweizer, Eduard. "The Spirit of Power: The Uniformity and Diversity of the Concept of the Holy Spirit in the New Testament." *Interpretation* (July 1952) 259–278.

Scobie, Charles H. H. "History of Biblical Theology." In *New Dictionary of Biblical Theology*, edited by T. Desmond Alexander, Brian S. Rosner, D. A. Carson, and Graeme Goldsworthy, 11–20. Downers Grove, IL: InterVarsity, 2000.

Scofield, William Campbell. *Holy Spirit in Both Testaments*. Chicago, IL: Fleming H. Revell, 1903.

Shepherd, Jr., William H. *The Narrative Function of the Holy Spirit as a Character in Luke-Acts*. SBL Dissertation Series 147. Atlanta, GA: Scholars Press, 1994.

Silva, Moisés. "Paul, The Apostle." In of *Baker Encyclopedia of the Bible*, edited by Walter A. Elwell and Barry J. Beitzel, 1622–34. Grand Rapids, MI: Baker Book House, 1988.

Simpson, Albert B. *The Holy Spirit*. New York: The Christian Alliance Publishing Company, 1895.

Smith, Gary. *Isaiah 1–39*. New American Commentary 15a. Nashville, TN: Broadman & Holman, 2007.

———. *Isaiah 40-66*. New American Commentary 15b. Nashville, TN: Broadman & Holman, 2009.

Snoeberger, Mark. "Tongues—Are They for Today?" *Detroit Baptist Seminary Journal* 14 (2009) 3–22.

Sontag, Frederick. "Should Theology Today Be Charismatic?" *Journal of the Evangelical Theology Society* 30 (1987) 199–203.

Spittler, R. P. "Spiritual Gifts." In *ISBE* 4:602–04. Grand Rapids, MI: Eerdmans, 1988.

Sproul, R. C. *The Mystery of the Holy Spirit*. Wheaton, IL: Tyndale House, 1990.

Stalder, Kurt. *Dask Werk des Geistes in der Heiligun bei Paulus*. Zürich, EVS-Verlag, 1962.

Stein, Robert H. *Luke*. New American Commentary 24. Nashville, TN: Broadman & Holman Publishers, 2001.

Steinmetz, David C. "Calvin and the Irrepressible Spirit." *Ex Auditu* 12 (1996) 94–103.

Stitzinger, James. "Spiritual Gifts: Definitions and Kinds." *Master's Seminary Journal* 14 (2003) 143–76.

Stott, John R. W. *The Message of Romans: God's Good News for the World*. Downers Grove, IL: InterVarsity, 1994.

BIBLIOGRAPHY

Strauss, Mark L. "David." In *New Dictionary of Biblical Theology*, edited by T. Desmond Alexander, Brian S. Rosner, D. A. Carson, and Graeme Goldsworthy, 435–43. Downers Grove, IL: InterVarsity, 2000.

———. "Jesus and the Spirit in Biblical and Theological Perspective: Messianic Empowering, Saving Wisdom, and the Limits of Biblical Theology." In *The Spirit and Christ in the New Testament & Christian Theology*, edited by I. Howard Marshall, Volker Rabens, and Cornelis Bennema, 266–84. Grand Rapids, MI: Eerdmans, 2012.

Tenelshof, Judy. "Encouraging the Character Formation of Future Christian Leaders." *Journal of the Evangelical Theology Society* 42 (1999) 77–90.

Theological Dictionary of the New Testament. Edited by G. Kittel and G. Friedrich. Translated by G. W. Bromiley. 10 vols. Grand Rapids, MI: Eerdmans, 1964–76.

Thielman, Frank. *Ephesians*. Baker Exegetical Commentary on the New Testament. Grand Rapids, MI: Baker Academic, 2010.

Thiselton, Anthony C. *The First Epistle to the Corinthians: A Commentary on the Greek Text*. New International Greek Testament Commentary. Grand Rapids, MI: Eerdmans, 2000.

———. *The Holy Spirit—In Biblical Teaching, through the Centuries, and Today*. Grand Rapids, MI: Eerdmans, 2013.

Thomas, Robert L. "Correlation of Revelatory Spiritual Gifts and NT Canonicity." *Master's Seminary Journal* 8 (1997) 5–28.

———. "The Mission of Israel and of the Messiah in the Plan of God." *The Master's Seminary Journal* (Fall 1997) 191–210.

———. "The Spiritual Gift of Prophecy in Rev 22:18." *Journal of the Evangelical Theological Society* 32 (1989) 201–16.

———. *Understanding Spiritual Gifts: A Verse-by-Verse Study of 1 Corinthians 12–14*. Grand Rapids, MI: Kregel, 1999.

Thomas, W. H. Griffith. *The Holy Spirit of God*. New York: Longmans, Green, and Co., 1913.

Thompson, Alan J. *The Acts of the Risen Lord Jesus: Luke's Account of God's Unfolding Plan*. New Studies in Biblical Theology 27. Downers Grove, IL: Intervarsity, 2011.

Thorsell, Paul R. "The Spirit in the Present Age: Preliminary Fulfillment of the Predicted New Covenant." *Journal of the Evangelical Theology Society* 41 (September 1998) 397–413.

Tidball, Derek. *Skilful Shepherds: Explorations in Pastoral Theology*. 2d ed. Leicester: Apollos, 1997.

Towner, Philip H. *The Letters to Timothy and Titus*. New International Commentary on the New Testament. Grand Rapids, MI: Eerdmans, 2006.

Treier, Daniel J. "The Fulfillment of Joel 2:28–32: A Multiple-Lens Approach." *Journal of the Evangelical Theology Society* 40 (1997) 13–26.

Turner, Max. "Holy Spirit." In *Dictionary of Jesus and the Gospels*, edited by Joel B. Green, Scot McKnight, and I. Howard Marshall, 341–51. Downers Grove, IL: InterVarsity, 1992.

———. "Holy Spirit." In *New Dictionary of Biblical Theology*, edited by T. Desmond Alexander, Brian S. Rosner, D. A. Carson, and Graeme Goldsworthy, 551–58. Downers Grove, IL: InterVarsity, 2000.

———. "Jesus and the Spirit in Lucan Perspective." *Tyndale Bulletin* 32 (1981) 3–42.

———. "Spiritual Gifts Then and Now." *Vox Evangelica* 15 (1985) 7–63.

———. "Spiritual Gifts." In *New Dictionary of Biblical Theology*, edited by T. Desmond Alexander and Brian S. Rosner, 789–96. Downers Grove, IL: InterVarsity, 2001.

———. "The Significance of Spirit Endowment for Paul." *Vox Evangelica* 9 (1975) 56–69.

———. *The Holy Spirit and Spiritual Gifts Then and Now*. Carlisle, Cumbria: Paternoster, 1996.

Vanhoozer, Kevin J. "Exegesis and Hermeneutics." In *New Dictionary of Biblical Theology*, edited by T. Desmond Alexander, Brian S. Rosner, D. A. Carson, and Graeme Goldsworthy, 52–64. Downers Grove, IL: InterVarsity, 2000.

Vidu, Adonis. "Habits of the Spirit: Reflections on a Pragmatic Pneumatology." *Journal of the Evangelical Theology Society* 50 (2007) 105–19.

Wallace, Daniel B. *Greek Beyond the Basics*. Grand Rapids, MI: Zondervan, 1996.

———. 2004. "Hebrews 2:3–4 and the Sign Gifts." Working Paper. https://bible.org/article/hebrews-23-4-and-sign-gifts.

———. "The Semantic Range of the Article-Noun-Καί-Noun Plural Construction in the New Testament." *Grace Theological Journal* 4 (1983) 59–84.

Waltke, Bruce. "Evangelical Spirituality: A Biblical Scholar's Perspective." *Journal of the Evangelical Theology Society* 31 (1988) 9–24.

Walvoord, John F. *The Holy Spirit*. Grand Rapids, MI: Zondervan, 1954.

Wanamaker, Charles A. *The Epistles to the Thessalonians: A Commentary on the Greek Text*. New International Greek Testament Commentary. Grand Rapids, MI: Eerdmans, 1990.

Ware, Bruce A. *Father, Son, & Holy Spirit: Relationships, Roles, and Relevance*. Wheaton, IL: Crossway, 2005.

———. "The New Covenant and the People(s) of God." In *Dispensationalism, Israel and the Church: The Search for Definition*, edited by Craig A. Blaising and Darrell L. Bock, 68–97. Grand Rapids, MI: Zondervan, 1992.

Warfield, B. B. *Counterfeit Miracles*. New York: Charles Scribner's Sons, 1918.

Warrington, Keith. *Discovering the Holy Spirit in the New Testament*. Peabody, MS: Hendrickson, 2005.

Watts, John D. W. *Isaiah 34–66*. Word Biblical Commentary 25. Dallas, TX: Word, 1998.

David W. Wead, "Hands, Laying on of." In *ISBE* 2:611–12. Grand Rapids, MI: Eerdmans, 1988.

Weisman, Ze'ev. "Anointing as a Motif in the Making of the Charismatic King." *Biblica* 57 (1976) 378–98.

———. "Charismatic Leaders in the Era of the Judges." *Zeitschrift für die alttestamentliche Wissenschaft* 89 (1977) 399–411.

———. "The Personal Spirit as Imparting Authority." *Zeitschrift für die alttestamentliche Wissenschaft* 93 (1981) 225–34.

White, R. Fowler. "Gaffin and Grudem on Eph 2:20: In Defense of Gaffin's Cessationist Exegesis." *Westminster Theological Journal* 54 (1992) 303–320.

———. "Richard Gaffin and Wayne Grudem on 1 Cor 13:10: A Comparison of Cessationist and Noncessationist Argumentation." *Journal of the Evangelical Theological Society* 35 (1992) 173–81.

Wilson, Andrew. "Apostle Apollos?" *Journal of the Evangelical Theology Society* 56 (2013) 325–35.

Windisch, Hans. *Die fünf johanneischen Parakletscprüche*. Tübingen: Verlag von J. C. B. Mohr (Paul Siebeck), 1927.

Wood, Irving Francis. *The Spirit of God in Biblical Literature*. New York: A. C. Armstrong & Son, 1904.
Wood, Leon J. *The Holy Spirit in the Old Testament*. Grand Rapids, MI: Zondervan, 1976.
Wright, Christopher J. H. *Knowing the Holy Spirit through the Old Testament*. Downers Grove, IL: InterVarsity, 2006.
Wright, N. T. *The New Testament and the People of God*. Minneapolis, MN: Fortress, 1992.
Young, Edward J. *The Book of Isaiah: Chapters 1–18*. Vol. 1 of *Isaiah*. 2nd ed. Grand Rapids, MI: Eerdmans, 1972.
———. *The Book of Isaiah: Chapters 40–66*. Vol. 3 of *Isaiah*. Grand Rapids, MI: Eerdmans, 1972.

www.ingramcontent.com/pod-product-compliance
Lightning Source LLC
Chambersburg PA
CBHW062043220426
43662CB00010B/1635